The Social Worker's Guide to Children and Families Law

The Social Worker's Guide
to Children and
Families Law

Lynn Davis

Jessica Kingsley Publishers
London and Philadelphia

MT

First published in 2009
by Jessica Kingsley Publishers
116 Pentonville Road
London N1 9JB, UK
and
400 Market Street, Suite 400
Philadelphia, PA 19106, USA

www.jkp.com

Library of Congress Cataloging in Publication Data
Davis, Lynn, 1962-
  The social worker's guide to children and families law / Lynn Davis.
    p. cm.
  ISBN 978-1-84310-653-1 (pb : alk. paper) 1. Children--Legal status, laws, etc.--England.
2. Parent and child--England. 3. Social workers--England--Handbooks, manuals, etc. I. Title.
  KD3305.D38 2009

  346.4201'70243613--dc22

                                          2008016023

British Library Cataloguing in Publication Data
A CIP catalogue record for this book is available from the British Library

ISBN 978 1 84310 653 1

Printed and bound in Great Britain by
Athenaeum Press, Gateshead, Tyne and Wear

2/9/10

Contents

Acknowledgements

Extracts from reported cases are reproduced by kind permission of Jordan Publishing, publishers of the indispensable Family Law Reports.

I am extremely grateful to my friends and colleagues Chris Simmonds and Debbie Aston for reading the draft of this book and for their helpful comments and suggestions. I am indebted to my editors Steve Jones and Lucy Mitchell for their help in guiding me through the publishing process. I am also grateful to my former clients, and the child care lawyers, social workers and Children's Guardians of Kent and Medway, for all they have taught me over the years.

Thanks go to Mum and to my friends for their support and encouragement.

This book is dedicated to Mark and the pack, with love.

Preface

This book is the product of my experience as a solicitor specialising in care proceedings and adoption cases, first for a local authority and then in private practice. It is also informed by my experience teaching the law module for social work students and providing legal update training for practising social workers. My aim is to make the essential principles of the law accessible and to show how to use the law in practice. I hope the book will be useful.

Of course, no book can ever be a substitute for proper legal advice on a particular case but I hope that it will give readers an understanding of the key principles and help them ask their lawyers the right questions.

The book is up to date as at 14 August 2008. The law has a habit of changing, so please be alert to the possibility of changes since that date.

To avoid repetition of he/she I have chosen one gender or the other throughout. Sometimes I have referred simply to English law, but intend no disrespect towards Welsh colleagues.

Any opinions expressed are entirely my own, and I take full responsibility for, and apologise for, any mistakes.

Introduction

Social workers rarely seem to regard the law with enthusiasm. Sadly, the law often seems to have the reputation of being intimidating, difficult, an obstacle, a complicating factor or, at best, a necessary evil.

In fact, the law can be fascinating, intellectually stimulating and – above all – of enormous practical value in providing a logical, disciplined analysis of even the most intractable case.

The law is the very foundation of social work practice in a profession surrounded by, even defined by, an intricate web of statutes, case law precedents and regulations. A sound working knowledge of the law is just as much a vital tool of the social worker's trade as an understanding of attachment theory or anti-discriminatory practice.

The law defines your role as a social worker. It empowers you to protect children and promote their welfare. It also defines the limit of those powers, striking the balance between state power and individual freedom. It confers duties and responsibilities, balanced against rights. A solid foundation of legal knowledge helps to protect and secure children. On the other hand, in many cases where mistakes have been made or opportunities missed, failures have not just been in social work skills but in the knowledge and correct application of legal principles.

Confident, competent social workers need a sound fundamental understanding of the law in context. They should be aware of the relevant Articles of the European Convention of Human Rights which underpin their every action. Their knowledge of the general legal provisions applicable to every family – concepts such as parental responsibility and children's autonomy – should be so deeply ingrained in their knowledge base that they apply them almost unconsciously. They need to know the remedies available from the courts to resolve disputes and problems within families. The key legal provisions relating directly to Children's Services – support, child protection and adoption – should come as second nature.

No book can give you all the answers. Not even the most specialist and experienced lawyer knows every single legal provision applicable to any case. The key for excellent practice is to embrace the law as part of your core knowledge base, to understand the fundamental principles and the key elements of the legal approach to problems and to apply that knowledge in context to your case work, identifying issues and asking the right questions. This book aims to help you do that, building your knowledge step by step.

Part 1

Fundamentals

Chapter 1

Human Rights

Why start here? Quite simply, since the Human Rights Act 1998 (HRA) came into force in 2000 every aspect of the law is subject to its provisions, so all the remaining chapters of the book must be read with this one in mind. Every action you take (or decide not to take) as a social worker is subject to the HRA.

What are human rights?

There are many definitions of human rights but, for our purposes, the term 'human rights' means those contained in the European Convention on Human Rights and Fundamental Freedoms 1950 (the Convention) because those are the rights incorporated into UK law by the HRA.

The Articles

The full text of each of the Convention Articles is set out in the HRA,[1] but they are commonly referred to by their shorthand titles.

Article 2	Right to life
Article 3	Prohibition of torture and inhuman or degrading treatment or punishment
Article 4	Prohibition of slavery and forced labour
Article 5	Right to liberty and security of person

1   Human Rights Act 1998. London: Stationery Office, available at www.opsi.gov.uk/ACTS/acts1998/ukpga_19980042_en_1, accessed 7 August 2008.

Article 6	Right to a fair trial
Article 7	Prohibition of retrospective legislation
Article 8	Right to respect for private and family life, home and correspondence
Article 9	Freedom of thought, conscience and religion
Article 10	Freedom of expression
Article 11	Freedom of assembly and association
Article 12	Right to marry and found a family
Article 14	Freedom from discrimination in the delivery of rights under the Convention
First Protocol	
Article 1	Protection of property
Article 2	Right to education
Article 3	Right to free elections
Sixth Protocol	
Article 1	Abolition of the death penalty
Article 2	Death penalty in times of war

Human rights in UK law

The HRA aims to ensure that all elements of our law are compatible with human rights. All new legislation must be drafted and all pre-existing law interpreted in a way which is compatible with Convention rights; everything is now viewed through the lens of human rights.

Courts try to make the existing law fit with the Convention; this sometimes demands some mental dexterity. For example, Article 5 guarantees the right to liberty, subject to exceptions when deprivation of liberty is justified (such as imprisoning criminals). The only exception specifically about children allows detention for 'educational supervision'. But s25 Children Act 1989 (CA89), dealing with secure accommodation, does not mention education at all – it is concerned with children who place themselves or others at serious risk. Whether this section is compatible with the HRA was considered by the Court of Appeal.[2]

The court was keen to find a solution and focused on the word 'education'. If it just means academic schooling, s25 CA89 is incompatible.

---

2   *Re K (A Child) (Secure Accommodation Order: Right to Liberty)* [2001] 1FLR 526 Court of Appeal.

However, 'education' can also be seen as a far broader concept, including social and emotional aspects of learning and development, and, the Court of Appeal found, is sufficiently wide to allow s25 CA89 to fit with the HRA.

If, despite mental gymnastics and verbal contortions, a statute cannot fit with the HRA, the higher courts can declare the legislation 'incompatible'. This does not make the statute invalid; if it did, there would then simply be a gap in the law. Instead, it can trigger a fast-track Parliamentary process to amend the law.

Public authorities

The HRA imposes a duty on public authorities (including local authorities) not to infringe the human rights of individuals. Every local authority must therefore consider the human rights implications of every decision, including those taken by social workers. The HRA impacts on every aspect of your work.

Someone whose human rights are breached or threatened by a public authority's actions can bring a free-standing human rights case or can plead human rights in a case which is primarily about something else; in care proceedings a mother might argue that the local authority proposes to breach her Article 8 right to a family life with her child.

Human rights cases and arguments can be taken in any UK court and, when all domestic remedies are exhausted, there may be a further appeal to the European Court of Human Rights (ECtHR) in Strasbourg. In a human rights case the court can use any remedy within its jurisdiction which is appropriate, including awarding compensation, granting an injunction or refusing to make an order sought by the public authority (for example, refusing to make a care order).

Human rights breaches by individuals

At first glance the HRA only covers actions by public authorities, not individuals – who, apparently, can breach each other's rights with impunity. In fact, the situation is more complicated. This is illustrated by the case of *A* v. *UK*,[3] which concerned a boy beaten with a cane by his stepfather.

---

3   *A* v. *UK* [1998] 2FLR 959 ECtHR.

The stepfather was prosecuted but acquitted on the defence of 'reasonable chastisement'.[4] The case went to the ECtHR which found that the UK system had failed to protect the child. The court said that states are:

> required to take measures designed to ensure that individuals within their jurisdiction are not subjected to torture or inhuman or degrading treatment or punishment, including such ill treatment administered by private individuals. Children and other vulnerable individuals, in particular, are entitled to state protection in the form of effective deterrence against such serious breaches of personal integrity.[5]

The implications for child protection authorities are obvious. It may be an individual who actually abuses the child, but a public authority has a positive duty to step in and protect the child. If it fails to do so, it is the public authority which becomes responsible, even though it was not the direct perpetrator of the abuse. Article 3 should be in the forefront of your mind in all child protection cases.

Understanding human rights – The 'living instrument'

To interpret the Articles which now form part of our law, we look to case law from the ECtHR as well as our own courts. The Convention is known as a 'living instrument', the interpretation of which can vary over time to reflect the changing understanding of society. As the ECtHR said, 'it is of crucial importance that the Convention is interpreted and applied in a manner which renders its rights practical and effective, not theoretical and illusory'.[6]

A v. UK (above) is a case in point. When the Convention was drafted in 1950 beating children with canes was widely accepted, but by the time A's case came to court in 1998 it was adjudged to constitute 'torture or inhuman or degrading treatment or punishment'.

The ECtHR can consider the same issue at different times and give different answers. For example, when the issue of transsexualism was raised in 1998 the applicant's claim to be recognised by the UK government as a woman (her post-operative gender) was unsuccessful.[7] The ECtHR found that there was no generally shared understanding of or approach to trans-

---

4   The defence of reasonable chastisement is no longer available.
5   A v. UK [1998] 2FLR 959 ECtHR, paragraph 22.
6   I v. UK [2002] 2FLR 519 ECtHR, paragraph 54.
7   Sheffield and Horsham v. UK [1998] 2FLR 928 ECtHR, paragraph 90.

sexualism, so each member state could decide for itself how to deal with such cases and UK law did not breach the applicant's human rights. Just four years later the same issue was raised again.[8] By then the ECtHR had moved on in its thinking and decided that 'the right of transsexuals to personal development and to physical and moral security in the full sense enjoyed by others in society cannot be regarded as a matter of controversy' and that 'the very essence of the Convention was respect for human dignity and human freedom'. The court decided that transsexual people had the right to be recognised and be allowed to marry in their post-operative gender. The House of Lords then declared UK law to be incompatible and this in turn led to the Gender Recognition Act 2004.[9]

A system that is not set in stone but can move flexibly with the times may seem attractive but it can be unsettling to live on shifting sands, not knowing whether an answer will be the same from one year to the next. Arguably the law should set standards, not follow society's whims. What happens if the prevailing mood moves in an unsavoury direction – should the courts reflect society's views in their decisions? How do judges determine what the prevailing view is? In practical terms, however, it is simply important to remember that Convention jurisprudence is flexible and can move on.

Approaching a human rights case

As always with the law, it is important to look at the exact words used. A close look at the various Articles shows that they may be:

- unqualified
- subject to specific exceptions
- subject to a general qualification.

Article 3 is an unqualified right. It simply outlaws torture and similar behaviour, full stop. It does not permit any exceptions, whatever the situation.

Article 5 (right to liberty of person) is subject to specific exceptions. It allows the state to deprive people of their liberty in certain listed circumstances such as imprisoning convicted criminals and compulsorily detaining mentally ill people.

---

8   *Goodwin* v. *UK* [2002] 2FLR 487 and *I* v. *UK* [2002] 2FLR 519, both ECtHR.
9   Gender Recognition Act 2004. London: Stationery Office, available at www.opsi.gov/uk/acts/acts2004/ukpga_20040007_en_1, accessed 7 August 2008.

Article 8, the most important for social workers as it deals with family life, contains not a list of specific exceptions but a general qualification which may justify interference with the right.

Article 8

1. Everyone has the right to respect for his private and family life, his home and his correspondence.

2. There shall be no interference by a public authority with the exercise of this right except such as is in accordance with the law and is necessary in a democratic society in the interests of national security, public safety or the economic well-being of the country, for the prevention of disorder or crime, for the protection of health or morals, or for the protection of the rights and freedoms of others.

In practice, courts analyse cases step by step as follows:

1. Does the complaint fall within the right claimed?
2. If so, has there been an interference with that right?
3. If so, is the interference lawful?
4. What are the aims of the interference?
5. Are those aims legitimate?
6. Are there relevant and sufficient reasons for the interference?
7. Are those reasons proportionate to the restrictions placed on the enjoyment of the right?

The last point raises the doctrine of 'proportionality'. Essentially, this means that the interference with someone's right may only go as far as is necessary and no further.

1.1 – Article 8 in care proceedings

Andrew, aged two, is subject to care proceedings due to neglect and failure to thrive. Since being in foster care he has caught up physically and developmentally. His mother Bianca has a learning disability and her lawyers argue that she received inadequate support. Bianca and Andrew both enjoy contact but the local authority plans to place Andrew for adoption with no ongoing direct contact. Bianca wants Andrew home. Her lawyers argue that Article 8 is breached.

1. *Does the complaint fall within the right claimed?*
    All care proceedings and adoption cases clearly fall within Article 8.

2. *If so, has there been or will there be an interference with that right?*
    The local authority cannot argue that taking a child from his mother and ending contact is anything other than an interference with family life.

3. *If so, is the interference lawful?*
    Assuming the relevant laws, court rules and procedures have been followed, the authority's actions are lawful.

4. *What are the aims of the interference?*
    The authority's objective is the protection of the child.

5. *Are those aims legitimate?*
    No one can seriously argue that the protection of vulnerable children is not a legitimate aim.

6. *Are there relevant and sufficient reasons for the interference?*
    At this point, the parties' cases diverge. The authority produces evidence to justify its case, while Bianca's lawyers might concede that the authority's reasons are relevant, but argue that they are not sufficient.

7. *Are those reasons proportionate to the restrictions placed on the enjoyment of the right?*
    Here the parties sharply disagree. The authority argues that its plans are the only way to meet Andrew's needs: nothing less will do. Bianca's lawyers argue that, even if the authority establishes some of its case, its proposals go too far. Each further step down the line restricting Andrew and Bianca's relationship requires extra justification. So, even if the case is made for a care order, termination of contact does not automatically follow – that must be justified separately. The further step of adoption (the most radical order of all) requires the clearest justification. The authority must explicitly justify every step it asks the court to take.

Depending on the evidence, the court may agree that Andrew cannot return home, but find that terminating contact (let alone adoption) would be a step too far. Interference with family life must be proportionate.

Key Articles

The most important Articles for children and families workers are 2, 3, 5, 6, 8 and 14. They should be as familiar to you as the provisions of CA89 and you should aim to become confident and fluent in using them in analysing cases and in presenting them to court.

Article 2

This protects the right to life, applicable at the extreme end of child protection.

Article 3

This Article prohibits torture and other similar treatment. The case *A* v. *UK* (above) shows that it has a broader ambit than the word 'torture' might at first imply. There is, however, a minimum level of severity below which the courts will not concern themselves.

Article 3 applies in all cases of physical abuse of children, but it is also possible to degrade someone or treat them inhumanly without touching them. This Article therefore goes beyond physical abuse to include physical neglect, emotional abuse and even emotional neglect.

The local authority has a positive duty to protect children and can be sued for failure to intervene when it knew (or should have known) that a child was being abused,[10] or, on the other hand, for taking unjustified action. The possibility of litigation heightens the need to keep careful records at every stage, noting decisions and the reasons for them. Decisions not to take action are just as significant as decisions to act. Court cases often take place many years after the event – if the case concerns events during the applicant's childhood, the time clock for litigation does not even start

---

10   *Z and Others* v. *UK* [2001] 2FLR 612 ECtHR.

running until he is an adult. By then, it will be miraculous if there is anyone left in the department who actually remembers his case. Everyone is dependent on the quality of the records kept at the time.

Article 5

The right to liberty is directly relevant to cases where children are placed in secure accommodation by the local authority. This right is subject to specified exceptions, all of which refer to 'lawful' detention, so if the detention does not comply with the letter of the law, it cannot be justified. For example, under CA89, a child cannot be detained in secure accommodation for more than 72 hours without court authority. If by some miscalculation a child is locked up for 73 hours before going to court, that detention is no longer lawful and cannot justify a breach of Article 5.

Article 6

The words 'right to a fair trial' immediately bring to mind thoughts of criminal cases, but the Article goes wider than that, also applying to any procedure which determines civil rights and obligations. Article 6 is relevant in emergency provisions under which children can be removed from home with no trial at all (via police protection) or after a court hears only one side of the story (via an emergency protection order made without notice).[11]

Article 6 also applies to decision-making processes, including those leading up to care proceedings and care planning after the making of a care order. The Court of Appeal has decided that the court must consider the fairness of the procedure as a whole,[12] so failure to invite parents to just one meeting did not make the whole process invalid. However, it is clear that properly involving and consulting people affected by local authority actions is a legal requirement, not just good practice. It is not just a question of reaching the right decisions but also of following the right procedures to get there.

Article 6 also guarantees the right to a fair and public hearing, but family cases are held in private. Does this breach the Convention? An

---

11   See Chapter 10 for more details.
12   *Re V (Care: Pre-birth Actions)* [2004] EWCA Civ 1575 [2005] 1FLR 627 and *Re J (Care: Assessment: Fair Trial)* [2006] EWCA Civ 545, both Court of Appeal.

argument that it does was rejected by the ECtHR which decided that a state can designate a whole class of case as an exception to the general rule where necessary to protect children's privacy.[13]

Article 8 – Privacy

The tension between confidentiality and openness in children's cases can bring into conflict the privacy element of Article 8 and the right to freedom of expression (Article 10). In one case during filming for a TV programme a young mother with a mental disorder whose child was to be placed for adoption was filmed in distressing circumstances.[14] The court weighed up her Article 8 rights against the BBC's right to freedom of expression on a subject of genuine public interest. The court found that the interest in freedom of expression did not outweigh the massive invasion of the mother's privacy and dignity.

Each case is different and depends on its own facts. In another case people who had been taken into care as children in an alleged ritual abuse case wanted to publicise their stories.[15] The proposed programme would reveal the identities of social workers involved. The court weighed up the competing rights of freedom of expression against privacy, and decided the breach of the social workers' rights was proportionate and pursued the legitimate aim of informed and open media discussion of matters of public interest.

The question of privacy also arises, for example, when you have to decide whether to inform a mother that her new partner has been investigated for allegations of child abuse. A balance has to be struck between the individual's right to privacy against the legitimate interest in protecting children. That balance depends in each case on factors including:

- the detailed information available

- its credibility

- the degree of risk

- the consequences of revealing the information

- the consequence of not revealing it

- how pressing is the need to disclose.

---

13   *B* v. *UK; P* v. *UK* [2001] 2FLR 261 ECtHR.

14   *T (by her Litigation Friend the OS)* v. *BBC* [2007] EWHC 1683 (QB) High Court.

15   *BBC* v. *Rochdale MBC* [2005] EWHC 2863 (Fam) [2007] 1FLR 101 High Court.

Article 8 – Family life

This element of Article 8 is engaged in every case of local authority intervention in family life. It should be second nature to consider and address Article 8 in your analysis and presentation of cases.

'Family life' is not limited to children and parents with parental responsibility. It continues beyond childhood and into adulthood and can include unmarried families, psychological (but biologically unrelated) parents, siblings, half-siblings and extended family members.

Everyone involved in a case is likely to have a separate Article 8 right, and these are often mutually incompatible so one person's rights have to be balanced against another's. Where the rights of parent and child conflict, the ECtHR determined that, if any balancing of interests is necessary, the interests of the child must prevail.[16]

The court often has to balance the parents' claim of a breach of their Article 8 right to family life against the authority's claim that it is acting to protect the child from a breach of his Article 3 right not to be ill treated.

Article 14

Article 14 prohibits discrimination on 'any ground such as sex, race, colour, language, religion, political or other opinion, national or social origin, association with a national minority, property, birth or other status'. The wording is broad enough to include issues which are not explicitly mentioned, such as disability or sexual orientation, and in future will no doubt cover other types of discrimination which we currently unknowingly practise.

At first glance it seems to go beyond all our discrimination legislation in one neat package, but in fact it outlaws discrimination only in the delivery of other Convention rights. In other words, 'free-standing' discrimination is not covered; the Article only applies if it can be allied to another Article. For example, the ECtHR considered a Portuguese court decision awarding residence to the child's mother on the grounds that the father's homosexuality was an 'abnormality' and the child should not grow up in an abnormal situation.[17] The father pleaded Article 14 allied

---

16   *Yousef* v. *Netherlands* [2003] 1FLR 210 ECtHR.
17   *Salgueiro da Silva Monta* v. *Portugal* [2005] 2FLR 596 ECtHR.

with Article 8, saying effectively: 'I am being denied my right to a family life with my child because I am gay and that is unjustified discrimination.' The ECtHR found no reasonable and objective justification for the Portuguese court's position, no legitimate aim was being pursued and there was no proportionality between the means and the aim. The discrimination was unlawful.

Points for practice

1. Make human rights considerations explicit in every aspect of your practice.

2. Have a checklist on the front of every file noting human rights points to consider. Include the topic in all reviews, in supervision and in all court reports.

3. Consider the rights of everyone involved in every decision to act – or not to act – and record reasons clearly. People have a right to see their own records[18] which should show that decisions (whether they proved in the event to be right or wrong) were made carefully and in good faith, trying to respect and balance everyone's rights.

4. Human rights demand that the process, not just the decisions made, must be fair, reinforcing good social work practice of involving and consulting service users throughout.

5. Don't be defensive: use human rights creatively and positively.

---

18   *Gaskin* v. *UK* [1990] 1FLR 167 ECtHR.

Chapter 2

Key Points in Children and Families Law

Sources of law

Finding the law is not a simple matter. There is no single point of reference: our law is a tapestry of primary legislation (statutes, or Acts of Parliament), secondary legislation (statutory instruments or regulations) and case law, together with guidance on how to apply it.

Statutes

Primary legislation is our starting point. Statutes, such as the Children Act 1989 (CA89), are passed by Parliament, receive Royal Assent and then come into force in due course. The date is part of the Act's title and can be important, for example, to distinguish between the Children Acts 1975, 1989 and 2004. The date records the year the Act was passed, not when it came into force – most of the Adoption and Children Act 2002 (ACA) only became law at the end of 2005. Some Acts are passed but never come into force, like much of the Family Law Act 1996. Finding a relevant statute is therefore only the first step.

Statutes can be wide-ranging and complicated, for instance CA89 re-wrote the law relating to children. Such a large volume of material has to be broken down into manageable chunks so statutes are divided into numbered sections. The letter 's' stands for the word 'section': s1 is the standard abbreviation for 'section 1'. Sections themselves can be broken down into subsections numbered first with a figure, (1), then a letter, (1)(a), and finally a roman numeral, all in brackets, (1)(a)(i).[1]

Statutes can be amended by later legislation repealing or adding sections, so it is important always to ensure that you are consulting the up-to-date version. A section number followed by a capital letter shows that the section has been inserted by a later statute such as s15A CA89 (dealing with special guardianship) which was added by the ACA. The added section has the same force as any other.

In major statutes like CA89, related sections are grouped together in 'Parts' numbered using capital roman numerals; for example CA89 Part III deals with local authority support for children and families and Part IV with child protection.

Complicated detail is often found in Schedules at the end of a statute, instead of in the body of the Act. For example s17 CA89 contains the essential principles of services to children in need, while the detailed services are listed in Schedule 2. Schedules have the same force as any other element of the statute.

Regulations

Secondary or 'delegated' legislation, often in the form of regulations, fleshes out the bones of a statute and authorisation for a statutory instrument is found in the statute itself. For instance, s23 CA89 says a looked after child can be placed at home with parents and that such placements are subject to regulations made by the Secretary of State. So to find the details, we must look to the Placement of Children with Parents etc. Regulations 1991.[2] All statutory instruments have a SI number – SI showing the year of issue and number, in this case SI1991/893.

Understanding statutes

The next challenge is to understand the relevant provision. Each word must be separately considered. Some words are defined in the statute itself in an

---

1   For an example of a section with all three subdivisions see Chapter 9, page 140.
2   Placement of Children with Parents etc. Regulations. London: Stationery Office, available at www.opsi.gov.uk/si/si1991/uksi_19910893_en_1.htm, accessed 7 August 2008.

interpretation section, like s105 CA89, or within an individual section, like the definition of 'harm' in s31(9) CA89.

If no definition appears in the statute itself, we look to see if the meaning of a word or section has been defined in case law – if not, we use the normal plain English meaning.

Case law

However carefully statutes and regulations are drafted, questions arise as to their meaning or application to a particular situation. Argument is put to the court which decides the question in the context of that case. If this decision is appealed, it could become a 'test case', determining the issue for all cases thereafter. This is because of the 'precedent' system whereby decisions of the highest courts (Court of Appeal and House of Lords) are binding on all lower courts, so a case ostensibly concerning one child potentially affects every child in the land as it decides a particular point of law.

To illustrate: in s31 CA89, one of the grounds for a care order is that the child is 'likely' to suffer significant harm. What does 'likely' mean – almost inevitable, anything slightly more than a vague possibility or somewhere in between? The House of Lords decided it means 'a real possibility, a possibility that cannot sensibly be ignored having regard to the nature and gravity of the feared harm in the particular case'.[3] That decided the question for all cases thereafter, as the House of Lords is the highest court in the land. The Court of Appeal, one stage lower in the hierarchy, sets binding precedents for courts below it, whereas High Court decisions are persuasive rather than binding. Whenever you see a reference to a case, note which court decided it.

When children's cases are reported, initials are used to preserve confidentiality with a brief description of the main subject in brackets. The 'likelihood' case mentioned above is *Re H & R (Child Sexual Abuse: Standard of Proof)*. The case reference for the full report of this case is [1996] 1FLR 80, that is, page 80 in volume 1 of the 1996 Family Law Reports. More recent cases also have a neutral case citation number, such as *Re C (A Child)* [2007] EWCA Civ 1206, the 1206th case decided by the Court

---

3   *Re H & R (Child Sexual Abuse: Standard of Proof)* [1996] 1FLR 80 House of Lords, Lord Nicholls at page 95D – affirmed by the House of Lords in *Re B (Children)* [2008] UKHL 35.

of Appeal for England and Wales (Civil Division) in 2007. In neutral citations, EWHL refers to the House of Lords and EWHC (Fam) to the Family Division of the High Court.

When judges' names are reported, their status in the court hierarchy is also given: Munby J is Mr Justice Munby of the High Court, Wall LJ is Lord Justice Wall of the Court of Appeal, while Lord Nicholls and Lady Hale sit in the House of Lords.

Guidance

Along with any legislation, the relevant government department often issues guidance. s7 Local Authority Social Services Act 1970 (LASSA) imposes a legal duty on local authorities to 'act under the general guidance' of the relevant Secretary of State. It is therefore important to be aware of the status of guidance as anything issued under s7 LASSA (including many important documents in child protection) must be followed unless there is an exceptional, clearly documented reason to justify doing otherwise. However, guidance itself never has the force of law so, if anything within it is inconsistent with statute or case law, it cannot prevail.

Key statutes

Children Act 1989

This is the starting point for all questions of children law and is the Act you need to know most intimately in your work. Its provisions are discussed in detail in the rest of the book, and key sections listed in Appendix 1.

Children Act 2004

This Act made structural and organisational changes to children's services and inter-agency working at national and local level. It established the Children's Commissioner and set up Local Safeguarding Children's Boards.[4] Its effects underlie your work, but you are unlikely to need to know its detailed provisions.

---

4   See Chapter 9 for more details.

Adoption and Children Act 2002

This completely reformed adoption law and made changes to the CA89. It is the key statute for all adoption cases.[5]

Children and Adoption Act 2006

This added provisions to CA89 relating to family assistance orders,[6] and private law contact disputes.

Children Act 1989 – Fundamental provisions

The fundamental principles of CA89 should be engraved on your heart. They apply whenever a CA89 case comes to court.

s1(1) – Welfare principle

People often recite the phrase 'the child's welfare is paramount' without analysing what the subsection actually says.

---

s1(1) When a court determines any question with respect to –

    (a)   upbringing of a child; or

    (b)   the administration of a child's property or the application or any income arising from it,

the child's welfare shall be the court's paramount consideration.

The statutory duty applies to courts considering children's cases, but only when the issue concerns the child's upbringing (or property). It does not apply,[7] for example, to an application to place a child in secure accommodation when the court simply determines whether the statutory grounds are met: the child's welfare is not paramount.

---

5   See Chapters 15 and 16 for more details.

6   See Chapter 6 for more details. Several provisions of this Act are not yet in force as at 7 August 2008. Implementation is anticipated in December 2008.

7   *Re M (Secure Accommodation Order)* [1995] 1FLR 418 Court of Appeal.

The welfare principle is also subject to other statutory provisions, so a court cannot make a care order, for example, unless the statutory grounds are met, even if it would be in the child's best interests to do so.

To some it comes as a surprise to realise that s1(1) CA89 applies only to courts – not to local authorities or other agencies. It may not be a bad ideal to adopt, but it cannot be used as a trite slogan. Local authorities have other statutory duties towards children and families and wider considerations including balancing the needs of everyone in their area and managing their budget. Unlike the courts, local authorities cannot place the needs of every individual child as their paramount consideration.

What does paramount mean? The child's welfare overrides that of others, but it is not the only consideration in a case. Lord McDermott's 1969 analysis is still helpful today:

> Reading those words in their ordinary significance…it seems to me that they must mean more than that the child's welfare is to be treated as the top item in a list of items relevant to the matter in question. I think they connote a process whereby, when all the relevant facts, relationships, claims and wishes of parents, risks, choices and other circumstances are taken into account and weighed, the course to be followed will be that which is most in the interests of the child's welfare… That is…the paramount consideration because it rules on and determines the course to be followed.[8]

But even this is not as clear as it might seem. How does the court decide when one child's needs conflict with those of another? If both children are the subject of applications, theoretically the needs of each are paramount but, in practice, the needs of one have to be weighed against the other.

2.1 – Half-siblings' conflicting interests

Charlie and David are half-brothers. Their mother cannot look after them. Charlie's father, Ed, wants Charlie (but not David) to live with him. Charlie wants to live with Ed. Maternal grandmother Frances wants to care for both boys. David wants to be with Charlie. Frances and Ed both apply to court and s1 CA89 applies to the applications. The court has a dilemma: for Charlie, the best solution is to live with

---

8   *J* v. *C* [1969] 1 All ER 788 House of Lords at pages 820–821 given in a case concerning an old piece of legislation under which the child's welfare was 'first and paramount'.

Ed, even if that means separation from his brother, but for David, the best solution is for the boys to be together. Each child's welfare may be paramount but the court cannot make an order which is ideal for each; it has to compromise. Charlie goes to live with Ed and David goes to live with Frances with extensive contact between the boys.

2.2 – Under-age mother and baby

George's mother Hannah is a troubled 14-year-old. George and Hannah are both subject to care proceedings. Hannah will be deeply distressed if George is permanently removed. It would be in her best interests for George to remain in foster care in the hope that one day she can care for him but George needs competent care and security now. Each child's welfare is paramount, but there is a conflict between them. Although Hannah is herself a child subject to proceedings, she is also George's mother, so his needs are likely to be put above hers. As Orwell might have put it, some interests are more paramount than others.

2.3 – Child applicant

Ian and Karen are siblings placed separately. Ian desperately wants to see Karen. If he applies to court for a contact order, he is the applicant, not the subject of the application: Karen is the child whose upbringing is in question. The court is not concerned with Ian's welfare, even though he is a child in some distress: Karen's welfare is the paramount consideration.

s1(3) – Welfare checklist

Declaring that the child's welfare is paramount is one thing; deciding what it means for a particular child is another. To guide the court on which factors to take into account, s1(3) CA89 gives a list of considerations, commonly known as 'the welfare checklist'. These apply whenever the court considers an application for an order under s8 CA89 (residence, contact, specific issue or prohibited steps orders), for a special guardianship order or care proceedings. They do not apply to emergency protection or child

> s1(3) ...a court shall have regard in particular to –
>
> (a)   the ascertainable wishes and feelings of the child concerned (considered in the light of his age and understanding);
>
> (b)   his physical, emotional and educational needs;
>
> (c)   the likely effect on him of any change in his circumstances;
>
> (d)   his age, sex, background and any characteristics of his which the court considers relevant;
>
> (e)   any harm which he has suffered or is at risk of suffering;
>
> (f)   how capable each of his parents, and any other person in relation to whom the court considers the question to be relevant, is of meeting his needs;
>
> (g)   the range of powers available to the court under this Act in the proceedings in question.

assessment applications when information is likely to be limited, although it is good practice to inform the court of any available details whether the subsection is obligatory or not. The items specified in the list are not exclusive, so other relevant factors should also be considered.

CHILD'S WISHES AND FEELINGS

The list is not in order of priority, but it is of symbolic significance that the child's views appear first. Children rarely go to court or write statements, so courts depend on professionals to state and explain the child's views. Social workers can help the court to understand what the child is really saying, through his words and behaviour. Is the child free to express his true views or is he under pressure to say the 'right thing'? How much weight should be given to his views?[9] What a child wants and what is best for him are not always the same, and sometimes the contents of item (a) on the checklist will be different from your recommendation to the court.

---

9   See Chapter 3 for more on competence.

PHYSICAL, EMOTIONAL AND EDUCATIONAL NEEDS

This heading falls squarely within social work competence. It is always important to identify the needs of the individual child concerned as opposed to the needs of any typical child of the same age.

EFFECT OF CHANGE

This is sometimes called the 'status quo' principle but that perhaps overstates its purpose. This heading reminds us that no intervention in a child's life is neutral; the very fact of change itself has an impact which must be taken into account. Unnecessary change should be avoided, but clearly a status quo which is harmful should not be preserved. The court may need to weigh short term adverse effects against long term benefits.

AGE, SEX, BACKGROUND AND CHARACTERISTICS

This heading includes such important factors as racial, cultural and linguistic heritage and any special needs. All of the child's characteristics need to be put into their proper perspective in the case; one element does not have greater importance than another. For example, in one case the child of orthodox Jewish parents was living with non-practising Catholics, so religion and culture were obviously important issues.[10] However, the Court of Appeal decided that the question of religion could only ever be one factor in a case, albeit in some cases a weighty one, and the child's overall welfare is always paramount. Butler-Sloss LJ said: 'No one would wish to deprive a Jewish child of her right to her Jewish heritage. If she had remained with a Jewish family it would be almost unthinkable, other than in an emergency to remove her from it.' However, the unusual circumstances of the case meant that the 'religious and cultural heritage cannot be the overwhelming factor in this case…nor can it displace other weighty welfare factors'.

HARM

This word is defined by s31(9) CA89 and can refer to abuse or neglect which impairs a child's health or development (see Chapter 9 for more detail on this).

---

10   *Re P (s91(4) Guidelines) (Residence and Religious Heritage)* [1999] 2FLR 573 Court of Appeal, pages 585H–586A and 586E.

CAPABILITY OF PARENTS AND OTHERS TO MEET THE CHILD'S NEEDS

This subheading assesses how the resources available within the child's network fit the child's needs already established in item (b). The child's parents are the first port of call but they are not the only relevant people to consider – the court may also look to the extended family, friends or other people in the child's life.

COURT'S POWERS

A key feature of the Act's design is the court's ability to use some of its powers creatively to do what is best for the child. The court is not limited to making or refusing the order sought and it can make some orders without any application if that is in the child's interests. Never limit your thinking to the application before the court – consider all available options.

2.4 – Residence or contact

Leon lives with his mother Millie, who prevents him from having contact with his father Nick. Nick wants Leon to live with him so he applies for a residence order. The court decides that Leon should remain with Millie and declines a residence order but it decides that contact must be secured so it makes a contact order of its own motion without any application being made.

2.5 – Care order or family placement

The local authority applies for a care order in respect of Oliver with a plan to place him for adoption. The court decides that it would be in his best interests to live with Patricia, his maternal grandmother. In spite of the local authority's submissions, the court declines the care order and instead makes a package of orders no one has applied for – residence order to Patricia, supervision order to the local authority, contact order to Oliver's mother and prohibited steps order preventing father from contacting Oliver.

s1(2) – 'No delay' principle

> s1(2) In any proceedings in which any question with respect to the upbringing of a child arises, the court shall have regard to the general principle that any delay in determining the question is likely to prejudice the welfare of the child.

Long delays in a child's case can make the decision almost a foregone conclusion; for example when one contact case took two years to go through court, by which time the mother had not seen her child for over three years, the ECtHR described the case as having 'a peculiar quality of irreversibility' and said 'in cases of this kind…there is always the danger that any procedural delay will result in the de facto determination of the issue submitted to the court before it had held the hearing'. [11]Article 6 of the Convention explicitly confers the right to a fair hearing 'within a reasonable time'.

However, there can be a tension between making a quick decision and making the right one. Delay is sometimes essential and the court may need social work advice on how to strike the right balance.

s1(5) – 'No order' principle

> s1(5) Where a court is considering whether or not to make one or more orders under this Act with respect to a child, it shall not make the order or any of the orders unless it considers that doing so would be better for the child than making no order at all.

This subsection has been widely misunderstood. At first it was thought that it meant that every single possible alternative must be explored before a case could even be taken to court, and that no order should ever be made if agreement could be reached. This was taking things too far.

More recently it was thought to be a presumption that no order would be made unless there was specific justification to make one. The Court of

---

11   *H* v. *UK* [1988] 10 EHRR 95 ECtHR.

Appeal has now clarified that the subsection means exactly what it says.[12] Ward LJ said:

> in my view this section is perfectly clear. It does not, in my judgment, create a presumption one way or the other. All it demands is that before the court makes any order it must ask the question: will it be better for the child to make the order than make no order at all? The section itself gives the test to be applied and the question to be asked. If judges in each case do just that they cannot go wrong, it being axiomatic that every case is different, and each case will depend on its own peculiar facts.[13]

No order might be the right outcome if the parties reach agreement, but the court should never simply rubber stamp any agreement (for no order or for a particular form of order) without assuring itself that it is appropriate. Agreements reached at court or under the threat of proceedings are not always what they seem, and the balance of power between the parties must be considered. s1(5) CA89 should never be used as an argument to force 'agreement', nor should a court accept any consent order without looking behind it to ensure it truly represents the child's best interests.

Even if the court approves the parties' agreement, an order can still be justified to embody that agreement if, for example, having a residence order makes the carer feel more secure.

s91(14) – Preventing repeated applications

Unlike s1 CA89, this is not a fundamental principle underlying all CA89 applications but it is a provision which can be used in any appropriate case under CA89. It gives the court dealing with one application power to exercise some control over future applications.

> s91(14) On disposing of any application for an order under this Act, the court may (whether or not it makes any other order in response to the application) order that no application for an order under this Act of any specified kind may be made with respect to the child concerned by any person named in the order without leave of the court.

---

12   *Re G (Children)* [2005] EWCA Civ 1283 [2006] 1FLR 771 Court of Appeal.
13   *Re G*, paragraph 10 (see note 12 above).

So once a s91(14) CA89 order is made, the person named in the order cannot apply for a specified type of order without first obtaining the court's permission, allowing the court to filter out unmeritorious applications. It adds an extra hurdle, but even if this is crossed it does not necessarily mean that the application itself will be successful.

This provision can prevent the continuation of a pattern of repeated and unreasonable applications, but it is not limited to that situation. The case of the Jewish child in a Catholic family (mentioned above) was not one of repeated applications but the court used s91(14) CA89 to prevent the disruption and upset of further applications, emphasising the importance of the child's welfare in considering making such an order. The provision has also been used to add security and permanence to residence or special guardianship orders, rather than choosing the more drastic option of adoption.

What about the human rights of the person subject to this restriction? The right to a fair trial is clearly relevant, but s91(14) CA89 does not deny access to the court, it simply adds another stage to the proceedings. Nonetheless, it is a power to be used sparingly and with great care. As a matter of justice, no such restriction should be imposed without giving the person concerned the opportunity to comment first, and any order should be proportionate to the need – the court must carefully consider what kind of applications should be restricted and for how long. The Court of Appeal confirmed that in exceptional cases a s91(14) order can be made without any time limit or until the child turns 16, but the court must clearly spell out its reasons for its order.[14] The order cannot include any other conditions, such as specifying what needs to change before the court will consider a further application, but the judge can make this clear to the person concerned,[15] and any later court will expect to see the issues addressed before allowing an application to proceed.

2.6 – Repeated applications

Queenie's parents separated ten years ago when she was two. Ever since, she has been subject to almost constant court applications by one parent or the other. Queenie is now so emotionally disturbed

---

14   *Re S (Permission to Seek Relief)* [2006] EWCA Civ 1190 [2007] 1FLR 482 Court of Appeal.

15   *Stringer v. Stringer* [2006] EWCA Civ 1617 [2007] 1FLR 1532 Court of Appeal.

that she is subject to care proceedings. The judge makes a care order and decides that Queenie needs a chance to settle in foster care without being disrupted by more court proceedings. He makes a s91(14) CA89 order stopping either parent from applying without court leave to discharge the care order, for residence or contact, for two years.

2.7 – Parental conduct

Rick has made repeated unsuccessful applications for direct contact to his daughter. The key problem is Rick's drug abuse. The judge decides to impose a s91(14) CA89 order. He cannot make treatment a condition of the order but he makes it very clear to Rick that, unless he addresses his addiction, he is most unlikely to obtain court permission to apply for contact again.

Points for practice

1. Always be aware of the legal context of your actions, powers and duties. Regularly reflect on the statutory basis for your actions and remind yourself of the applicable legal principles.

2. Have a copy of s1 CA89 to hand to ensure you are considering relevant factors.

3. Use the law creatively. Embrace it as a tool of your trade, not something to be wary of or intimidated by. Having a command of legal principles and available options can help you to analyse cases clearly.

Chapter 3

Parental Responsibility and Children's Autonomy

Parental responsibility

Parental responsibility (PR) is a key concept underlying children and families law. When the term was introduced by the Children Act 1989 (CA89), it was seen as an important symbolic change from the old terminology of parental rights: parents now have responsibility for their children, rather than rights over them.

In normal life we rarely consider the legal relationships between children and their parents, but as a social worker you often have to deal with families in difficulty where quick decisions have to be made. You need to know who has the right to make those decisions.

What is PR?

We might instinctively know what PR entails but defining it is a surprisingly difficult task. s3(1) CA89 does not even try to define PR: it simply tells us that PR consists of 'all the rights, duties, powers, responsibilities and authority which by law a parent of a child has in relation to the child and his property'. It includes:

- naming the child
- feeding, housing and maintaining him
- securing his education

- arranging and consenting to health care
- choosing his religious upbringing.

PR diminishes as a child's autonomy grows. A newborn baby is totally dependent on his parents, whereas 17½ years later, they are doing well if he still listens to them.

Who has PR?

Despite its name, PR is not necessarily connected with parenthood. It is possible to be a parent but not have PR or to have PR but not be a parent.

MOTHERS

The easiest starting point lies with a child's mother who automatically has PR.[1] As long as the child has not been adopted and she was not a surrogate mother, you can safely assume she has full legal rights and responsibilities towards the child, even if she herself is still under 18.

COUPLES

Married parents

The law copes most easily with conventional families. Married parents both have PR,[2] whether they married before or after the child's birth.[3] Marriage refers only to a formal marriage evidenced by a marriage certificate as, contrary to persistent popular opinion, 'common law marriage' does not exist: a couple can live together for a lifetime without acquiring married status. Anyone who refers to their 'common law husband/wife' is probably unmarried.

If a married woman gives birth, there is a strong presumption that her husband is the child's father but this is overridden if there is evidence to the contrary.

---

1   s2(1) and 2(2)(a) CA89.
2   s2(1) CA89.
3   This is because of the effect of s2 Legitimacy Act 1976.

Unmarried parents

Unmarried mothers, like all mothers, automatically have PR,[4] but unmarried fathers do not;[5] they have to take action to acquire it. Essentially there are three options, each of which can be easily substantiated by documentary evidence:

1. Registration: if mother and father jointly register the father's name on the child's birth certificate, this confers PR if and only if the birth was registered (or re-registered) on or after 1 December 2003. Before that date, even if the father's name appears on the birth certificate, it has no legal effect.

2. Agreement: if mother and father jointly enter a PR agreement[6] this confers PR on father. To be effective, the agreement must be in a prescribed form, signed and witnessed at court and registered at the Principal Registry of the Family Division.[7]

3. Court order: the father can seek a PR order from the court.[8] Only the child's biological father can seek this order; the mother cannot apply to force the father to take on responsibility. If paternity is disputed, the court can require DNA testing to establish the truth. The court then considers the evidence given by both parties applying s1 CA89 and the following factors:

    • commitment – this might be shown by financial support, contact and involvement in the child's education

    • attachment – what is the relationship between father and child?

    • reasons for application – does father genuinely want to take responsibility for his child or is he motivated more by his relationship with the mother, be it a desire to get back together with her or to make her life difficult?

---

4   s2(2)(a) CA89.
5   s2(2)(b) CA89.
6   s4 CA89.
7   Full details and the relevant forms can be found on the Courts Service website at www. hmcourts-service.gov.uk/courtfinder/forms/cpral.pdf, accessed on 21 April 2008.
8   s4 CA89.

The courts' general approach is that a father who shows enough interest in his child to want PR usually merits it, to put him in the same position as a married father.[9] Butler Sloss LJ said:

> a father who has shown real commitment to the child concerned and to whom there is a positive attachment, as well as a genuine bona fide reason for the application, ought…to assume the weight of those duties and cement that commitment and attachment by sharing the responsibilities for the child with the mother. This father is asking to assume that burden as well as that pleasure of looking after his child, a burden not lightly to be undertaken.[10]

The question of whether a father should have PR is not the same as whether he should see the child: a father can be granted PR but refused contact.[11]

STEP-PARENTS

The term 'step-parent' refers to a person who marries a child's parent not a parent's unmarried partner. A step-parent does not gain PR just by marrying a child's parent and many step-families live together without legal formalities, probably unaware that only one of the people playing the role of parent in fact has PR.

There are three options for step-parents wishing to acquire PR:

1. PR agreement entered into by the step-parent and the birth parents who already have PR (i.e. always the mother, and sometimes the father).[12] The agreement gives PR to the step-parent, shared with those who already had it. The format and procedures for this agreement closely follow that for unmarried fathers.

2. Court order – an option if an agreement is not possible, because a parent with PR opposes the step-parent's desire to have PR, or cannot be found.[13] s1 CA89 applies and courts will probably consider factors like commitment, attachment and motivation as for unmarried fathers. Just as for PR agreements, an order adds another person with PR without eliminating anyone else.

9   Re S (Parental Responsibility) [1995] 2FLR 648 Court of Appeal.
10   Re S (A Minor) (Parental Responsibility) [1995] 3FCR 225 at page 236.
11   Re H (A Minor) (Parental Responsibility) [1993] 1FLR 484 Court of Appeal.
12   s4A(1)(a) CA89.
13   s4A(1)(b) CA89.

3. Adoption. This is the only way for a step-parent actually to become the child's parent, rather than just obtaining PR. Under step-parent adoption orders made before the Adoption and Children Act 2002 (ACA) came into force, somewhat bizarrely, not only the married step-parent but also the birth parent adopted the child.[14]

    Thankfully the ACA introduced a new form of step-parent adoption allowing just the 'step' half of the couple to adopt. Interestingly (and unlike the step-parent provisions of the CA89) such adoptions are available to the birth parent's unmarried partner, not just to his/her spouse.[15] It is perhaps unfortunate that only the most drastic step-parent order is available to unmarried couples.

    An adoption order terminates previous PR (except that of the birth parent half of the 'step' couple). So, where a stepmother adopts a child, in law she becomes the child's mother, replacing the birth mother who loses her PR and all legal relationship with the child. Clearly, adoption is a drastic step with profound human rights implications.

Step-parents also have available the other provisions for 'non-parents' set out below, but married step-parents are more likely to use the provisions specifically designed for their situation.

Same sex couples

Assuming one of the partners in a same sex relationship is the child's birth parent, the normal rules apply to determine his/her PR. Just as for heterosexual couples, the other partner has no automatic entitlement to PR simply because s/he is in a relationship with the child's parent, so has to take positive steps to acquire PR.

Since 5 December 2005 same sex couples have been able to enter into a Civil Partnership under the provisions of the Civil Partnership Act 2004.[16] Although the legislation shies away from using the term 'marriage', in fact the rights and responsibilities of civil partners are very similar to those of married couples. The step-parent provisions described above are available to a parent's civil partner just as to a spouse, so s/he can acquire PR by

---

14 Under the Adoption Act 1976 only single people or married couples could adopt, so the birth parent and step-parent had to adopt jointly.

15 s51(2) ACA.

16 Civil Partnership Act 2004. London: Stationery Office, available at www.opsi.gov.uk/acts/acts2004/ukpga_20040033_en_1, accessed 9 August 2008.

agreement or court order or become the child's parent by adoption.

Partners who have not entered into a civil partnership are in the same position as unmarried heterosexual cohabitants so they can seek to adopt the partner's child or to look at the 'non-parent' provisions below.

Non-parents

Children often live with people other than their parents under informal arrangements, the parties involved giving no real thought to the legal situation. In fact the carers are acting on behalf of the person with PR who, consciously or otherwise, has delegated that responsibility.[17]

However, such people can acquire PR in their own right by making an appropriate application to court, a sensible step where the arrangement is long term, there are tensions between the parties or the person with PR is unreliable or cannot always be found. Which type of order is appropriate depends on the circumstances of each case. The orders are discussed in detail later in the book, but in terms of PR their effects are as follows:[18]

- Residence order[19] – confers PR for the duration of the order on the person the child is to live with, shared equally with others who have PR.

- Special guardianship order[20] – grants PR to the special guardian (who cannot be a birth parent) for the duration of the order. The special guardian can act without reference to others with PR.

- Adoption order (ACA)[21] – grants exclusive PR to the adopters, extinguishing birth parents' PR.

LOCAL AUTHORITY

'Looked after' children may be:

- 'in care', subject to a care order made by the court[22]

---

17   s2(9) CA89.
18   Other aspects of the orders are discussed in Chapters 4 and 5 (residence and special guardianship) and 15 and 16 (adoption).
19   s8 CA89.
20   s14A CA89.
21   Or Adoption Act 1976 for applications commenced before 31 December 2005.
22   s31 CA89.

- 'accommodated' under a voluntary arrangement.[23]

When a child is in care, the local authority (not the social worker or foster carer) has PR. Birth parents do not lose their PR but, if necessary for the child's welfare, the local authority can restrict how they exercise it.[24]

Accommodated children are looked after under a purely voluntary arrangement by which a parent delegates PR to the local authority to the extent and for so long as s/he chooses.[25] Neither the local authority nor the carer has PR.

ORPHANS

If a child is orphaned, the position depends on whether any advance provision has been made. Parents can appoint a 'testamentary guardian' to have PR for their children in the event of their death,[26] but if they die without making such provision, someone wishing to become the child's guardian can apply to court.[27] The s1 CA89 principles apply to the application and the court's order gives the guardian PR for the child.

If no one is appointed as guardian for an orphan, the local authority must accommodate and maintain him,[28] but it does not acquire PR: local authorities can only acquire PR through a care order and simply having no one with PR does not of itself give grounds for a care order. Some children therefore have no one at all with PR for them, a small but important gap in the law.

SURROGACY

The details of the law relating to surrogacy[29] are beyond the scope of this book, but it is useful to know that in surrogacy cases a 'parental order' means that the child is treated in law as the child of the commissioning couple (at least one of whom has provided sperm/eggs), not of the surrogate

---

23   s20 CA89.
24   s33(3) CA89.
25   s2(9) CA89.
26   s5(3) CA89.
27   s5(1) CA89.
28   s20 CA89.
29   See the Human Fertilisation and Embryology Act 1990. London: Stationery Office, available at www.opsi.gov.uk/acts/acts1990/ukpga_19900037_en_1, accessed 9 August 2008.

mother. The commissioning couple gain exclusive PR for the child and the woman who actually gave birth has no legal relationship with the child.

DONORS

People who donate eggs, sperm or embryos through a formally licensed clinic may be genetic parents of any resulting child but they are not named on birth certificates, do not gain PR and do not have any other rights, responsibilities or legal relationship towards that child, who is treated in law as the child of the family into which he is born. However, for donations made since 1 April 2005, the child when adult will be entitled to know the donor's identity, date and place of birth and last known address.[30]

These rules do not apply to informal, 'DIY' sperm donations, where the biological father is treated in law in exactly the same way as any other unmarried father.

3.1 – Who has PR?

These children are in the same class. Who can sign consent for a school trip?

Their home situations are as follows:

Abdul – married parents – *both parents have PR.*

Britney – unmarried parents – *her mother has PR. Her father has PR if his name was entered on her birth certificate on or after 1 December 2003, if he and her mother have entered into a formal agreement registered at court or if he has a court order.*

Colin – mother – *his mother has PR. If his parents were married, even if they are now separated or divorced, the father has PR. If not, his father's position is the same as Britney's father.*

Daisy – mother and stepfather – *her mother has PR. Her father's situation is the same as Colin's father. If her stepfather has a step-parent PR agreement or order, he also has PR which may be shared three ways. If he has adopted Daisy, only he and Daisy's mother have PR. If he is just living with Daisy's mother without being married, he could have PR if he has a residence order for Daisy or has adopted her.*

Ellie – father and father's male partner – *her mother has PR*

---

30   For more information on surrogacy, donations, IVF, etc. see the Human Fertilisation and Embryology Authority website at www.hfea.gov.uk, accessed 9 August 2008.

whether or not she was married to Ellie's father and even if she is no longer on the scene. Even though Ellie lives with her father, he may or may not have PR depending on his status. If Ellie's father and partner are civil partners, the partner is in the same position as Daisy's married stepfather; if not, he is like Daisy's unmarried stepfather.

Fergal – grandparents – *unless his grandparents have adopted him, Fergal's mother still has PR as may his father. The grandparents may be acting under the parents' delegated PR or they may have PR in their own right. If they have a residence order, PR is shared with the parent(s); if they have a special guardianship order, PR is shared but they can exercise it to the exclusion of the parents.*

Georgia – foster parents – *if she is accommodated, her parent(s) retain full PR and delegate elements to the local authority. If she is in care, the local authority has PR and can limit the parents' exercise of their PR if necessary in Georgia's best interests.*

Henry – adoptive parents – *the adoption order terminated Henry's birth parents' PR. His adoptive parents have exclusive PR.*

Idris – is an orphan who lives with family friends – *his carers have PR if they were appointed as guardians in his parents' wills or by the court. However, he may live with them on a purely informal basis.*

How does PR end?

Once acquired, PR is not easily lost. It is not ended by divorce or dissolution of a civil partnership, nor by abandonment, nor can a parent relinquish PR except by consenting to an adoption order.[31]

PR can end as follows:

- child attains 18

- child or parent dies

- child is adopted (ending birth parents' PR)

- an unmarried father's PR order or agreement is revoked by the court

- a parental order is made in a surrogacy case (ending the surrogate mother's PR)

---

31   s2(9) CA89.

- a step-parent PR order, residence order or special guardianship order is discharged by the court (ending the PR of the person who acquired it through the original order)

- a care order is revoked by the court (ending the local authority's PR).

A father who obtained PR by agreement or court order can have his PR removed by the court.[32] This happens only in extreme circumstances such as a case where the father had gravely injured the child and was said by the judge to have forfeited his PR.[33] There is no equivalent provision for mothers or married fathers, whose PR cannot be removed by the court no matter how appallingly they behave or how much the child wishes to disown them.

Exercising PR

You may not be aware of it, but every time you consent to a school trip or take your child to the GP, you are exercising PR. In day to day life, most PR is exercised almost unconsciously.

DELEGATING PR

PR cannot be surrendered or transferred, but some or all of it can be delegated.[34] Every time your child has a babysitter, you are temporarily delegating aspects of your PR. When a child is voluntarily accommodated, the parent(s) delegate the day to day exercise of PR to the local authority.

SHARING PR

As we have seen, many children have more than one person with PR at the same time.[35] If everyone with PR had to confer and agree on every decision, however minor, it would be unwieldy in the most harmonious family and no decisions at all could be taken for a child whose separated parents had lost contact with each other. The law therefore sensibly allows for PR to be exercised in almost all cases by any one person who has it.

---

32   s4(3) CA89.
33   *Re P (Terminating Parental Responsibility)* [1995] 1FLR 1048 High Court.
34   s2(9) CA89.
35   s2(5) CA89.

> s2(7) CA89 Where more than one person has PR for a child, each of them may act alone and without the other (or others) in meeting that responsibility...

As a social worker, it is useful to be aware that you can usually act on the basis of consent from one person with PR. Others with PR should of course still be consulted and involved in the process, but if one parent is more accessible and co-operative than the other, that parent's consent suffices.

However, there are some exceptions to the general rule. Where there is a residence order, the consent of everyone with PR or court leave is needed for the child to leave the UK for more than a month or to change the child's surname.[36] The courts have applied the same rule to surname change even where there is no residence order.[37] Case law decisions also mean that consent of everyone with PR is required for non-medical circumcision,[38] and for immunisations.[39]

As most decisions can be made by one parent without the other, there is the potential for conflict. What happens if separated parents disagree on a child's schooling, religious upbringing or medical treatment? As a matter of practical reality, a resident parent often effectively makes all the decisions and takes all the responsibility for the child but even having a residence order does not give that right in law. The courts confirmed in the case concerning immunisations that the parent with whom the child lives has no greater rights than the absent parent, unlike a special guardian who has power to override others or the local authority which has 'senior partner' status under a care order. Where people with equal rights and responsibilities cannot agree, ultimately the matter can go to court for decision, using the private law provisions of CA89.[40]

---

36   s13(1) CA89.
37   *Re PC (Change of Surname)* [1997] 2FLR 730 High Court.
38   *Re J (Specific Issue Orders: Child's Religious Upbringing and Circumcision)* [2000] 1FLR 571 Court of Appeal.
39   *Re C (Welfare of Child: Immunisation)* [2003] 2FLR 1054 (High Court) and 1095 (Court of Appeal).
40   See Chapters 4–6 for more detail.

PEOPLE WITHOUT PR

Fathers

Although PR is an important concept, under the CA89 a father without PR is still a 'parent', albeit one without PR. It is always important to be aware of the precise wording of the law. If a CA89 provision applies to people with PR, he is not included, but if it applies to 'parents', he is (for example the right to apply for a s8 order and the presumption of reasonable contact with a child in care). Unfortunately, in the Adoption and Children Act (ACA) the word 'parent' only means parents with PR. So a father without PR is a 'parent' under CA89 but not if the case moves on to adoption.

However, even where the law clearly refers to parents with PR, a birth father cannot simply be ignored – he may still have a right for his family life with the child to be respected under Article 8 of the European Convention on Human Rights. So while the consent of a father without PR is not required for an adoption order, he may nevertheless have to be involved in the process. A series of cases recognised that fathers without PR range from fully committed parents on the one hand to one-night stands or even rapists at the other extreme,[41] so the question must be asked in each case as to where the particular father lies on that spectrum to determine whether he has a right to a family life with the child.

Others

You might think that someone who is not a parent and has no PR cannot have any responsibility for or authority over a child, but this is not always so (see subsection 3(5) in the box on the next page).

This subsection does not go into detail about what action is or is not permitted – it is specifically designed to cover a myriad of unpredictable circumstances, so the wording leaves a lot to common sense.

3.2 – Babysitter's actions

Sally is babysitting for baby Tom, who is taken ill. Sally cannot contact Tom's parents, so she decides to take Tom straight to hospital. It does not occur to her to ponder her legal authority to do this, but if it did, she could rely on s3(5) CA89. The doctors at the hospital

---

41 Cases heard under the old legislation but equally applicable to the new. Discussed further in Chapter 13.

can also treat Tom on the same basis or rely on the legal doctrine of necessity.

> s3(5) CA89 A person who –
>
> (a)   does not have parental responsibility for a particular child; but
>
> (b)   has care of the child,
>
> (c)   may (subject to the provisions of this Act) do what is reasonable in all the circumstances of the case for the purpose of safeguarding or promoting the child's welfare.

3.3 – Foster carer's actions

Ursula is a foster carer looking after Vivien, who is accommodated. Vivien's mother Wanda arrives unexpectedly, saying that she has decided to take Vivien home. Neither Ursula nor the local authority have PR, but instead of simply handing Vivien over, Ursula asks Wanda to wait while she telephones Vivien's social worker. She is using her common sense and unwittingly relying on s3(5) CA89. Clearly she could not keep Vivien against Wanda's wishes for hours on end, but it is sufficient to allow Ursula to buy herself some time.

Points for practice

1.   As soon as you start work with a new family work out who has PR and note it clearly on the file – you need to be able to find it at short notice.

2.   Remember the answer may be different for each child of the family and may change over time – keep the note up to date.

3.   Ask to see relevant certificates and court orders – take copies for your file.

Children's autonomy

The law sometimes prescribes a precise age at which a person can do a particular thing. For example, he can consent in his own right to medical, surgical or dental treatment at the age of 16,[42] he is criminally liable for his actions from the age of ten and can get a licence to drive a car from the age of 17. If there is a specific statute, the law applies to all, whatever the characteristics of the individual child.[43]

But what about situations where there is no such provision? Then, we have to look at the more flexible (and therefore less clear) concept of competence. The name of Gillick has, ironically, become synonymous with a principle which is the polar opposite of that which Mrs Gillick sought to establish. The Gillick case was a landmark decision.[44] In itself, it concerned only the issue of provision of contraceptive advice for those under 16 without parental knowledge or consent but the principles established in the case have been applied in many other situations. Lord Templeman said:

> It is, in my view, contrary to the ordinary experience of mankind…to say that a child or a young person remains in fact under the complete control of his parents until he attains the definite age of majority, now 18 in the United Kingdom, and that on attaining that age he suddenly acquires independence. In practice, most wise parents relax their control gradually as the child develops and encourage him or her to become increasingly independent. Moreover, the degree of parental control actually exercised over a particular child does in practice vary considerably according to his understanding and intelligence and it would, in my opinion, be unrealistic for the courts not to recognise these facts.[45]

He described a parent's legal right as 'a dwindling right which the courts will hesitate to enforce against the wishes of the child, and the more so the older he is'. His Lordship went on to say:

> once the rule of the parents' absolute authority over minor children is abandoned, the solution to the problem in this appeal can no longer be found by referring to rigid parental rights at any particular age. The solu-

---

42   s8 Family Law Reform Act 1969.

43   For full details see the Children's Legal Centre's (2008) publication *At What Age Can I…? A Guide to Age-based Legislation* updated by Joanne Claridge.

44   *Gillick* v. *West Norfolk and Wisbech Area Health Authority and Another* [1986] 1 AC 112 [1986] 1FLR 224 House of Lords.

45   Page 9 B.

tion depends upon a judgment of what is best for the welfare of the particular child. Nobody doubts...that in the overwhelming majority of cases the best judges of a child's welfare are his or her parents. Nor do I doubt that any important medical treatment of a child under 16 would normally only be carried out with the parents' approval. That is why it would and should be 'most unusual' for a doctor to advise a child without the knowledge and consent of the parents on contraceptive matters.[46]

The principles established by the Gillick case apply beyond medical issues to other fields, including social work, and can be of vital importance. If you believe a child needs a medical examination or an interview as part of a child protection investigation, can the child herself give consent? The problem is that there is no simple rule. You cannot say 'she is 12, therefore she can do x but cannot do y': the answer can be different for different children in the same situation, or for the same child in different situations. For example, an average 14-year-old might be able to consent to a medical examination; but what about a 14-year-old with a learning disability, or who is emotionally disturbed and vulnerable? An intelligent, well-balanced 15-year-old may be competent to decide most things, but is she able to take on board the issues involved and refuse to have medical treatment without which she will die? A child may be intellectually able, but emotional turmoil may impede her decision-making.

The question of competence involves the following elements:

- the child's age – as a rule of thumb, generally the older the child the more likely she is to be competent

- the child's level of understanding – what are the intellectual, cognitive and emotional characteristics of this child affecting her ability to understand the issues?

- the nature and implications of the decision in question – how complicated are the issues involved, and how far-reaching or long-lasting are its effects?

- the information available to the person being asked to decide

- the young person's freedom of choice – are there any feelings of pressure or loyalty affecting her capacity to make a truly voluntary decision?

---

46   Page 11 B.

It is important also to realise that competence or otherwise is not determined by the decision made. Making a bad choice does not of itself make a child incompetent – just as for adults, freedom of choice sometimes includes the right to make mistakes. There can be a tension between autonomy and welfare.

Points for practice

1. Whenever you work with a child, note any factors relevant to his competence. This will stand you in good stead if an issue arises at short notice.

2. Record your assessment of a child's competence and your reasons for it whenever you decide to act (or not act) on a child's consent, for example to an interview or medical examination.

Part 2
Private Law

Chapter 4

Section 8 Orders, Specific Issues and Prohibited Steps

Private law orders

We often talk of 'private law' or 'public law' cases under the Children Act 1989 (CA89). As the terms suggest, they involve private individuals or a public authority (particularly the local authority in care proceedings) respectively. Private law orders are grouped together in Part II CA89.

Where a child lives, who he sees and what steps are taken in his life (schooling, medical treatment, choice of surname) are aspects of parental responsibility (PR). Such decisions are taken day in, day out as part of normal family life. However, if there is a dispute, the court can step in and make those decisions for the child by using one or more of the four s8 orders:

1. residence order – determining who the child is to live with

2. contact order – an order directing the person with whom the child lives to allow contact with named person

3. specific issue order (SIO) – directing a particular exercise of PR

4. prohibited steps order (PSO) – forbidding a particular exercise of PR.

The court can also make a special guardianship order (SGO) conferring PR which is shared but can be exercised exclusively.[1]

---

1   s14A CA89, added to the CA89 by the Adoption and Children Act 2002.

Local authorities and private law orders

Private law proceedings involve individuals. The local authority is not a party to the proceedings, can never apply for or be awarded residence or contact orders,[2] and can only apply for a PSO or SIO with court leave, which would only be given in very unusual circumstances. Nevertheless, as a social worker you need to understand private law orders because:

- the local authority may be requested by the court to provide a welfare report in a s8 application[3]

- a report from the local authority is mandatory in a SGO application

- the court can make private law orders in public law proceedings (care proceedings, for example, could end in the making of a residence order or SGO). These options need to be considered when making recommendations to the court and addressed under paragraph (g) of the welfare checklist[4] (the range of powers available to the court)

- the court can make a family assistance order[5] requiring the local authority to assist a child or family involved in private law proceedings

- children caught up in private law disputes may be 'children in need' requiring support services from the local authority

- children in private law disputes may be at risk of suffering significant harm – there can be an overlap between private and public law. The local authority may be directed to prepare a report if the court suspects significant harm.[6]

s8 orders and care orders are incompatible; they cannot live alongside each other. If a care order is made, it automatically discharges previous s8 orders. If a residence order is made in respect of a child in care, the care order is discharged. Contact for children in care is dealt with under s34, not s8 CA89. Public and private law orders do not mix.

---

2   s9(2) CA89.
3   s7 CA89.
4   s1(3)(g) CA89.
5   s16 CA89.
6   s37 CA89 – see below for more information.

Grounds

No specific grounds are prescribed for a s8 order or SGO, so the court bases its decisions on the criteria set out in s1 CA89,[7] the child's welfare being the court's paramount consideration, and taking into account all the elements of the welfare checklist.

Who can apply?

Some people can apply as of right for s8 or SGOs; others need court permission. The court can also make these orders of its own motion with no application if it is in the child's best interests to do so.[8]

APPLICATION AS OF RIGHT

Any of the four s8 orders can be applied for by:

- the child's parent (including a father without PR)
- the child's legal guardian
- anyone who already has a residence order for the child.

In addition, residence or contact orders (but not SIOs or PSOs) can be applied for by:

- a parent's spouse or civil partner (current or ex) where the child is treated as a child of the family
- anyone with whom the child has lived for at least three years
- anyone who has the consent of:
  - ◦ the person with a residence order (if any)
  - ◦ or the local authority if the child is in care
  - ◦ or, in any other case, everyone with PR.

SGOs are not available to the child's parents. People entitled to apply are:

- the child's legal guardian
- anyone with a residence order

---

7   See Chapter 2 for more details.
8   s10(1)(b) and s14A(6)(b) CA89.

- anyone with whom the child has lived for three years
- anyone who has the consent of:
    - ° the person with a residence order (if any)
    - ° or the local authority if the child is in care
    - ° or, in any other case, everyone with PR.

Three months' prior notice has to be given of the intention to apply for a SGO.

4.1 – Child of the family

Yasmin's son, Zack, has always been treated by Yasmin and her civil partner Annie as their child. The couple separate acrimoniously. Zack stays with Yasmin, who refuses to allow him to see Annie. Annie has the automatic right to apply for a contact order as Zack was a child of the family. She could not, however, seek a SIO or PSO to control Yasmin's exercise of PR without court leave.

4.2 – Father without PR

Brigitte's father Christophe is French. He has no PR. He wants to pay for Brigitte to go to a bilingual school so she can learn French. Brigitte's mother wants her to go to the local school with her friends. As a parent, even without PR, Christophe has the right to apply for a SIO to determine where Brigitte should go to school.

APPLICATION WITH COURT PERMISSION

Anyone without the automatic right to apply for the order they want has to obtain court permission before they can proceed. There are two separate stages to the process. The first stage is seeking permission just to apply; only if this is granted does the case proceed to the application itself. The fact that permission has been granted does not mean that the application will be successful – the court could allow the application to be made but then refuse to make the order.

The child's welfare is not paramount in deciding whether to give permission to apply because this is not a question of the child's upbringing. Instead, the factors for the court to consider are listed in s10(9) CA89:

- the nature of the proposed application
- the applicant's connection with the child
- any risk that the application itself (whether or not the order sought is finally made) might disrupt the child's life to a harmful extent
- if the child is looked after by a local authority (in care or accommodated), the authority's plans for the child and the parents' wishes and feelings.

The court also considers the merits of the proposed action (without pre-judging it) – if there is no realistic prospect of success, leave will not be granted. However, the chances of success should not be dismissed lightly. In one case a grandmother wanted to apply for a residence order for her grandchild during care proceedings.[9] The judge refused, accepting the local authority's and Children's Guardian's views that the grandmother was too old and she had no realistic prospect of success. The grandmother appealed successfully. Her rights under Articles 6 (fair trial) and 8 (family life) of the European Convention on Human Rights meant that her application should not have been dismissed without proper enquiry. The Court of Appeal said that greater appreciation should be given to what grandparents had to offer.

CHILD APPLICANTS

A child has no automatic right to apply for his own s8 order. He has to seek the court's permission before he can even set out his case and there are specific provisions to apply. First, the court must be satisfied that the child has sufficient understanding to make the proposed application.[10] However, even then, permission does not automatically follow; the court still has a discretion. It will consider whether there is any realistic chance of the order sought being granted, and why the child, rather than someone else, is seeking to make the application.

4.3 – Child's application for leave

Georgina, aged 14, is estranged from her parents and lives with her friend's parents. She wants them to be able to sign consent forms for

---

9   *Re J (Leave to Issue Application for Residence Order)* [2003] 1FLR 114 Court of Appeal.
10   s10(8) CA89.

her and to have PR so she wants them to have a residence order. She must seek court leave as she has no automatic right to apply. Even assuming the court finds that she is competent to make the application, it may well refuse leave, considering that it is more appropriate for the carers to make their own application. Unless they have Georgina's parents' agreement, or Georgina has been there for at least three years, they too will need to seek leave to apply for a residence order.

If a child wants an order in respect of another child he is treated as any other applicant for court permission to apply.

4.4 – Child's application in respect of another child

Holly is in long term foster care. Her sister Ivy has been adopted. Holly wants to see Ivy, but Ivy's adoptive parents oppose contact, saying it would disrupt Ivy and threaten her security as Holly is still in contact with the girls' birth mother. Holly needs court leave before she can apply for a contact order. As she is the applicant, not the subject, of the proposed application, the court considers the factors in s10(9) CA89. The application itself (let alone any contact order) may disrupt Ivy directly by seeking her wishes and feelings and indirectly because of its effect on her adopters. The court may consider the prospects of success to be limited as if the application went ahead, Ivy's welfare, not Holly's, would be paramount. The court is likely to refuse Holly permission to make the application.

FOSTER CARERS

There are special provisions for local authority foster carers. Like anyone else, they can apply for residence or contact as of right if:

- the child has been living with them for at least three years
- the child is in care and the local authority agrees
- everyone with PR agrees.

Otherwise, they must seek court permission first but there is an extra hurdle for foster carers to prevent the plans for the child being impeded inappropriately.[11] Before they can even apply for court leave they must either:

- have the local authority's consent

---

11   s9(3) CA89.

- be relatives of the fostered child ('relative' means a grandparent, sibling or uncle/aunt)
- have had the child living with them for at least a year preceding their application.[12]

4.5 – Foster carer's application

Jane is a local authority foster carer. Baby Kevin is placed with her under a plan for him to move when a permanent placement is found. Carers are identified, but Jane has fallen in love with Kevin and wants to keep him. The local authority does not consider Jane a suitable long term carer for Kevin. Can Jane apply to court for a residence order or SGO to stop the local authority's plans? She has no automatic right to apply for an order because Kevin has lived with her for less than three years and the local authority does not support her application. She cannot even apply for leave if Kevin has been with her for less than a year. For a SGO she would have to give three months' notice of her intention even to apply for leave, giving the authority plenty of time to move Kevin. The answer is different if:

- Kevin is not in care but only accommodated and his birth parents support Jane, in which case she can apply for a residence order

- care proceedings take so long that Kevin has been in placement for over a year. Then Jane has the right to apply for leave and the court will look at the tests under s10(9) CA89 including the local authority's plans for Kevin and the risk of the application disrupting him (one factor being the delay a court application would cause)

- in care proceedings the court could make a residence order to Jane of its own motion.

BIRTH RELATIVES OF ADOPTED CHILDREN

An adoption order terminates all of the adopted child's previous legal relationships, so birth parents are no longer 'parents' in the eyes of the law and have no automatic right to apply for a s8 order. No one in the birth

---

12   This period was reduced from three years to one by the ACA.

family can apply for an order without court leave first. Except in unusual cases, they are likely to have an uphill struggle even to obtain court leave, let alone an order.[13]

Reports to court

s7 reports

A court dealing with a s8 CA89 application is often faced with warring parties and high emotions. Parties are often unrepresented, appearing in person without lawyers. The court may find itself short of objective information and in need of professional advice on the child's welfare. For that reason, s7(1) CA89 gives the court power when 'considering any question with respect to a child under this Act' to ask the Children and Family Court Advisory Support Service (CAFCASS) or the local authority for a report 'on such matters relating to the welfare of the child as are required to be dealt with in the report'. The court will probably ask the local authority rather than CAFCASS to report if the family is already known to the authority.

The court can request an oral or written report.[14] Once a direction is made, the authority has a statutory duty to provide a report.[15] It is important to note that, although s7 reports are most commonly sought in residence and contact disputes, the court's power goes further than that and could apply to other cases such as a PR application under s4 CA89 or an application for leave to apply for a s8 order, especially in a case where the proposed applicant is a child.

A welfare report can include hearsay (that is, second-hand information) and opinion evidence and the court can take this into account as long as it is relevant.[16] Indeed, the court will often be grateful for a well-informed professional opinion to assist it in determining the child's best interests.

The order is likely to specify exactly what topics the court wants to be addressed in each case. These issues should be carefully addressed, but the reporter should also cover anything else relevant to the child's welfare which comes to light in the course of enquiries. Rather than simply leaving

---

13 See Chapter 16 for more on post-adoption contact.
14 s7(3) CA89.
15 s7(5) CA89.
16 s7(4) CA89.

any new matter to appear in the report, it may be appropriate to ask the court for further directions, perhaps to broaden the scope of enquiries or order the parties to file further evidence.

4.6 – New information

Lily's father has applied for contact. The court requests a s7 report on Lily's wishes and feelings about contact. The social worker goes to see Lily and becomes aware that Lily's mother apparently has a serious alcohol problem which has not previously been mentioned. It would be wholly wrong not to bring this swiftly to the court's attention.

s37 reports

s37 CA89 reports are completely different from s7 reports. The court only has power to direct a s37 report when 'it appears that it may be appropriate for a care or supervision order to be made'. This section is therefore a way for the court to refer possible abuse or neglect to the local authority for investigation.

The report must set out whether the local authority intends to apply for a care or supervision order, provide services or assistance or take other action. A s37 order is not made lightly, so if the local authority decides not to take proceedings, the report must give reasons for the decision and details of what the authority proposes to do for the child and family instead.[17] If it is really concerned about the child's welfare, the court can even make an interim care order when it issues the s37 direction and, if it does so (or considers doing so), it also appoints a Children's Guardian to represent the child. Ultimately, however, the court cannot force the authority to commence care proceedings.

4.7 – s7 report

Laurence applies for a residence order in respect of Molly who currently lives with his ex-partner Nigel. Laurence says Molly wants to come to live with him; Nigel says she wants to stay with him.

---

17   s37(3) CA89.

This is a classic case for a s7 report. The court needs independent assistance to understand Molly's true wishes and feelings (it is quite possible that Molly is trying to keep both men happy by telling each that she wants to be with him).

4.8 – s37 report

Oliver lives with his mother Pauline and her partner Quentin. Pauline has refused all contact between Oliver and his father Rodney, claiming that Oliver has disclosed sexual abuse by Rodney. Rodney seeks a residence order, denies the allegations and says that Quentin is a known paedophile.

This is not a straightforward residence dispute. The allegations and counter-allegations raise child protection concerns. If the court thinks that a care or supervision order could be needed a s37 direction is appropriate.

Local authority's reporting role

When the local authority reports to court (under s7 or s37 CA89) it is not a party to the proceedings – it is neither making nor defending an application – its role is to provide impartial expert advice to the court. Only parties to the proceedings are entitled to legal representation, so the social worker who compiles the report does not have a lawyer at court. However, she should be able to obtain legal advice from her legal department and should not have to go to court unsupported. Unfortunately, the least experienced social workers are often asked to compile s7 reports, sometimes in cases where emotions between the parties are running high and where there are complex welfare issues. They can feel badgered by lawyers on both sides without having their own lawyer to protect them. s7 and s37 reports should be given proper priority within Children's Services Departments.

Status of reports to court

The court must take the report into account, although it is not bound to follow its recommendations – the court decides the case, not the person who compiles the welfare report, but, if it reaches a different conclusion, the court must give its reasons for doing so.

Family assistance orders

In family proceedings, the court has power to make a family assistance order (FAO) whether or not it makes any other sort of order.[18] CAFCASS or the local authority can be directed to provide a worker to advise, assist and befriend anyone named in the order, who may be:

- a parent or guardian of the child
- anyone the child is living with
- anyone who has an order for contact with the child
- the child himself.

Until 1 October 2007 there had to be exceptional circumstances to justify making a FAO, but that requirement was removed.[19] The maximum duration for a FAO was also extended from 6 to 12 months.

FAOs can be allied to contact orders, for example to secure supervision of contact. The court can direct the CAFCASS officer or social worker involved to give advice and assistance about establishing, improving and maintaining contact. It can also require the officer to report to the court on any matters relating to any s8 order in force at the same time as the FAO, including whether the order should be varied or discharged.

If a CAFCASS officer is implementing a FAO, and considers that a child is at risk of harm, she should make a risk assessment and can apply to the court to revive the previous proceedings, for the court to consider the risk assessment and give directions. This applies only to CAFCASS officers because a local authority social worker does not need a special provision: if she is concerned that children subject to a FAO may be at risk, she can simply invoke the local authority's child protection powers.[20]

Prohibited steps and specific issue orders

These orders are mirror images of each other. Their names are self-explanatory: a prohibited steps order (PSO) prevents a particular step from being taken whereas a specific issue order (SIO) directs one. They are to be used

---

18   s16 CA89.
19   CA89 as amended by the Children and Adoption Act 2006.
20   See Chapter 9 for further details.

for matters other than a child's residence or contact,[21] which have their own specially designed s8 orders.

The range of issues covered by these orders is as wide as the spectrum of decisions taken in children's lives – education, health, religion, surnames – all can be the subject of court action if there is a dispute. Increasingly, reported cases reveal the courts struggling to find the right way forward where there is a clash of cultures or beliefs between the child's parents. As always under s8, the court's concern is the child's welfare which is paramount. It considers the factors set out in the welfare checklist to help determine where the child's best interests lie.[22]

However much the court may wish to encourage parents to take responsibility and reach agreement, ultimately it is the court's job to make a decision. In one case about education, the latest bitter dispute between the divorced parents of two children, the judge directed that the mother should make future decisions about schooling, following consultation with the father. The Court of Appeal said that, while the judge had the best possible motives, he had effectively failed to adjudicate.[23] The parents had a right to judicial determination of the question and the court could not abdicate its responsibility.

Prohibited steps orders

> s8(1) CA89…'a prohibited steps order' means an order that no step which could be taken by a parent in meeting his parental responsibility for a child, and which is of a kind specified in the order, shall be taken by any person without the consent of the court.

Although the section refers to steps which are an exercise of PR, the order can prevent that action by 'any person', so these orders are not only addressed to parents. A PSO can be made, for instance, to prevent any named person from seeking contact with a child. In appropriate cases, this can be made in conjunction with a 'no contact' order addressed to the child's carer.

---

21   s9(5) CA89.
22   s1(3) CA89 – see Chapter 2.
23   *Re P (Parental Dispute: Judicial Determination)* [2002] EWCA Civ 1627 [2003] 1FLR 286 Court of Appeal.

4.9 – PSO to stop contact

Rosie's mother's ex-boyfriend Steve is violent. The court wants to stop Steve having contact with Rosie. A no contact order can stop Rosie's mother from allowing Steve to have contact, but it is not addressed to Steve. A PSO, however, can order Steve not to seek any contact with Rosie.

PSOs have been used to address many and varied issues including:

- preventing a child being taken out of the country
- preventing a person arranging for a child to appear in a TV programme
- stopping a parent from changing a child's school
- preventing a change of surname
- barring certain elective surgery.

However, PSOs must relate to some sort of exercise of PR so cannot deal with aspects of an adult's own life rather than an action towards a child. Thus a PSO cannot be used to exclude someone from the family home;[24] instead, an application should be made for a Family Law Act 1996 injunction.

Specific issue orders

s8(1) CA89…'a specific issue order' means an order giving directions for the purpose of determining a specific question which has arisen, or which may arise, in connection with any aspect of parental responsibility for a child.

Like PSOs, SIOs cover the whole range of issues and can see the courts grappling with complex and delicate matters, trying to find where the child's best interests lie.

---

24   *D* v. *D* [1996] 2FLR 273 Court of Appeal.

RELIGION

In *Re J* first the High Court then the Court of Appeal were faced with questions arising from the separation of a couple from very different backgrounds with contradictory plans for their five-year-old son.[25] The Muslim father, opposed by the non-Muslim mother with whom the boy lived, first sought an order that the boy should be brought up as a Muslim.

Choosing a child's religion is an aspect of PR, so the court has the power to order that a child should be brought up in a particular religion. This could even be a different religion from that of the resident parent although that would be highly exceptional. In this case, the reality was that the child was not brought up in Muslim circles, and the father himself did not actively practise his religion or mix in Muslim circles. The court decided that the father could provide knowledge of his religion on contact visits, so declined to make the order.

Another case concerned the children of a Muslim mother and Hindu father.[26] After their separation, the mother wanted to bring the children up as Muslims, saying that they would otherwise be excluded from their community. These children knew about their dual heritage and until their parents' separation had been involved in the practice of both religions. Baron J said that children of mixed heritage should be able to choose for themselves which religion to follow and should be allowed to have the best of both worlds. To present these children to the world as anything other than children of mixed heritage would be to practise an 'impermissible deception'.

CIRCUMCISION

The father in the *Re J* case (above) also applied for an order that the boy should be circumcised. This was normal practice in the father's culture, but was vigorously opposed by the mother. Interestingly, this was the first case ever to examine whether ritual (as opposed to medical) circumcision of boys was lawful at all.[27] The High Court – later backed by the Court of Appeal – found that ritual circumcision with parental consent is lawful, but in the case of disagreement, in spite of s2(7) CA89, it is not a decision

---

25 *Re J (Specific Issue Order: Muslim Upbringing & Circumcision)* [1999] 2FLR 678 High Court and *Re J (Specific Issue Orders: Child's Religious Upbringing and Circumcision)* [2000] 1FLR 571 Court of Appeal.

26 *Re S (SIO: Religion)* [2005] EWHC 2769 (Fam) High Court.

27 Female circumcision is illegal under the Prohibition of Female Circumcision Act 1985.

to be made by one parent alone and any disputes should be referred to the High Court.

Carefully balancing all of the arguments and the facts of the case, the judge decided not to make a SIO because the child was experiencing a secular upbringing in England, not mixing in circles where circumcision was the norm, the intervention was irreversible, painful and involved some physical and psychological risk and, importantly, the mother would be unable to present it positively to the child. Wall J said 'it is a strong thing to impose a medically unnecessary surgical intervention on a resident parent who is opposed to it'.[28]

IMMUNISATIONS

However, the resident parent does not always have the final say, even in the case of non-essential and invasive treatment. In *Re C* the court confirmed that parents have equal rights before the court.[29] The resident parent does not have greater rights than the separated parent, who is entitled to be consulted about major decisions in the child's life.[30]

In that case, applications were made by two fathers for orders that their children should have the MMR immunisation. Both mothers, who had residence orders, opposed the applications. The High Court judge (later upheld by the Court of Appeal) heard expert evidence and decided that the immunisations were in the children's best interests. The benefits outweighed the risks, including the mothers' emotional distress which, it was argued, would impact on the children.

The court stressed this was not a general approval of immunisation. Refusing to have a child immunised is a legitimate exercise of PR where both parents agree. But if they disagree, neither parent can decide alone, notwithstanding s2(7) CA89, and the court should decide.

TELLING CHILDREN THEIR ORIGINS

In one case, the mother of eight-year-old twins and her partner (who the twins thought was their father) did not want the children to be told about

---

28   *Re J*, page 700C at paragraph 4 (see note 25 above).

29   *Re C (Welfare of Child: Immunisation)* [2003] 2FLR 1054 (High Court) and 1095 (Court of Appeal).

30   *Re C*, paragraph 367 (see note 29 above).

their true paternity.[31] The Court of Appeal confirmed that the family courts are entitled to take responsibility for this decision in the event of adult dispute and directed that the children should be told the truth. In a similar case, DNA testing was ordered to determine whether twins were the product of an extra-marital affair or the children of the mother's husband.[32] The Court of Appeal said that there are few cases where the interests of children are served by the suppression of the truth.

EDUCATION

Disputes about the choice of schools can also be the subject of SIO applications. One case centred on whether a child should have a voice test, a necessary preliminary to going to the cathedral school the father wanted him to attend, contrary to the mother's wishes.[33] The court ordered that the voice test should go ahead, without pre-judging the decision on schooling if the test proved successful.

POLICE INTERVIEWS OF CHILD WITNESSES

If police want to interview witnesses who are too young to consent for themselves, they usually need parental agreement. In one case seven-year-old twins were the only eye witnesses when their 16-year-old brother shot dead their 12-year-old sister.[34] Their mother, the only person with PR, declined consent for the police to interview the twins, arguing it would have a detrimental effect on them. In fact, psychiatric evidence was that it would be beneficial for them to speak and they should be interviewed. The police (supported by CAFCASS and the local authority) applied for leave to seek an order giving them permission to interview the children.

Ryder J decided that giving or withholding permission for a police interview is an aspect of PR so it can be controlled by the court by a SIO (or by using the High Court's inherent jurisdiction). Interestingly, he decided that in this case the child's welfare was not paramount. Normally, s8 orders

---

31 *Re F (Children: Declaration of Paternity)* [2007] EWCA Civ 873 Court of Appeal.
32 *Re H and A (Paternity: Blood Tests)* [2002] EWCA Civ 383 [2002] 1FLR 1145 Court of Appeal.
33 *M v. M (SIO: Choice of School)* [2007] EWHC 2769 (Fam) [2007] 1FLR 251 High Court.
34 *Chief Constable of Greater Manchester v. KI and KW (by their Children's Guardian, CAFCASS Legal) and PN* [2007] EWHC 1837 (Fam) High Court.

are governed by s1 CA89 because s8 applications usually concern a child's 'upbringing'. Here, the judge found that giving evidence to the police is not just a question of upbringing but part of the role of a citizen, bringing into play considerations of the rights of others, including the general public interest in the investigation of possible crimes. This was a case in which a balancing exercise had to be undertaken, weighing up the children's welfare against wider considerations. In the event, there was no conflict – the public interest required an interview but it was also the best thing for the children who needed to talk. The distress they suffered stemmed from the terrible event they had witnessed, not being interviewed about it. The judge gave the police leave to apply for a SIO, but no order was needed as the mother backed down and gave her consent.

NAMES

The issue of children's names is an emotive one. Choosing a child's name is one of the first steps taken by new parents in exercising their PR, and there is a statutory duty to register the birth. Names signal where a child belongs, signify family connections and can be an integral part of a child's identity, reflecting aspects of the child's heritage, religion or ethnic background. Changing the name by which a child is known (the name on the Register of Births cannot be changed) can give rise to bitter disputes which find their way into the courts.

If there is a residence order in force, a child's surname cannot be changed without written consent of everyone with PR or a court order.[35] There is no statutory provision about what happens if there is no residence order, but in spite of s2(7) CA89, the High Court decided that this is such a significant decision that all those with PR must agree.[36]

If there is a dispute, the matter can be brought to court under s13 CA89 if there is a residence order or, if not, in an application for a SIO (to authorise a change of name) or PSO (to prevent a change of name). As a father without PR has the right to apply for any s8 CA89 order, somewhat paradoxically, he can go to court about a change of name even though his lack of PR means he has no right to choose the child's name in the first place.

---

35   s13(1) CA89.
36   *Re PC (Change of Surname)* [1997] 2FLR 730 High Court.

The House of Lords was clear that a child's name is a very serious and profound issue, whatever the child's age.[37] The child's welfare is the court's paramount consideration, looking not just at the present situation but also future implications. Each case must be decided on its own facts and circumstances.

Courts are not generally impressed by an argument that a child's name should be changed to be the same as the person caring for him or siblings, or by any emotional or proprietorial claiming of parental rights through a surname. The length of time a child has used a particular name and practical difficulties of change may be significant factors.

A case in which a change was permitted was where a Bangladeshi Muslim mother had married an Indian Sikh against her family's wishes.[38] When the marriage broke down, the mother was allowed to change her son's name from a Sikh name to a Muslim one so that she and her son would be accepted back into her Bangladeshi community.

s8 and human rights

When the court decides what should happen to a child contrary to the parents' wishes, is this not a breach of their human rights? In the immunisation case, the High Court recognised that ordering an exercise of PR against a parent's wishes is indeed a breach but, because the Article 8 right to respect for family life is a qualified right, breaches can be justified provided they are in accordance with the law, necessary for the protection of the interests of children and the interference with the right is proportionate to the need.

Points for practice

1. s8 orders should be used flexibly (singly or in combination) to meet the needs of any case. Consider all the options in any court case (private or public law).

2. Work through the welfare checklist step by step to keep your focus on the child's welfare, not the adults' emotions and demands.

3. Never overlook human rights issues. Always address Article 8.

---

37   *Dawson* v. *Wearmouth* [1999] 1FLR 1167 House of Lords.
38   *Re S (Change of Names: Cultural Factors)* [2001] 2FLR 1005 High Court.

Chapter 5

Residence and Special Guardianship

Residence orders

> s8(1) CA89 ...'a residence order' means an order settling the arrangements to be made as to the person with whom a child is to live.

Grounds

There are no specific grounds to be proven for any of the orders under s8 Children Act 1989 (CA89). A child's residence is clearly a question concerning his upbringing, so s1 CA89 applies in an application for a residence order (RO). The child's welfare is paramount and the court uses the welfare checklist[1] to help analyse the case.

Effect of a residence order

The main function of a RO is to decide who a child lives with, so these orders often follow a relationship breakdown. Generally, the court's concern is who the child lives with, not where. However, in exceptional cases the court can attach a condition to a RO prescribing the area where the child is to live.[2] This obviously constitutes a restriction on the rights of

---

1   s1(3) CA89.
2   s11(7) CA89.

the person with residence, so is not lightly done. For example, the mother of a child with Down's syndrome and heart problems was not allowed to move her daughter to Cornwall, due to the child's medical problems, her limited understanding and the difficulties of maintaining contact if the family moved.[3] In another case, the mother's plan to move to Newcastle was designed to thwart the father's contact so the court imposed a condition requiring the child to remain within an area around London.[4]

Parental responsibility

It makes sense that those looking after a child should have the power and responsibility to make decisions for him – they need parental responsibility (PR). For this reason, a RO confers PR on the person awarded residence for the duration of the RO.

---

s12(2) CA89 Where the court makes a residence order in favour of any person who is not the parent or guardian of the child concerned that person shall have parental responsibility for the child while the residence order is in force.

5.1 – PR for grandparents

Tammy's parents cannot care for her, so she lives with her grandparents, with her parents' blessing. Although everyone is in agreement, and the parents can delegate PR to the grandparents, it makes sense for them to have PR in their own right. They can apply for a RO without court leave with the parents' consent. The court considers s1 CA89 including the 'no order' principle in s1(5) CA89. Although there is no dispute about where Tammy lives, the fact that an order will give the grandparents PR is a good reason to make the order.[5] Tammy now has four people with PR: her parents and her grandparents.

---

3   *Re S (A Child) (Residence Order: Condition) (No. 2)* [2002] EWCA Civ 1795 [2004] 1FLR 651 Court of Appeal.

4   *B v. B (Residence: Condition Limiting Geographic Area)* [2004] 2FLR 979 High Court.

5   This was the situation in *B v. B (A Minor) (Residence Order)* [1992] 2FLR 327 High Court.

If a father who does not already have PR obtains a RO, the court must make a PR order under s4 CA89 at the same time.[6] His PR then lasts until the child turns 18, even if the RO is discharged earlier.

Limits on PR

The PR obtained under a RO is shared with everyone else who has PR and, other than the question of residence, there is no priority between them. This is very different from a special guardianship order (SGO), where the special guardian can exercise PR exclusively.[7]

When a RO is in force, the child's name cannot be changed nor can the child be taken out of the UK for more than a month without either the consent of everyone with PR or the court's permission.[8]

A RO confers PR but does not make the person the child lives with a 'parent', so it does not give power to take decisions which are restricted to parents, such as consenting to adoption or appointing a guardian for the child.

Shared residence

The court can make a RO to more than one person at a time. This is obviously sensible if a child is living with a couple who would not otherwise have PR. In scenario 5.1 it would make no sense to give a RO to one or other of the grandparents – the child lives with both, so there should be a joint RO.

5.2 – Same sex partners

Uta has a baby, Victoria. Uta and her partner Wendy plan to bring Victoria up together. Uta and Wendy are not in a registered civil partnership, so Wendy cannot seek a step-parent PR agreement or order. Instead, she seeks a RO. The court makes a joint RO, recognising that Victoria is to live with both partners together, and conferring PR on Wendy, which she would not otherwise have.[9]

---

6   s12(1) CA89.
7   For a summary of differences between residence, special guardianship and adoption see Appendix 2.
8   s13 CA89.
9   The facts of this scenario mirror the case of *Re C (A Minor) (Residence Order: Lesbian Co-parents)* [1994] Fam Law 468 High Court.

Joint ROs can be made even where a couple has separated, if this reflects the reality of the situation better than residence to one ex-partner and contact to the other. There may be a psychological benefit to the child from knowing that he lives with both parents even though they live apart, rather than living with one and just seeing the other. If necessary, the court can add a condition to the order specifying how a child's time is to be split between the two households.[10] A joint RO may be particularly appropriate for a separated couple if it allows one ex-partner to have PR s/he would not otherwise have.

5.3 – Half-siblings

Xavier and his wife separate, agreeing that the two children of the family, Yvonne and Zachary, will share their time between their mother and Xavier. Xavier has always treated the two children equally but Yvonne is not his biological child so he has PR only for Zachary. Xavier has a right to apply for a RO in respect of both children (he is Zachary's father and Yvonne is treated as a child of the family). The court decides that a joint RO reflects the position better than a RO to one partner and contact to the other. An order is better for the children than no order as the RO gives Xavier PR for Yvonne so the children have a more equal status.[11]

Duration of residence orders

Most s8 orders do not last beyond the child's sixteenth birthday unless there are exceptional circumstances. However, the court can make a RO in favour of a non-parent until the child reaches the age of 18 without the need for the circumstances to be exceptional.[12] This power is not necessary for a RO to a parent as his/her PR already lasts to 18.

Variation and discharge

The court can vary or discharge a RO, like any other s8 order. An application for variation or discharge is made under s8(2) CA89 and is governed

---

10   s11(4) CA89.

11   The facts of this scenario mirror the case *Re H (Shared Residence: Parental Responsibility)* [1995] 2FLR 883 Court of Appeal.

12   By virtue of an amendment to CA89 introduced by the Adoption and Children Act 2002.

by s1 CA89 principles, so the question is whether it is in the child's best interests to alter or end the arrangements made by the original order.

Certain people (including the child's parents) can apply as of right to vary or discharge a RO. This is not, therefore, a permanent order, and can be insecure as ongoing disagreements can repeatedly be brought back to court. This is one of the key differences between ROs and SGOs, and, to an even greater extent, between ROs and adoption.[13] In the case of actual or feared repeated applications, or where there is a need for added security, the court can consider making an order under s91(14) CA89 limiting future applications for variation or discharge.[14]

Local authority support

The local authority does not have a duty to support anyone with a RO. It has a discretionary power (the exercise of which is often subject to a means test) to give financial support towards the cost of the child's accommodation and maintenance, unless the person with the RO is one of the child's parents or a parent's spouse/civil partner.[15] In reality, local authorities are only likely to allocate scarce resources to people with ROs if the RO is a way to take the child out of care.

There are no specific provisions for other types of service or support for those with residence orders; they fall simply within the authority's general duties under s17 CA89.[16] This is in contrast to SGOs and adoption where the right to support is much more extensive.

Special guardianship orders

Special guardianship orders (SGOs) were added into the CA89 to provide another weapon in the court's armoury, an order which is stronger than a RO, but not as drastic as adoption.[17]

---

13   See the 'at a glance' chart highlighting the difference between ROs, SGOs and adoption in Appendix 2.

14   See Chapter 2 for more details on s91(14) CA89.

15   Schedule 1 paragraph 15 CA89.

16   See Chapter 7 for more details.

17   s14A–G CA89, inserted into the CA89 by the Adoption and Children Act 2002.

What is so special?

Two key features of SGOs mark them out from ROs, making them more attractive to people looking after children who are not their own. These are:

1. greater autonomy in exercising PR

2. greater security.

PARENTAL RESPONSIBILITY

A special guardian (SG) obtains PR. Others with PR do not lose it (as they do if an adoption order is made) but it is not an equal partnership. The SG can act totally independently; effectively he has autonomy. This includes deciding who the child should live with as, unlike a RO, a SGO does not dictate a child's residence.

> s14C(1)(b) CA89 Subject to any other order in force with respect to the child under this Act, a special guardian is entitled to exercise parental responsibility to the exclusion of any other person with parental responsibility for the child (apart from another special guardian).

Interestingly, the SG has more power to override the parents than a local authority with a care order. Unlike the local authority, the SG's power to overrule parents is not dependent on being able to show it is necessary to do so for the child's welfare.

There are some limits on the SG's powers. He cannot change the child's surname or take him out of the UK for more than three months without either the consent of all those with PR or court permission, nor is he a 'parent', so he cannot agree to the child's adoption or appoint a guardian.

SECURITY

SGOs have an element of security built in. They are not irrevocable (as adoption orders are) but neither are they subject to parents' automatic right to apply for variation or discharge like ROs. The child's parents cannot apply to revoke a SGO without showing the court at a preliminary hearing that there has been a significant change in circumstances.[18] When a SGO is in force, no one can apply for a RO without court leave,[19] not even birth parents and others who normally have an automatic right to apply for s8 orders. This means that SGs and children subject to a SGO are freed from the prospect of repeated court applications to change the child's residence. There is no restriction on other applications under s8 CA89, although this could be added if appropriate by making an order under s91(14) CA89.

Who can apply?

SGOs differ from ROs in the important respect that the child's parents cannot apply.[20] The philosophy of the CA89 is that parenthood is for life. Much as one parent might like to be able to exercise PR to the exclusion of the other, they cannot do so and must find a way to share PR.

People with an automatic right to apply for a SGO (excluding a parent in each case) are:

- a child's guardian

- anyone with a RO

- anyone with whom the child has lived for at least three years

- anyone with the consent of either:

  ° anyone with a RO

  ° the local authority if the child is in care

  ° everyone with PR

- a local authority foster carer with whom the child has lived for at least a year.

Other people can only apply with court leave. The court can also make a SGO if it thinks it appropriate even if no one has applied.[21] The court could therefore make a SGO in an application for a s8 order, care order or adoption order.

---

18   s14D CA89.
19   s10(7A) CA89.
20   s14A CA89.
21   s14A(6)(b) CA89.

Grounds

There are no specific grounds set out in the Act so the court must consider s1 CA89. The child's welfare is paramount, and the elements in the welfare checklist set out in s1(3) CA89 must be considered.

The local authority's role

SGOs are not a local authority placement, even though they may be seen as a way of achieving permanence for children who are in care, sometimes as an alternative to adoption. Unlike adoption, the local authority does not screen or select applicants, approve children for placement or match applicants and children with each other.

Anyone seeking a SGO must give the local authority three months' written notice of his intention to apply. If he needs court leave, he must obtain that first before giving notice. The authority must then investigate the application and prepare a thorough report for the court. The court cannot make a SGO without a report from the local authority,[22] although if most of the information is already before the court (for example in reports for care proceedings), the authority does not have to duplicate effort by filing a whole new report; instead, the information can be cross-referenced.[23]

The required contents of the report are set out in detail in regulations,[24] and include:

- full details of the child

- full details of his family

- wishes and feelings of the child and his family

- full details of the proposed SG including:

  ° his/her health

  ° an assessment of his/her capacity as a carer

  ° a report of interviews with three referees

- an analysis of the implications of a SGO for:

---

22   s14A(11) CA89.

23   *Re S (Adoption or Special Guardianship Order) (No. 2)* [2007] EWCA Civ 90 [2007] 1FLR 855 Court of Appeal.

24   Special Guardianship Regulations 2005 SI 2005/1109, available at www.opsi.gov.uk/si/si2005/20051109.htm, accessed 11 August 2008.

- ° the child
- ° his parent(s)
- ° the prospective SG
- ° any other relevant person
- an assessment of the relative merits of a SGO and any other order under CA89 or the Adoption and Children Act 2002
- a recommendation as to whether:
  - ° a SGO or any other order should be made
  - ° there should be contact arrangements.

Other orders

Before making a SGO, the court must consider whether to make a contact order under s8 CA89 at the same time and whether to discharge or vary any existing CA89 order. The court can also give leave for the child to be known by a new surname.[25]

SGOs and adoption

Adoption is a life-long order which changes the child's whole identity, terminating all pre-existing legal relationships, terminating birth parents' PR and making the child in all respects a member of the adoptive family, including an automatic change of name.[26] SGOs do none of these things: they simply add another person with a powerful version of PR.

Local authority support for special guardians

The idea of SGOs as a long term provision for children is reflected in the duty placed on local authorities to provide support services for SGs.[27] On request, the authority must assess the need for services, report on the outcome of the assessment and draw up a package of support which may

---

25   s14B(2)(a) CA89.
26   See Chapters 15 and 16 for more details on adoption.
27   Details are set out in the Special Guardianship Regulations 2005 SI 2005/1109 (see note 24 above).

include counselling, advice and information as well as financial support, respite care and meeting children's therapeutic needs. The precise details of the support to be provided are a matter for the local authority's discretion. These support provisions closely resemble those for adopters and are considerably stronger than the discretionary provisions for financial support of non-parents with ROs.

The choice of orders

The first step is to be clear which orders are available (whether on application or of the court's own motion). Then the needs of the case should be considered against the characteristics of the possible orders to find which best fits the child's best interests. The child's welfare is paramount and there are no presumptions one way or the other as to which order should be made in any particular case.

Where does the principle of minimum intervention or proportionality fit in? Clearly a RO is less intrusive than a SGO, which in turn is far less intrusive than an adoption order. However, this does not mean that a RO should automatically be preferred; the key point to remember is that the child's welfare comes first. Only then, if there is a choice of orders which might be equally applicable, is it appropriate to choose the less interventionist approach.

Messages from case law

Although SGOs are still in their infancy, some cases have arisen illustrating some of the factors the courts take into account particularly in choosing between SGOs and adoption.

In *Re S* the question was whether, assuming S could not return to her mother, she should stay with her foster mother under a SGO or adoption order.[28] The significant factors included:

- the mother had made a remarkable change in her life since the care proceedings began

- the relationship between the mother and the foster mother was excellent, each recognising the other's significance to S

---

28   *Re S (Special Guardianship Order)* [2007] EWCA Civ 54 [2007] 1FLR 819 Court of Appeal.

- there was a well-established pattern of contact
- S herself wanted to preserve her relationship with both, by living with the foster mother and seeing her mother regularly.

The court made a SGO with a s91(14) CA89 order to add extra security by preventing further applications without court leave. A SGO matched S's needs better than adoption.

Re AJ concerned a boy who had been living with his aunt and uncle since he was six months old.[29] The care plan was for him to remain there permanently. Significant factors included:

- the parents were unreliable and had not maintained regular contact
- there was a substantial possibility that the mother would seek the child's return to her at some stage
- the aunt and uncle did not feel that a SGO would be strong enough to control the parents, who they saw as unpredictable and difficult
- the aunt and uncle were committed to promoting contact and ensuring AJ was aware of his identity.

The court made an adoption order. This was in spite of arguments that in a family placement adoption distorts family relationships (aunt becomes mother; mother becomes aunt). The Court of Appeal did not consider this to be a major or negative distortion. It was clear that there was no intention to use the change in legal relationships to conceal his true origins from the child.

In Re M-J, the boy was placed with his mother's half-sister who wanted to adopt him, whereas his mother argued that (if he could not return to her) a SGO should be made.[30] Factors included the following:

- the half-sister was very anxious and insecure about the mother's application to have M-J returned to her
- the mother never accepted that the placement would be permanent and always hoped for his return
- the child was securely attached to his aunt

---

29   Re AJ (Special Guardianship Order) [2007] EWCA Civ 55 [2007] 1FLR 507 Court of Appeal.
30   Re M-J (Special Guardianship Order) [2007] EWCA Civ 56 [2007] 1FLR 691 Court of Appeal.

- the mother had made considerable progress in addressing her own problems.

The court made an adoption order. The need for total security of the placement was a key factor.

Re L involved a girl whose parents had problems of drug addiction and domestic violence and who lived with her grandparents from the age of three months.[31] They wanted to adopt her. The local authority was concerned about the grandparents' reluctance to be clear with the child about who her parents were so favoured a SGO. The grandparents accepted this but wanted leave to change the child's surname. The court refused permission, a decision upheld by the Court of Appeal. Ward LJ said:[32]

> Sympathetic though I am to their predicament, their concerns overlook the value of the lesson we are all taught at our mother's knee: honesty is the best policy. This family must honestly face up to its fractured constitution. E must learn to live with the fact that she is being brought up by her grandparents.

In *S* v. *B* grandparents had cared for the child (now aged six) since the age of six months.[33] Everyone agreed on permanent placement with them and need to remove the child from the care system. The High Court made a package of orders: a SGO, a PSO preventing parental contact, an order under s91(14) CA89 and order giving leave for child to be known by the grandparents' surname. In explaining his thinking, Hedley J said:[34]

> Given that in a case such as this adoption would significantly skew otherwise perfectly comprehensible and not unusual family relationships and structures, this is a case where, in my judgment, the court should prefer special guardianship unless special guardianship really cannot meet the needs of the child concerned bearing in mind that the child's welfare will be the court's paramount consideration.

He continued:

> One purpose of adoption is of course to give lifelong status to carers where otherwise it would not exist. In a familial placement that is not necessary because family status exists for life in any event. That is not to

---

31   *Re L (Special Guardianship: Surname)* [2007] EWCA Civ 196 [2007] 2FLR 50 Court of Appeal.

32   *Re L*, paragraph 39 (see note 31 above).

33   *S* v. *B and Newport City Council; Re K* [2007] 1FLR 1116 High Court.

34   *S* v. *B*, paragraphs 21–23 (see note 33 above).

say that a familial placement may never be secured by adoption... I am, however, satisfied that this is not such a case. In my judgment this is one of those cases for which special guardianship was specifically designed, as it permits familial carers, who are not parents, to have all the practical authority and standing of parents, whilst leaving intact real and readily comprehensible relationships within the family. It avoids K...having to learn that apparent relationships are not the real ones, without in any way restricting the role of the maternal grandparents effectively to parent K as the sole exercisers of parental responsibility.

Points for practice

1. In any court case, make a list of the possible orders available to the court. Keep the key characteristics of each order clearly in mind.

2. Always start with an analysis of the child's needs and find the order which best fits the case.

3. List advantages and disadvantages for each possibility to help find the most suitable option.

4. Remember other s8 CA89 orders and/or a s91(14) CA89 order can be added – a package of orders might be appropriate.

Chapter 6

Contact

Contact orders

> s8(1) CA89 ...'a contact order' means an order requiring the person
> with whom a child lives, or is to live, to allow the child to visit or stay
> with the person named in the order, or for that person and the child
> otherwise to have contact with each other.

Contact orders under s8 Children Act 1989 (CA89) can be made together
with a residence order, special guardianship order or adoption order and
in combination with prohibited steps orders and specific issue orders. They
are not compatible with care orders; contact for children in care falls under
s34 CA89.

Although contact disputes often arise from relationship breakdown,
contact is not just an issue for separating partners – a child may also need
contact with his grandparents, siblings, extended family members or others. Non-parents usually need court leave before they can make an application but parents, including fathers without parental responsibility (PR),
have the automatic right to apply. Contact gives rise to some of the most
harmful, long-running and bitter disputes before the court.

What is contact?

Contact is a wider concept than access. Not limited to face to face visits, it can include staying contact, telephone calls, letters/emails, cards and presents, and the provision of information through school and other reports. It can be as direct, open and flexible or as indirect, controlled and limited as circumstances require.

Contact orders can be expressed in broad terms leaving the parties to make their own arrangements or, if necessary, can be prescriptive, even setting out the precise day, time, length and venue of visits, dictating arrangements for handing the child over and setting pre-conditions before contact can occur. An order can provide for contact to build up gradually over time, or an interim contact order can be made, allowing the situation to be reviewed and revised as necessary. The court can use its power under s11(7) CA89 to attach whatever conditions to the order as are necessary to make it work.

The term 'contact order' is also wide enough to include a 'no contact order', stating that the child's carer is not to allow contact between the child and a named person, although such orders are rare.

6.1 – Broad contact order

Anna and Ben separate. After mediation, they agree that the children should live with Anna and see Ben regularly. The court is satisfied that the couple can make their own practical arrangements so its order is broadly expressed, giving Ben contact to include weekly visits, an overnight stay once a month and staying contact for half of each school holiday.

6.2 – Detailed contact order

Connie and Diana separate acrimoniously. They argue over every detail of arrangements. The court decides to avoid potential for more argument by ordering the exact dates, times, duration, venue and conditions for contact visits.

6.3 – Interim contact order

Eric's visiting contact with his children has gone well and he wants them to stay overnight. The children are happy about this but their mother is not. The court makes an interim order allowing for two overnight stays followed by a further hearing to review progress.

When new amendments to the CA89 come into force,[1] the court will also have the option of a contact activity condition.[2] This condition, available for parents only, directs an activity designed to promote contact such as attending for anger management or for advice on establishing, maintaining or improving contact.

Is contact compulsory?

A contact order requires the person the child lives with to 'allow' the child to have contact. S/he clearly cannot set up obstacles (such as conveniently arranging for the child to be out at contact time, or tearing up letters); indeed, s/he should respect the court's order and try to make it work, but s/he is not obliged to force a kicking and screaming child to attend and instead should take the matter back to court.

A contact order is not addressed to the child; it only concerns the carer who is compelled to allow another person to have contact. The person with the benefit of the contact order is not obliged to take it up and the child is not ordered to do anything himself, so does not breach an order by refusing to co-operate. Obviously, in practice, the older the child the more effectively he can vote with his feet.

Presumption of contact

There is no statutory presumption of contact for parents in private law cases (unlike public law cases where parents whose children are in care have a statutory presumption of 'reasonable contact').[3] However, in practice the courts work on the basis succinctly expressed by Ward LJ:[4] 'every child is entitled to know its parents and to have contact with them unless there are cogent reasons to refuse it'.

The starting point is direct contact. Only if this is not possible, even with conditions and caveats, should contact be limited to indirect contact. It is only in the most exceptional case that the courts will refuse all contact between a child and a parent. The Court of Appeal stressed that all options

---

1   Introduced into CA89 by the Children and Adoption Act 2006 (CAA06). At the time of writing implementation of these provisions is anticipated in December 2008.
2   s11A CA89.
3   s34(1) CA89.
4   *Re L (Special Guardianship: Surname)* [2007] EWCA Civ 196 [2007] 2FLR 50 Court of Appeal, paragraph 58.

should be explored before effectively terminating or impeding children's relationship with their father.[5] In that case, a referral was made to anger management and a supervised contact service to see if help could be given to make contact work.

This is of course consistent with Article 8 of the European Convention on Human Rights (the right to respect for family life). As well as the adults' rights to contact with their children, children also have a right to a relationship with both of their parents and other family members. Restrictions on Article 8 rights are justified only if they are in accordance with the law, necessary in the child's interests and proportionate to the need. This means that contact should be restricted only to the extent that is necessary and no further.

Even in an exceptional case, the court will usually allow some sort of contact, however limited. For example, although one father was affectionate towards his child, his extreme behaviour is illustrated by his imprisonment for 68 breaches of a defined contact and non-molestation order, and again for harassing the maternal grandparents.[6] Mother and child had changed identities and moved ten times to get away from him. The Court of Appeal rejected his application for direct contact, revoked his PR (previously obtained through a s4 CA89 order) and made a s91(14) CA89 order. Even so, it still granted indirect contact, all communications to be sent through CAFCASS Legal who were to vet the contents. The order set out exactly what the father could send and when, and the mother was to ensure that the child received the communications, encourage her to acknowledge receipt and provide an annual written report to the father (via CAFCASS Legal) on the child's progress at school.

If you are advising the court, start your analysis by considering whether unrestricted direct contact is in the child's best interests and work down the list of increasing restrictions until you get to the point which best meets the needs of the case. The checklist in Appendix 3 might help.

---

5   *Re W (Contact)* [2007] EWCA Civ 753 [2007] 2FLR 1122 Court of Appeal.
6   *Re F (Indirect Contact)* [2006] EWCA Civ 1426 [2007] 1FLR 1015 Court of Appeal.

Is there a presumption of equal contact?

The issue of contact for separated parents – particularly fathers – is politically sensitive. It is alleged that the system favours mothers over fathers, but the courts are keen to stress that parents have equal rights before the court. However, as there are more non-resident fathers than mothers, when the system fails it disproportionately fails fathers and their children. Campaigners argue that the court should start not just with a presumption of contact, but of equal contact. This idea did not find favour with Butler-Sloss P who said:[7]

> this would not be in the best interest of children whose welfare is the issue before the courts. The court is not and should not be tied to a certain number of days which would automatically be ordered to be spent by the absent parent with the child... It is, in my judgment, crucial that the court has the greatest flexibility in deciding on the type and quantum of contact according to the circumstances of each individual case.

Welfare considerations

How, then, does the court decide what type and level of contact should be ordered? As with all orders under s8 CA89, there are no specific grounds to be proven and the court has to consider the child's welfare as paramount,[8] using the factors in the welfare checklist to guide it.[9] The court is likely to request help in the form of a welfare report.

WISHES AND FEELINGS[10]

Ascertaining the child's true wishes and feelings requires skilled social work, including understanding the child's unspoken messages. Children caught up in contact disputes may not speak readily; they may be acutely aware of parental emotions and animosity, experience torn loyalties, try to say the 'right thing' and in some cases are coached as to what to say. In just such a case the children, aged 15 and 13, lived with their father, had not

---

7   In *Re S (Contact: Promoting Relationship with Absent Parent)* [2004] 1FLR 1279 Court of Appeal, paragraph 26.

8   s1(1) CA89.

9   s1(3) CA89.

10   s1(3)(a) CA89.

seen their mother for over eight years and said they did not want contact.[11] The Court of Appeal found it was a case of irrational and implacable hostility and the children's views had to be seen in that context. Ward LJ said teenagers' views:

> ordinarily carry great weight, but we have to bear in mind not only their age, but their understanding. Their understanding in this case is corrupted by the malignancy of the views, with which they have been force-fed over many years of their life, until so blinded by them that they cannot see the truth either of their mother's good qualities or of the good it will do them to have some contact with her.[12]

EFFECT OF CHANGE OF CIRCUMSTANCES[13]

In a contact case, this should not be seen as a presumption that the status quo is best for the child; the fact that one parent might have successfully blocked contact between the child and the other parent is not a good reason to maintain that situation. The court may need expert advice on how to balance short term harm against long term benefit.

NO DELAY[14]

This takes on particular significance in contact cases. The longer a child goes without having contact, the harder it is to re-establish a relationship. If you are involved in a contact case, it is part of your responsibility to ensure that the case is not allowed to drift.

Problems in the court system

There are undeniably cases in which the system has failed parents – often fathers – and their children. In one such case, Re D, Munby J expressed himself in terms which are unusually heartfelt for a High Court judge.[15] The case had gone on for five years over 43 hearings conducted by 16 different judges with evidence running to 950 pages. The judge criticised

---

11   *Re M (Contact: Long-term Best Interests)* [2005] EWCA Civ 1090 [2006] 1FLR 627 Court of Appeal.

12   *Re M*, paragraph 26 (see note 11 above).

13   s1(3)(c) CA89.

14   s1(2) CA89.

15   *Re D (Intractable Contact Dispute: Publicity)* [2004] 1FLR 1226 High Court.

the proliferation of paper, adjournments, delay in seeking expert assistance and in appointing a Children's Guardian, the lack of an overall timetable, and the court's failure to deal with the mother's defiance of court orders. He described the last two years of litigation as 'an exercise in absolute futility... The system has failed him... I feel desperately, desperately sorry for him. I am very sad that the system is as it is.'[16] He continued: 'Responsible voices are raised in condemnation of our system. We need to take note. We need to act. And we need to act now.'[17]

Munby J's view was that, when there is a problem with contact, too often the court lists the matter for further directions, reduces contact in the meantime (and/or imposes supervision), obtains experts' reports and directs further evidence, all of which compounds delay, and the court only wakes up to the fact that the case is intractable when it is too late for effective intervention.

He gave a stark warning: 'We can no longer simply complacently assume that our conventional domestic approach to such cases meets the standards required by Articles 6 and 8',[18] suggesting that a challenge in the European Court of Human Rights is only a matter of time away.

Many people consider that an adversarial court system is not the best way to resolve such disputes. Wall J said:[19]

> the court process is stressful for both parents and for children, it is expensive for those who are not publicly funded, it is slow and adversarial. It tends to entrench parental attitudes rather than encouraging them to change. It is ill adapted to dealing with the difficult human dilemmas involved notably when it comes to the enforcement of orders... Contact in my experience works best when parents respect each other and are able to co-operate; where the children's loyalties are not torn and where they can move between their parents without tension, unhappiness or fear of offending one parent or another.

However, he pointed out that parents must also take responsibility for the situation they create – it was not enough for the father to blame 'the system' where he bore a substantial share of the responsibility for the breakdown of contact.

---

16   *Re D*, paragraph 2 (see note 15 above).
17   *Re D*, paragraph 4 (see note 15 above).
18   *Re D*, paragraph 35 (see note 15 above).
19   *Re O (Contact: Withdrawal of Application)* [2003] EWHC 3031 (Fam) [2004] 1FLR 1258, paragraph 6(6). Quoted with approval by Butler-Sloss P in *Re S* (see note 7 above).

After these cases, the President of the Family Division of the High Court introduced the Private Law Programme aiming to improve the way courts handle contact disputes,[20] including:

- early professional intervention
- early identification of safety issues
- dispute resolution
- effective court control including active case management, judicial continuity, and transferring cases to the appropriate level of court
- monitoring outcomes
- ensuring court orders are enforced.

Child's role in the process

Children are not automatically parties in private law cases, unlike care proceedings. There is no obvious logic to the different treatment of the two groups of children caught up in litigation. Private law proceedings can be just as bitter, complex and protracted as care proceedings and the issues for the child (who he lives with, who he sees) are just as profound. In care proceedings the court always has both the local authority and Children's Guardian as objective professional parties: in private law cases it may have neither. Some worry that making a child a party to the case sets him up against his parents and exposes him to evidence about the difficult aspects of the family's life; however, this is no different from a child in care proceedings who is a party as a matter of course.

In *Mabon* v. *Mabon* children aged 17, 15 and 13 wanted to instruct a solicitor, but the judge refused, fearing that the litigation process would cause them emotional damage.[21] The Court of Appeal allowed their appeal saying it was 'unthinkable' to exclude educated, articulate and mature young people from proceedings which affected them so fundamentally and that there needed to be a keener appreciation of the children's autonomy and right to participate in the process.

Courts are now more willing to use the provision in the court rules which allows a child to be made party to the proceedings in the County

---

20   Available at www.dca.gov.uk/family/plpguide.pdf, accessed 11 August 2008.
21   *Mabon* v. *Mabon* [2005] 2FLR 1011 Court of Appeal.

Court or High Court (not in the Family Proceedings Court (FPC)).[22] Even so, this only happens in exceptional circumstances, for example where:

- the child's views or interests are inconsistent with those of any of the adult parties
- the child may be suffering harm as a result of the dispute
- there are complex medical or mental health issues
- there is an international element
- the interests of one child in the case conflict with those of another.

A child party is represented by a solicitor and a CAFCASS Guardian (unless he is capable of giving his own instructions to the solicitor), rather than simply having his interests reflected in a welfare report. If you are involved in a complex case, feel free to raise the issue of whether the child should be made a party and separately represented.

Even if made a party, the child is unlikely to attend court. A child's role in court proceedings is a delicate question, under much discussion. In one case, where the father alleged that mother had deliberately alienated the children,[23] the judge wondered whether judges should see children themselves, and if so, what training they would need.[24]

Judging parents' allegations

Sometimes the court has to consider allegations by one parent about the other's behaviour (perhaps alleged child abuse or domestic violence), which has a bearing on contact. Simply making an allegation of misbehaviour cannot be enough to deny the other parent contact; sadly people have been known to make false allegations and even to coach their children to do so. On the other hand, if the allegations are true they cannot be ignored. So the court must hear evidence to decide whether the allegations are true before it can decide on contact. It may have to do this as a preliminary issue, remembering to make provision for what happens in the meantime.

If you are the social worker compiling a report in a case where allegations are made and denied, it is not for you to decide who is telling the

---

22   Rule 9.5, Family Proceedings Rules 1991.
23   *Re T (Contact: Alienation: Permission to Appeal)* [2003] 1FLR 531 High Court.
24   For more discussion, see L. Davis (2007) 'Children in Court' and 'Children in Court: A Postscript.' *Family Law Journal 37*, 65 and 434.

truth; that is the court's job. You may therefore have to formulate alternative sets of recommendations.

6.4 – Recommendations where there are allegations

Fergal seeks contact with his son George. George's mother Helen alleges that Fergal was violent to her in front of George, that Fergal's application is motivated by a desire to resume his relationship with her and that George is frightened of his father. Fergal emphatically denies all the allegations. The worker compiling the welfare report cannot decide whether Helen is telling the truth – only the court can do that – but her recommendations depend on the truth of the allegations. If they are true, contact should be supervised and the parents must not come face to face at contact time. If they are false, such conditions are not necessary and George must not be given the impression that Fergal needs supervision. The worker therefore gives the court two alternative recommendations, explaining that her final view depends on the court's conclusions about the allegations.

Contact and domestic violence

Domestic violence in contact cases has become a high profile issue. In the past, it seemed that contact was presumed to be in the child's interests regardless of parental conduct, that violence not aimed directly at the child was an issue between the adults not affecting the child, and parents (usually mothers) resisting contact to their ex-partners were labelled as implacably hostile without considering whether there was good reason for their attitude. Things have changed.

This was demonstrated in *Re M* where the FPC refused a father direct contact due to his violence including incidents at the child's school and at hospital.[25] He appealed, but Wall J found that the magistrates had good reasons for their decision. He commented:

often in these cases where domestic violence has been found too little weight in my judgment is given to the need for the father to change. It is often said that, notwithstanding the violence, the mother must nonetheless bring up children with full knowledge and a positive image of their natural father and to arrange for the children to be available for contact.

---

25   *Re M (Contact: Violent Parent)* [1999] 2FLR 321 High Court, page 333B-C.

Too often it seems to me the courts neglect the other side of the equation, which is that a father like this father must demonstrate that he is a fit person to exercise contact; that he is not going to destabilise the family; that he is not going to upset the children and harm them emotionally.

There then followed the Court of Appeal case of *Re L*, which considered four appeals all involving contact and domestic violence.[26] Key factors in a court's decision include:

- both parties' conduct towards each other and child
- extent of violence
- effect on the carer
- effect on the children
- offender's ability to recognise and to attempt to change the behaviour
- the motivation of the parent seeking contact.

The Court of Appeal set out the following principles:

- there needs to be a heightened awareness of the existence of, and consequences on children of, exposure to domestic violence between parents or other partners
- where an allegation of domestic violence is made which might affect the outcome of the case, it should be adjudicated on and found proven or not
- as a matter of principle, domestic violence is not a bar to contact but it is one factor in a delicate balancing exercise of discretion
- in the interim, until the issue has been adjudicated on, the court should consider the likelihood of harm to the child if contact were granted or refused. The court should ensure as far as it can that the safety of the child and residential parent is secured before, during and after such contact.

Courts must now follow a Practice Direction in contact or residence cases where there are allegations of domestic violence. The court must identify factual and welfare issues, consider allegations of violence and their significance to the likely outcome if proven, and give directions to deter-

---

26   *Re L (Contact: Domestic Violence); Re V (Contact: Domestic Violence); Re M (Contact: Domestic Violence) Re H; (Contact: Domestic Violence)* [2000] 2FLR 334 Court of Appeal.

mine factual disputes.[27] The definition of 'harm' in s31(9) CA89 has been amended to add the words 'including, for example, impairment suffered from seeing or hearing the ill-treatment of another', clearly covering a situation of domestic violence where the child himself is not the direct victim. This is directly relevant in private law cases as, under item (e) of the welfare checklist, the court must consider any harm the child has suffered or is at risk of suffering. Arguably the new wording does not represent a change in the law, it merely makes explicit something that might have seemed obvious in any case – violence to other family members harms children.

Violence between partners can lead on to violence towards the children themselves. The Family Justice Council (FJC) addressed the court's approach to such cases in a 2006 report,[28] prompted by the shocking Women's Aid Federation report on 29 children from 13 different families who were killed by their fathers on contact visits over ten years.[29] Five of those cases involved contact orders, three of which were made by consent.

One of the FJC's main conclusions was that a cultural change is required, moving from the idea that 'contact is always the appropriate way forward' to 'contact *that is safe and positive for the child* is always the appropriate way forward'. There should be increased emphasis on safety when considering whether contact is in the child's best interests. The FJC considered research and concluded: 'contact with a loving and supportive parent is in the best interests of children; contact with violent and unstable parents may not be'.

The FJC report recommended that, whenever domestic violence is alleged or admitted, a risk assessment should be carried out before an order is made by consent. The issue of s1(5) CA89, and its misinterpretation as a presumption of no order, is raised again. The laudable aim of reducing discord and promoting co-operation between the parties can unwittingly lead to pressure being put on parties (even by their own legal advisers) to reach agreement. Victims of violence or intimidation may be too ready to try to appease the

---

27   Practice Direction (2008) *Residence and Contact Orders: Domestic Violence and Harm.*
       Available at www.judiciary.gov.uk/docs/judgments_guidance/pd_domestic_
       violence_090508.pdf, accessed 11 August 2008.

28   Family Justice Council (2006) 'Report to the President of the Family Division on the
       approach to be adopted by the Court when asked to make a contact order by consent,
       where domestic violence has been an issue in the case.' Available at www.family-
       justice-council.org.uk/docs/Reportoncontact.pdf, accessed 11 August 2008.

29   H. Saunders (2004) *29 Homicides: Lessons for Domestic Violence and Child Protection.*
       Women's Aid Federation of England. Available at www.womensaid.org.uk/page.asp?
       section=000100010009000500050009000004, accessed 11 August 2008.

perpetrator by agreeing or too lacking in self-esteem to raise the issue. Courts are often reluctant to interfere with agreements, instead welcoming them as being within the spirit of the CA89. If you are involved in a private law case, make sure that what is presented as an agreement is freely entered into and that, in your efforts to reduce conflict and promote conciliation, you do not unwittingly add to pressure already felt by a vulnerable party.

The FJC also suggested that care should be taken before removing safeguards put in place to make contact safe. If there are no incidents, it may not mean that the safeguards are unnecessary: it may mean that they are working.

Enforcing contact orders

One of the most difficult problems in long-running contact disputes is the willingness of some parents to disobey the court's orders, often for reasons more to do with the parental relationship than the child's welfare. The European Court of Human Rights held that states have a positive obligation under Article 8 to take action to enable parents to be reunited with their children and simply fining a father breaching contact orders was not enough.[30]

There should be no doubt that a contact order is a court order and defiance of it is contempt of court. When new provisions of the CA89 come into force,[31] the court will attach a notice to a contact order warning of the consequences of failure to comply with the order,[32] and will have the option of asking a CAFCASS officer to monitor compliance with the order and report back to court.[33]

At present, there is no provision for monitoring a contact order. If it does not work, it is up to the aggrieved party to take the matter back to court and s/he should do so as soon as possible. Ultimately the court has power to imprison recalcitrant parties – this happened for example in the case of *A* v. *N* where the mother was imprisoned for repeatedly flouting a contact order.[34] Imprisoning the person with whom the child lives may have a detrimental effect on the child, but the child's welfare is not the court's paramount consideration in this decision. Imprisonment is a last resort, but there has to be a limit to how long the court can tolerate contempt.

---

30   *Hansen* v. *Turkey* [2004] 1FLR 142 European Court of Human Rights.
31   Introduced by the Children and Adoption Act 2006. At the time of writing implementation of these provisions is anticipated in December 2008.
32   s11I CA89.
33   s11H CA89.
34   *A* v. *N (Committal: Refusal of Contact)* [1997] 1FLR 533 Court of Appeal.

When the new CA89 provisions are in force the court will also have the option of making an enforcement order,[35] which will require anyone proven beyond reasonable doubt to have breached a contact order to do unpaid work. Unlike imprisonment, this will allow the court to punish the defaulting party without also effectively punishing the child. A further option will be an order making the defaulting party compensate the other for any financial loss (such as wasted travel costs, lost wages or the cost of a cancelled holiday).[36]

An option already available to the court in an appropriate case is to consider changing the child's residence. In *Re C*, the Court of Appeal upheld a judge's decision to transfer a five-year-old girl's residence from her mother to her father.[37] This was despite the fact that the child had lived all her life with her mother, who had refused contact to the father for over three years, meaning that he had become a 'virtual stranger' to his daughter. The father was given a residence order and ancillary orders were made for contact, therapy for the child and family assistance. The Court of Appeal stressed the need for courts to act robustly in cases of failing or failed contact.

There may also come a point at which the hostility between the parties and repeated litigation itself starts to harm the child, even to the level of significant harm. Private law disputes can then cross over into child protection issues.

Points for practice

1. Remain clear-headed and focused on the child. Constantly refer back to the welfare principle and welfare checklist.

2. Be mindful of the adults' agendas and relationships and the effect they have on the child. Take extra care in establishing the child's true wishes and feelings. Consider whether the child should be separately represented.

3. Do not give up. Contact disputes can be intractable. Dogged determination is required, as well as the imagination to consider new ways forward or options not yet attempted.

4. Make sure any apparent agreement is freely entered into and is in the child's best interests.

---

35   s11J CA89.
36   s11O CA89.
37   *Re C (Residence Order)* [2007] EWCA Civ 866, Court of Appeal.

Part 3

The Local Authority's Support Role

Chapter 7

Children in Need

One mother is struggling to cope: she needs advice and guidance; another has no money for food or nappies until she receives her benefits: she needs help to get by. Another family needs a break from caring for their seriously disabled child: they need respite care. All come to Social Services for help.

Under the Children Act 1989 (CA89), the local authority's first role is not child protection but supporting children and their families using the relevant sections which are grouped together in Part III of the Act. Child protection provisions are a safety net when the family and support services have failed; prevention is the first port of call.

Statutory duties

The local authority's preventive duty is spelt out in Schedule 2 CA89. It must take 'reasonable steps' to:

- prevent children suffering ill-treatment or neglect[1]

- reduce the need for care proceedings or criminal proceedings against children[2]

- avoid the need to place children in secure accommodation[3]

- discourage children in their area from committing criminal offences.[4]

---

1   CA89 Schedule 2 paragraph 4.
2   CA89 Schedule 2 paragraph 7(a)(i) and (ii).
3   CA89 Schedule 2 paragraph 7(c).
4   CA89 Schedule 2 paragraph 7(b).

These statutory duties are striking in their breadth and vagueness, leaving the authority considerable discretion to decide how to achieve them. For example, paragraph 9, dealing with the provision of family centres, starts with the words 'every local authority shall'. In legal language, 'shall' means 'must', so this is a statutory duty. However, the duty is for the authority to provide 'such family centres as they consider appropriate' so each authority can decide for itself how many and what type of centres to provide.

Similarly Schedule 2 does not actually impose a duty to prevent children from suffering ill-treatment or neglect, but a duty to 'take reasonable steps through the provision of services' to do so. 'Reasonable' is the lawyer's favourite word. It blurs the edges, allowing room for judgment, argument and justification. A local authority must do something to stop children being ill-treated or neglected – doing nothing is unlikely to be 'reasonable' – but beyond that it is up to the authority's discretion, bounded only by the requirement not to behave irrationally. This allows each authority to manage its own budget and respond to local needs but it also means that provision can be remarkably different on either side of a local authority boundary.

Provision of services is one thing; their quality is another, and depends on the authority's strengths at the strategic as well as grass-roots level. The strategic role is led by the Children's Services Director,[5] who must ensure that his authority publishes a children and young people's plan after consultation with partner agencies. Unfortunately, despite the best of intentions and a plethora of government initiatives to promote children's welfare through inter-agency working, financial considerations seem to have led to ever-tightening criteria for preventive services in order to preserve the child protection budget. However, the broad wording of the Schedule 2 CA89 statutory duties means such budget-driven decisions are unlikely to be susceptible to legal challenge.

Children in need

How do these broad strategic duties relate to real children and their families who need help and support? The keystone in the statutory structure is s17 CA89.

---

5   A post created by the Children Act 2004.

> s17 (1)CA89 It shall be the general duty of every local authority (in addition to the other duties imposed on them by this Part) –
>
> (a) to safeguard and promote the welfare of children within their area who are in need; and
>
> (b) so far as is consistent with that duty, to promote the upbringing of such children by their families, by providing a range and level of services appropriate to those children's needs.

Section 17 in practice

1. IS THIS CHILD 'IN NEED'?

The duty under s17 CA89 only applies to children 'who are in need', a term with a precise statutory meaning defined in s17(10) CA89.

> s17(10) CA89 For the purposes of this Part a child shall be taken to be in need if –
>
> (a) he is unlikely to achieve or maintain, or to have the opportunity of achieving or maintaining, a reasonable standard of health or development without the provision for him of services by a local authority under this Part;
>
> (b) his health or development is likely to be significantly impaired, or further impaired, without the provision for him of such services; or
>
> (c) he is disabled.

The definition signals the section's preventive intention – it looks ahead to what is likely to happen if nothing is done. So children do not have to already be falling behind to qualify – it is enough if it is clear they are likely to do so unless services are provided. As with any statutory definition, it gives rise to further questions.

What do 'health' and 'development' mean?

s17(11) CA89 defines 'health' and 'development' broadly to include physical and mental health and physical, intellectual, emotional, social and behavioural development.

What does 'disabled' mean?

'Disabled' is defined in terms matching those of the National Assistance Act 1948, the key statute for services for adults with disabilities, so there should be a seamless transition from childhood to adulthood services. Unfortunately the outmoded terminology seems less than sensitive today.

> s17(11) CA89 For the purposes of this Part, a child is disabled if he is blind, deaf or dumb or suffers from mental disorder of any kind or is substantially and permanently handicapped by illness, injury or congenital deformity...

A disabled child is automatically a 'child in need', even if he is happy, healthy and thriving in the care of excellent parents.

The authority also has a duty to maintain a register of disabled children in its area.[6] This is intended to be helpful, not stigmatising, and must not be confused with the Child Protection Register. Registration is neither compulsory nor a pre-condition to receiving services.

What is a 'reasonable standard' and what does 'significantly impaired' mean?

These words are not defined in CA89 so they must be given their ordinary and natural meaning. Clearly the section was deliberately drafted in broad terms, so each case can be judged in its own context.

Identifying children in need

The authority must take reasonable steps to identify the extent to which there are children in need in its area and to publish information about available services, doing its best to ensure that the publicity reaches the people who need the services.[7]

---

6   Schedule 2 CA89 paragraph 2.
7   Schedule 2 CA89 paragraph 1.

2. IS THE CHILD WITHIN OUR AREA?

This is a simple question of fact. If a child is physically present in the area, whether he lives there, goes to school there or arrives there as an unaccompanied minor seeking asylum, he is the responsibility of the local authority for that area.

3. WHAT SERVICES SHOULD WE PROVIDE?

The objective is to safeguard and promote children's welfare by providing appropriate services. Part I of Schedule 2 to CA89 sets out the types of services the authority has a duty or power to provide to meet this general duty. These include providing:

- services for advice, guidance and counselling[8]
- occupational, social, cultural or recreational activities[9]
- family centres.[10]

There is a specific duty to provide services designed to 'minimise the effect on disabled children…of their disabilities' and 'to give such children the opportunity to lead lives which are as normal as possible'.[11]

These services are provided for children in general. The Act does not specify what should be provided in each individual case: that depends on an assessment of each child's needs and the proper exercise of discretion to decide what services to provide, if any.

The authority can (and should) assess the child's needs and entitlements under other relevant legislation (such as education and/or disability legislation) at the same time, avoiding duplication of assessment and allowing a co-ordinated response.[12] This requires joint working arrangements with other teams and agencies, using tools such as the Common Assessment Framework.[13]

The Act does not specify how to assess a child's needs; instead, this is found in guidance, in particular the Framework for Assessment of Children in Need and their Families (the Framework).[14] This authoritative

---

8   Schedule 2 CA89 paragraph 8(a).
9   Schedule 2 CA89 paragraph 8(b).
10   Schedule 2 CA89 paragraph 9.
11   Schedule 2 CA89 paragraph 6.
12   Schedule 2 CA89 paragraph 3.
13   Available at www.everychildmatters.gov.uk/deliveringservices/caf, accessed 11 August 2008.
14   Department of Health (2000) *Framework for Assessment of Children in Need and their Families.* London: Stationery Office, available at www.dh.gov.uk/en/Publicationsandstatistics/Publications/PublicationsPolicyAndGuidance/DH_4003256, accessed 11 August 2008.

document was issued under s7 Local Authority Social Services Act 1970, so must be followed unless there is extremely good reason otherwise. This was confirmed when the High Court ordered a local authority to carry out an assessment under s17 CA89, giving it 35 days to do so, matching the timescale for an initial assessment under the Framework.[15]

4. WHO RECEIVES THE SERVICES?

Services can be given direct to the child in need himself, for example he can attend a playgroup. But often it is not the child, but a parent, who needs help such as advice on parenting. As long as this is provided with a view to safeguarding or promoting the child's welfare, it still falls within s17 – services can be given to the family or any family member.[16]

Before deciding what services to provide, the authority must (so far as practicable and consistent with the child's welfare) ascertain and give due consideration to the child's wishes and feelings about services.[17]

5. WHO PROVIDES THE SERVICES?

It is the local authority's job to secure the requisite services whether by delivering them itself or by delegating the task to others.[18] Authorities can and frequently do contract with other bodies, especially the voluntary sector, to provide s17 services.

6. CAN WE ASK OTHER AGENCIES TO HELP?

Often meeting a child's needs involves other agencies – a child might have special educational needs, or the family's difficulties might be exacerbated by housing problems. These issues require inter-agency co-operation.

Children's services authorities have a statutory duty to promote children's well-being through co-operation with relevant bodies and partner agencies.[19] Other agencies with responsibilities towards children have their

---

15   R (ota AB and SB) v. Nottinghamshire County Council [2001] 3FCR 350 High Court.
16   s17(3) CA89.
17   s17(4A) CA89, added to CA89 by the Children Act 2004.
18   s17(5) CA89.
19   s10 Children Act 2004.

own statutory duty to ensure that 'their functions are discharged having regard to the need to safeguard and promote the welfare of children'.[20]

There is also a duty to assist imposed by s27 CA89 on:

- other departments of the authority
- other local authorities (not limited to Children's Services functions)
- any local education authority
- any local housing authority
- health authorities in their various forms.

---

s27(2) CA89 An authority whose help is...requested shall comply with the request if it is compatible with their own statutory or other duties and obligations and does not unduly prejudice the discharge of any of their functions.

If you need help from another agency which is not forthcoming despite the spirit of mutual co-operation, you can make a formal request for help under s27 CA89. A formal letter citing a statutory duty can often unblock channels and secure assistance when a polite request fails.

The duty to assist is not unconditional. It is qualified by reference to the other agency's own functions. So, the House of Lords found that, where a housing authority had already quite properly applied its own statutory criteria and rejected a family's homelessness application, it was not obliged to house the family at the request of Social Services under s27 CA89.[21]

Inter-agency co-operation depends on sharing information, some of which may be confidential. If so, refer to the helpful government guidance on sharing information.[22]

---

20   s11(2) Children Act 2004.

21   *R v. Northavon District Council ex parte Smith* [1994] 2FLR 671 House of Lords.

22   HM Goverment (2006) *Information Sharing: Practitioneers' Guide. Integrated Working to Improve Outcomes for Children and Young People.* Available at www.everychildmatters.gov. uk/informationsharing/, accessed 11 August 2008.

7. CAN WE GIVE MONEY INSTEAD OF SERVICES?

s17 CA89 is primarily about services, 'assistance in kind' in the words of the Act,[23] but sometimes a cash donation is the most practical way of helping out, and this is permitted in 'exceptional circumstances'. What counts as 'exceptional' is a matter for judgment, but clearly there must be something out of the ordinary. s17 CA89 does not envisage regular or repeated payments. Responsibility for financial support for impoverished families lies with the benefits system: local authorities are not there to subsidise or replace the Benefits Agency.

8. CAN WE PROVIDE ACCOMMODATION UNDER S17 CA89?

At one stage, the answer to this question was unclear, so s17(6) CA89 was amended to state explicitly that services can include providing accommodation, not just helping a family find accommodation by providing a deposit or the first month's rent.

Like any other s17 service, this can be provided to the child's family, so s17 CA89 can be used to house the whole family, not just the child. A child provided with accommodation under s17 is not 'looked after' (unlike a child accommodated under s20 CA89).[24] However, an authority cannot get out of its duties to looked after children simply by declaring that accommodation is provided under s17 CA89 not s20 CA89.[25]

How does this power fit with the Housing Department's duties? Under homelessness legislation there comes a point at which the Housing Department is no longer obliged to house families, even those with young children. Can those families then claim a right to be housed under s17 CA89?

This very question came to the House of Lords where it was decided (by the narrowest of margins, a 3:2 majority) that Social Services are not legally obliged to accommodate families so that children can be housed with their parents.[26] s17 CA89 imposes a general duty. Providing accommodation is not its primary function but just one service which might be provided, subject to the local authority's discretion. So, the local authority

---

23   s17(6) CA89.
24   See Chapter 8 for more details.
25   *R (H)* v. *Wandsworth LBC; R (Barhanu)* v. *Hackney LBC; R (B)* v. *LB Islington* [2007] EWHC 1082 (Admin) [2007] 2FLR 822 High Court.
26   *R (G)* v. *Barnet LBC; R (W)* v. *Lambeth LBC; R (A)* v. *Lambeth LBC* [2003] UKHL 57 [2004] 1FLR 454 House of Lords.

has the power to provide accommodation for families but no duty to do so and neither parents nor children can claim this as a right. Otherwise, Social Services would turn into a substitute housing department.

The local authority also has a power (not a duty) to assist a person to obtain alternative accommodation if he is living in the family home and causing or likely to cause a child significant harm.[27] In principle the idea that, instead of removing the child from home, you can move the abuser is attractive, but in practice questions arise as to how you ensure first that the abuser really has left, and second that s/he is not continuing to abuse the child in spite of living elsewhere.

9. CAN WE CHARGE FOR SERVICES?

Assistance under s17 CA89 can be given unconditionally or subject to repayment or other conditions (for example, providing day care as long as the mother uses the time to attend for drug counselling). But before providing a service or imposing conditions the authority must consider the family's means; repayment cannot be demanded from anyone on income support or certain other benefits.

10. CAN THE FAMILY SUE IF WE DO NOT PROVIDE THE SERVICES THEY WANT?

The House of Lords decided s17 CA89 imposes a 'general duty' owed by the authority to children in need overall, not a specific duty towards individuals.[28] This means that a particular family has no statutory right to any specified service and cannot claim a breach of statutory duty if it is not provided.

The only legal remedy realistically available for those with complaints under s17 CA89 is judicial review, a procedure under which the High Court regulates the exercise of administrative powers. This is a rather odd and limited kind of remedy as the court does not actually judge the merits of the decision in question but instead looks at the procedures adopted and considerations taken into account. It can quash decisions which are:

---

27   Schedule 2 CA89 paragraph 5.
28   *R (G)* v. *Barnet LBC*; *R (W)* v. *Lambeth LBC*; *R (A)* v. *Lambeth LBC* [2003] (see note 26 above).

- taken improperly
- beyond the authority's legal powers
- taken considering the wrong factors
- plain unreasonable.

The 'unreasonableness' test is a high hurdle to surmount – the decision made must not only be wrong but so wrong that no reasonable authority could ever have come to that conclusion. The court can then quash the decision and direct the authority to reconsider the matter, doing it properly this time. It is possible for the authority to reach the very same decision but in a manner which is not open to further challenge.

Some judicial review applications do succeed. One case, *Re T*, concerned a seriously troubled 14-year-old boy.[29] A victim of sexual abuse himself, he was also an abuser, excluded from school, violent and involved in theft, arson and drug and alcohol abuse. A risk assessment found that he needed to live in physical safety and emotional security before therapeutic work could be carried out. It recommended a specialist residential placement. The local authority decided instead that his needs could be met by mainstream educational provision and placement in a children's home previously rejected as unsuitable.

On judicial review the court found that the authority was not bound to follow the assessment, but the decision was based on inadequate information and was fundamentally flawed. Inter-agency working had failed, and no reference was made to the boy's own wishes and feelings. The whole process was irrational and unreasonable, so the decision was quashed and the local authority was directed to reconsider.

Another case concerned a 15-year-old girl with quadriplegic cerebral palsy and registered blind.[30] A support package had included regular respite care (up to five nights a week) with foster carers for the last ten years. Despite adaptations, the foster home was not and could not be made suitable. The carers wanted to move to a more suitable property but needed a loan from the housing association for which they needed the local authority's support. Instead, the local authority planned for the child to board at school four nights a week and spend one weekend a month at a residential facility. The child and her mother were strongly opposed to any more than

---

29   *Re T (Judicial Review: Local Authority Decisions Concerning Child in Need)* [2003] EWHC 2515 (Admin) [2004] 1FLR 601 High Court.

30   *R (CD) v. Isle of Anglesey County Council* [2005] 1FLR 59 High Court.

two nights a week boarding and to the end of her ten-year relationship with the carers.

On judicial review, the judge held that the care plan was unlawful. The authority had failed to consider the child's clear and consistent wishes, the mother's physical and emotional inability to provide the care needed, or the very strong links between carers and child. Having encouraged the child to make a second home with the carers the authority could not de-register them because their accommodation did not meet the child's needs. The court urged the authority to reconsider supporting the carers' application to the housing association but it would not order it to do so – the authority had to make its own decision, but do so properly.

Prevention and protection

Services under Part III of CA89 are voluntary and supportive, aiming to enhance the family's role, and are quite different from the interventionist child protection provisions which appear later in the Act. However, the boundary can become blurred. The *Re T* case above illustrates how, at the most serious end of the s17 CA89 spectrum, children can be 'in need' because of abuse or neglect. Some cases start with a child protection referral but are resolved by registering the child as a child in need and providing services; other cases start with a request for services but, on assessment, child protection issues become apparent. In the past, some abuse or neglect of disabled children was missed because they were seen only as children in need, provided with support by a specialist team whose mindset was not one of child protection. It is important to remain alert to the need to move from one set of legal provisions to another when appropriate.

Points for practice

1. The children in need provisions are the bedrock of the statutory scheme. Support services should be given proper priority and funding.

2. Inter-agency co-operation is essential to prevent both gaps and duplication in services. Build links with other agencies and call on their help, reminding them of their legal duties if necessary.

3. Always ensure that s17 CA89 decisions are made properly, fairly, with appropriate consultation, and are carefully recorded.

Chapter 8

Accommodation

Accommodation – Not care

Aaron and Barry are both in foster care. They are both 'looked after' children, their placements made and maintained by the local authority. Each has a social worker and regular reviews, and they will have the same rights when they leave the foster home. However, legally speaking, their cases are profoundly different. Aaron is 'in care': the local authority has parental responsibility (PR) for him because he is subject to a care order, made by a court on the basis of significant harm. Barry is 'accommodated':[1] his parents retain full PR, some of which they have delegated to the authority under a voluntary arrangement. No court has been involved and there is no significant harm. The local authority is providing a service to help Barry and his family.[2]

Accommodation appears in s20 Children Act 1989 (CA89), in the same Part of the Act as s17 CA89 as it is one of the local authority's support services for children and families. The Department of Health said:

> Partnership with parents and consultation with children on the basis of careful joint planning and agreement is the guiding principle for the provision of services within the family home and where children are provided with accommodation under voluntary arrangements. Such arrangements are intended to assist the parent and enhance, not undermine, the parent's authority and control.[3]

---

1   The old fashioned term 'voluntary care' is inaccurate and should never be used.

2   For a summary of similarities and differences between a child in care and an accommodated child, see Appendix 4.

3   Department of Health (1991) *The Children Act 1989 Guidance and Regulations Volume 2: Family Support, Day Care and Educational Provision for Young Children.* London: Stationery Office, paragraph 2.1.

Requesting accommodation for a child should not be stigmatised as parental failure but seen as a responsible action, seeking help when it is needed.

The duty to accommodate

When parents request accommodation for their child, does the local authority have a duty to provide it? The answer lies in the precise wording of s20 CA89.

---

s20(1) CA89 Every local authority shall provide accommodation for any child in need within their area who appears to them to require accommodation as a result of –

   (a)   there being no person who has parental responsibility for him;

   (b)   his being lost or having been abandoned; or

   (c)   the person who has been caring for him being prevented (whether or not permanently, and for whatever reason) from providing him with suitable accommodation or care.

A step-by-step approach must be followed, first to establish whether the child's situation falls within the section, and then to decide whether offering accommodation is the most appropriate response or whether other options (such as providing services to the child and family or calling on support from the wider family or social network) might be better.

As the duty to accommodate only arises in respect of a 'child in need', the first step is to determine whether a particular child falls within s17 CA89.[4] If so, the next question is whether his circumstances fit any of the definitions in s20(1) CA89.

8.1 – Unaccompanied minor

David arrives alone in the UK claiming asylum. He may or may not have parents elsewhere in the world but there is no one with PR for him in the UK so he falls within s20(1)(a) CA89.

---

4   For further details see Chapter 7.

8.2 – Orphan

Ethan's parents die in an accident, so there is no one with PR for him. The local authority steps in and places him in foster care under s20(1)(a) CA89. If Ethan's parents are appointed testamentary guardians or if anyone is willing to apply to court to become his guardian, he will swiftly move out of accommodation. If not, he may remain accommodated long term.

s20 CA89 never gives the local authority PR, so a child accommodated under s20(1)(a) CA89 could remain a child for whom nobody has PR for the rest of his childhood.

8.3 – A lost child

Felicity, aged three, is found wandering alone. As she is lost or abandoned, the local authority takes her in under s20(1)(b) CA89 until her parents are traced. Depending on how Felicity became lost, she may go straight home or her case may turn into a child protection matter.

s20(1)(c) CA89 is wider than the other two subsections and is the most common ground for accommodation. The statutory draftsman did not even try to anticipate all the possible situations which might arise, so instead expressed the subsection in broad terms to cover all eventualities.

8.4 – Circumstances prevent continued care

Seven children need the authority's help:

- Greg's mother has to go into hospital for an operation.
- Harry's mother cannot care for him until her mental health improves.
- Ian's father is in prison.
- Jane's father is going into residential rehabilitation.
- Keith's parents are about to be evicted and will be homeless.
- Leon's disabilities mean his parents cannot meet his needs at home.
- Martin's parents cannot cope with his aggressive behaviour.

s20(1)(c) CA89 could apply to all seven.

The local authority must decide whether a child falling into any of the three categories appears to need accommodation (as opposed to any other service). If so, there is a duty to accommodate. So it is for the authority to judge whether providing accommodation is the right way forward. Department of Health guidance[5] says that the authority should first carry out an assessment under the Framework for Assessment,[6] then:

> It should use the findings of that assessment, which will take into account the wishes and feelings of the child (as required by s20(6) of the Children Act), as the basis for any decision about whether he should be provided with accommodation under s20 (and therefore become looked after) or whether other types of services provided under s17 of the Act are better suited to his circumstances.

Exasperated parents of a rebellious teenager, for example, might want their offspring to be accommodated, but you might judge that it is better to try to work with the family with him staying at home. That is an entirely legitimate response within the terms of s20 CA89.

16- and 17-year-olds

There is a specific duty towards a 16- or 17-year-old in need where the local authority considers his welfare is 'likely to be seriously prejudiced' if he is not accommodated.[7] This is a stronger test than for younger children, who must simply 'appear' to require accommodation.

Young people needing accommodation may go to the Housing Department, not Children's Services, so co-operation between departments is vital. The *Framework for Assessment* says:

> Homeless young people may frequently come to the attention of both housing and social services and will need to be assessed to establish whether they should be provided with accommodation. There is a danger that in these circumstances young people may be passed from one agency

---

5   Department of Health Circular (2003) 'Guidance on Accommodating Children in Need and their Families', LAC (2003)13, available at www.dh.gov.uk/en/ Publicationsandstatistics/LettersandCirculars/LocalAuthorityCirculars/ AllLocalAuthority/DH_4003946, accessed 11 August 2008.

6   Department of Health (2000) *Framework for Assessment of Children in Need and their Families.* London: Stationery Office, available at www.dh.gov.uk/en/ Publicationsandstatistics/Publications/PublicationsPolicyAndGuidance/ DH_4003256, accessed 11 August 2008.

7   s20(3) CA89.

to another and it is important therefore that joint protocols are agreed between housing and social services in the matter of how and by whom they are to be assessed.[8]

The interaction of the two duties (housing and accommodation) was considered by the House of Lords. Their Lordships confirmed the decision made by the Court of Appeal,[9] when Wall LJ said: 'it is self evident that most troubled 16 and 17 year old children will be unaware of the services available to assist them, and it is equally self evident that the onus is not on children in need to identify and request the services they require'.[10]

However, he also said that not every homeless 17-year-old is automatically a child in need.[11] In that particular case, although the young woman was clearly troubled following a 'wretched' childhood, there was nothing in the evidence to require the Council to have designated her as a 'child in need'.

This decision was of vital practical importance. If she had been a child in need and accommodated by the authority it would have had an ongoing duty, including providing after care services. As it was, she was housed under homelessness legislation, the Council had fulfilled its duty and had no further responsibility to her. The court was, however, anxious to emphasise that this case was not a precedent in any way limiting or relaxing the duties to investigate the circumstances of young people who may be in need and provide services or accommodation for them where appropriate.

The power to accommodate

There is a power to accommodate a child even if there is no duty to do so.[12] This power covers 'any child' within the area, in need or not, even where a person with PR is able to care for the child, if the local authority considers that accommodating the child would safeguard and promote his welfare. However, as a power, not a duty, it is entirely discretionary.

---

8   Paragraph 5.72.
9   *R(M)* v. *LB Hammersmith and Fulham* [2006] EWCA Civ 917 [2007] 1 FLR 256 Court of Appeal; *R (ota M)* v. *London Borough of Hammersmith and Fulham* [2008] UKHL 14 House of Lords.
10 *R (M)* v. *LB Hammersmith and Fulham* (Court of Appeal), at paragraph 73 (see note 9 above).
11 *R (M)* v. *LB Hammersmith and Fulham* (Court of Appeal), at paragraph 49 (see note 9 above).
12 s20(4) CA89.

s20 CA89 and PR

The detailed provisions of s20 CA89 flow naturally from the local authority's role to support, not replace, the child's parents.

Even if the child's usual carer requests accommodation, it makes sense that someone with PR who is able and willing to look after the child should do so, instead of the authority stepping in. In this situation, the local authority is not allowed to accommodate the child[13] – a child's primary place is with a parent, not in substitute care. This does not apply, however, if there is a residence order or special guardianship order in force,[14] because the court's decision displaces the normal equality between those with PR in deciding where the child should live. Court orders (such as s8 CA89 contact orders) are unaffected by a child being accommodated.

Once a child is accommodated, again it is logical that anyone with PR can remove him from accommodation at any time and without notice.[15] In practice you may ask a parent to give notice before discharging the child from accommodation to allow arrangements to be made, including preparing the child, but such agreements have no legal force.

The child's views

It is not only good practice but a statutory duty to consider the child's views, although his consent to accommodation is not required.

Once the child turns 16, he can agree to be accommodated instead of someone with PR taking over his care,[16] and he can refuse to be discharged from accommodation against his will.[17] The Act is, however, silent about what happens when a young person refuses to be accommodated or purports to discharge himself from accommodation. This Part of the Act gives no power to detain a young person against his will and in reality over 16-year-olds, who can leave school and support themselves, can vote with their feet. For under 16s, if persuasion is unsuccessful, the authority has to consider whether the grounds exist for care proceedings or, in an extreme case, a secure accommodation application under s25 CA89.

---

13   s20(7) CA89.
14   s20(9)(a) CA89.
15   s20(8) CA89.
16   s20(7) CA89.
17   s20(11) CA89.

> s20(6) CA89 Before providing accommodation under this section, a local authority shall, so far as is reasonably practicable and consistent with the child's welfare –
>
> (a) ascertain the child's wishes and feelings regarding the provision of accommodation; and
>
> (b) give due consideration (having regard to his age and understanding) to such wishes of the child as they have been able to ascertain.

8.5 – Accommodation in action

Nigel, aged 12, lives with his mother, Olivia. His parents are separated and he is registered as a child in need. Olivia is going into a three-month residential drug rehabilitation programme and she asks the local authority to arrange foster care for Nigel while she undertakes her rehab.

Social worker Peter consults Nigel who says he is 'OK' about going into foster care. The local authority has a duty to accommodate Nigel under s20(1)(c) CA89 because:

- he is a child in need
- Olivia is temporarily prevented from looking after him
- he appears to need accommodation.

Peter draws up an agreement with Olivia which says:

- Nigel is to be accommodated for at least the three months of Olivia's treatment
- Olivia will give at least a week's notice before removing Nigel from the foster home
- Olivia delegates to the local authority aspects of her PR, including giving day to day care, arranging routine and emergency medical treatment and agreeing to school trips.

Variation 1 – Nigel's father, Quentin, has PR. When Peter tells him of the accommodation plan, Quentin says he can care for Nigel and opposes foster care.

Peter may try to work with Quentin but he has no right to accommodate Nigel against Quentin's wishes – even if Quentin hardly knows his son and Nigel does not want to live with him. If Peter has evidence that Nigel is likely to suffer significant harm in Quentin's care, he must invoke child protection procedures but, if not, can only offer advice and support.

Variation 2 – Quentin has PR, but Olivia has a residence order.

The residence order changes the situation: Quentin cannot now veto Nigel's accommodation. He must go to court to discharge or vary the residence order before he can oppose accommodation.

Variation 3 – Quentin has no PR. He is able and willing to care for Nigel, who wants to live with him, but Olivia objects.

Without PR, Quentin cannot veto accommodation. Only Olivia has PR so, even if Nigel would be better off with Quentin, he cannot be placed there against Olivia's wishes. Quentin must seek a PR order or residence order.

Variation 4 – Quentin has a contact order.

Quentin's contact order is unaffected by Nigel's accommodation and must be honoured.

Variation 5 – Olivia leaves rehab without completing her programme. She demands Nigel's immediate return.

Even though Olivia agreed to give notice before resuming Nigel's care, this has no legal force and she has the right to remove him at any time. Peter can only block Nigel's return if circumstances justify emergency compulsory action.

Variation 6 – Olivia arrives at the foster home at 3 am in an unfit state to care for Nigel, demanding his instant return.

The foster father does not want to be pushed into an immediate decision. He can fall back on s3(5) CA89, as he is a person without PR but with the actual care of the child. He can 'do what is reasonable in all the circumstances of the case for the purpose of safeguarding or promoting the child's welfare'. This buys him enough time to try to persuade Olivia to wait until morning and talk to Peter, or to phone the out of hours service or police for them to decide whether to take emergency action to prevent Nigel's removal.

Variation 7 – Olivia's drug problem worsens and she is unable to care for Nigel in the foreseeable future.

Nigel can remain accommodated long term, for the rest of his childhood if necessary. s20(1)(c) CA89 still applies as his mother is now permanently prevented from caring for him.

Variation 8 – Nigel is now 16 and settled in his foster home. Olivia is better and wants to have Nigel back home. He refuses to go.

As Nigel is 16, Olivia no longer has an automatic right to discharge him from accommodation. He can refuse to leave, and the local authority can continue to look after him even against Olivia's wishes. Even a month before Nigel's sixteenth birthday, the provision would not apply and Olivia would have the right to discharge him against his wishes in the absence of a court order.

A looked after child

An accommodated child is a 'looked after' child, just as his counterpart who is in care. The local authority's duties to such children are spelled out in detail in CA89 and accompanying Regulations and are summarised in Appendix 5.

Disagreements

The statutory scheme assumes that everyone will work in partnership and harmony. But what if there is a disagreement about what is best for the child? For a child in care, the answer is simple as the local authority has the final say. Not so where a child is accommodated: the parent(s) have PR but are not caring for the child while the local authority is caring for the child, but has no PR. Just such a situation arose in the case of a 12-year-old girl with multiple severe disabilities and other difficulties.[18] She had been accommodated by the local authority for three years in a residential placement as her parents were unable to meet her needs. The local authority then proposed to move her to a foster home. Her parents opposed the move, but the local authority went ahead and commenced introductions.

The parents sought a judicial review of the local authority's actions. The High Court found that the authority had no right to move the child against the parents' wishes as it had no PR, but the parents had no right to dictate to the local authority how it used its resources or to demand a particular placement: there was a legal impasse. The local authority could not place the girl in the foster home and the parents could not insist that she stayed in the residential home.

Because this was judicial review, the court's job was done in simply declaring the authority's planned actions unlawful – it did not have juris-

---

18   *R v. Tameside BC ex parte J* [2000] 1FLR 942 High Court.

diction to make an order resolving the problem. However, three options were suggested:

- the parties could negotiate a solution (a little optimistic when the dispute had already gone to court)

- the local authority should consider whether there were grounds to seek a care order, which would give it power to determine the child's placement

- the authority could say to the parents 'this is the service we are offering. If you are not happy, you can exercise your PR by taking on or arranging her care yourself.'

This case shows the potential practical difficulties arising from the legal characteristics of accommodation especially if the arrangement continues long term.

Ending accommodation

The CA89 says very little about how accommodation ends. The presumption is that the child simply returns to a parent's care, automatically ending the period of accommodation by the authority.

Sometimes, a child spends a brief period in foster care, then a family member comes forward for him and the authority happily hands the child over to that person's care. There are two possible legal interpretations of such an arrangement, with very different consequences for all concerned:

1. The child is discharged from accommodation to the new carer.[19] The local authority has fulfilled its duty, and the child is no longer 'looked after'. The new carer could care for the child as a private foster carer or seek a residence order/special guardianship order.

2. The local authority places the child with the new carer.[20] The carer must be assessed and registered as a local authority foster parent, even if he is a relative. The child remains 'looked after' and the local authority remains responsible for his accommodation and maintenance and in due course may have to provide after care services.

---

19   Under s23(6) CA89.
20   Under s23(2) CA89.

The London Borough of Southwark had cause to rue its failure to be explicit about the legal basis of just such a placement.[21] A social worker arranged for a girl (who had previously spent some time in foster care) to live with her father's ex-partner. The carer was told the local authority would assist her and she received financial help on four occasions. Later help was refused, so she took the matter to court. Southwark argued that it had not placed the girl with the carer, it had simply facilitated a private fostering arrangement, acting as a broker between private individuals. It denied further responsibility. The Court of Appeal disagreed, saying that, if a local authority takes a major role in making arrangements for a child, the most likely conclusion is that it is exercising its powers and duties to accommodate the child – private fostering arrangements are usually made direct between individuals. If an authority wants to side-step its duty to accommodate by arranging private foster care it must be explicit to all those involved, including giving clear information about financial arrangements – otherwise both the carer and the court are likely to conclude that the local authority is making the placement.

The High Court considered three cases where councils argued that unaccompanied minor asylum seekers had been housed under s17 CA89, not accommodated under s20 CA89.[22] The practical importance was that under s20 CA89 the young people would have been 'looked after' and entitled to ongoing services; not so if they were given services under s17 CA89. The court decided that, where the authorities had a duty to accommodate under s20 CA89 and did provide accommodation, they could not escape their responsibilities by giving the arrangement a different label. The only authority which escaped liability was Islington, which had assisted a 16-year-old girl to sign a tenancy agreement direct with a private landlord and to fund her rent from housing benefit.

Accommodation and child protection

In the scheme of the CA89, there is a clear distinction between support services, including accommodation, and child protection measures. In practice, boundaries are more blurred. Where a child needs to be accommo-

---

21 *Southwark London Borough Council* v. *D* [2007] EWCA Civ 182 [2007] 1FLR 2181 Court of Appeal.

22 *R (H)* v. *Wandsworth LBC*; *R (Barhanu)* v. *Hackney LBC*; *R (B)* v. *LB Islington* [2007] EWHC 1082 (Admin) High Court.

dated because of serious inadequacies in parental care, a support service starts to blend into a protective measure.

Sometimes parents are asked to agree to have their child accommodated to avoid care proceedings. Reaching an agreement rather than resorting to compulsory measures is often said to be 'partnership with parents', consistent with the idea of minimum intervention and the 'no order' principle in s1(5) CA89. But is an agreement secured by an implicit threat really an agreement at all? The idea of 'partnership' is stretched to breaking point when the balance of power is so unequal. Accommodation, designed to be a truly voluntary measure, does not have the safeguards of care proceedings: legal advice for parents, separate representation for the child and independent adjudication on the evidence by a court. All the cards are in the local authority's hand.

If the parents agree to have the child accommodated, this is only the start. Thereafter, their co-operation has to be secured at every stage as they retain exclusive PR – the local authority has no power to dictate to them or to make long term plans, a particular problem if the parents are not always predictable or reasonable. The ultimate problem is that they have the power to remove the child at any time and without notice. The authority is then forced to fall back onto the compulsory measures it was trying to avoid.

Child protection cases should be taken through the mechanisms designed specifically for such situations, not shoe-horned into a legal model which does not fit. Accommodation is there to help and support children and their families who are in need and should be kept for situations where agreement truly exists.

Points for practice

1. Always be clear whether a looked after child is accommodated or in care.

2. Make sure you know who has PR for an accommodated child.

3. Even if you are making arrangements at short notice, be clear with all concerned the exact legal basis on which they are made.

4. Record everything in writing, specifying the legal basis for your actions.

5. Use accommodation for cases of true agreement, not for child protection cases.

Part 4

Child Protection

Chapter 9

Child Protection Investigations

Introduction

Child protection hits the headlines when authorities fail a child in desperate need of rescue (like Victoria Climbié) or when over-reactions lead to children being removed unnecessarily (as in Cleveland). There are inquiries, reports and law reforms (the Cleveland report informed the Children Act 1989;[1] the Climbié report influenced the Children Act 2004.)[2] Then the fuss dies down, politicians and media assume that problems are resolved and social workers struggle on doing their best to protect children. Success goes unreported and unnoticed.

McFarlane J summed up the situation eloquently:[3]

> The child protection system depends upon the skill, insight and sheer hard work of front line social workers. Underlying those key features, there is a need for social workers to feel supported and valued by the courts, the state and the general populace to a far greater degree than is normally the case. Working in overstretched teams with limited resources, social workers frequently have to make crucial decisions, with important implications,

---

1   E. Butler Sloss (1989) *Report of the Inquiry into Child Abuse in Cleveland 1987.* London: HMSO.

2   Lord Laming (2003) *The Victoria Climbié Inquiry. Report of an Inquiry by Lord Laming,* available at www.victoria-climbie-inquiry.org.uk, accessed 11 August 2008.

3   *Re X (Emergency Protection Orders)* [2006] EWHC 510 (Fam) [2006] 2FLR 701 High Court, at paragraph 20.

on issues of child protection; often of necessity these decisions must be based upon the available information which may be inchoate or partial. There are often risks to the child flowing from every available option (risk of harm if the child stays at home, risk of emotional harm at least if the child is removed). It is said that in these situations social workers are 'damned if they do, and damned if they don't' take action. Despite these difficulties, it is my experience that very frequently social workers 'get it right' and take the right action, for the right reasons, based upon a professional and wise evaluation of the available information. Such cases sadly do not hit the headlines, or warrant lengthy scrutiny in a High Court judgment. I say 'sadly' because there is a need for successful social work, of which there are many daily examples, to be applauded and made known to the public at large.

Ironically, this passage appeared in a judgment about a case of disastrously poor practice.

Ensuring that your cases fall in the category of unnoticed success requires clear thinking, good judgment and a sound knowledge of the relevant law.

Strategic responsibilities

The Children Act 2004 (CA04)[4] transferred key responsibility for child protection to Directorates of Children's Services (effective from 1 April 2008) under the leadership of a Director of Children's Services.

It also set up the multi-agency body for implementing child protection procedures in each area, the Local Safeguarding Children Board (LSCB). The local authority appoints the Chair, and partner agencies are represented by people senior enough to speak authoritatively for their agencies, commit them to policy and practice and hold them to account. Represented agencies include the police, health authorities, probation, CAFCASS, Connexions and Youth Offending Teams.

The LSCB is to co-ordinate the represented bodies' actions to safeguard and promote children's welfare in their area.[5] To this end, its main functions (set out in CA04 and regulations[6]) are:

---

4   Children Act 2004. London: Stationery Office, available at www.opsi.gov.uk/acts/acts2004/ukpga_20040031_en_1, accessed 11 August 2008.

5   s14(1) CA04.

6   Local Safeguarding Children Boards Regulations 2006 SI 2006/90, available at www.opsi.gov.uk/si/si2006/20060090.htm, accessed 11 August 2008.

- devising policies and procedures covering:
  - ° action to be taken in case of concerns about a child's safety or welfare including:
- thresholds for intervention (for support services and child protection)
- inter-agency procedures for enquiries (such as joint police and social work investigations)
  - ° recruiting, training and supervising people working with children
  - ° investigation of allegations against people working with children
  - ° safety and welfare of privately fostered children
  - ° co-operation with neighbouring authorities
- communication and raising awareness about child protection
- monitoring and evaluating actions of the local authority, LSCB and partner agencies and encouraging improvement
- participating in planning and commissioning children's services
- reviewing child deaths
- conducting serious case reviews where abuse or neglect is known or suspected, a child has died or been seriously harmed and there is concern about the work of the local authority or partner agencies.

Significant harm

The key term in all Children Act 1989 (CA89) child protection provisions from initial investigation through to care orders is 'significant harm'. Understanding this term is fundamental.

Harm

The statutory definition in s31(9) CA89 states that 'harm' means 'ill-treatment or the impairment of health or development'. 'Ill-treatment' includes 'sexual abuse and forms of ill-treatment which are not physical', thus including emotional abuse. Physical abuse itself is not explicitly included, but this is taken as read. Just as in s17 CA89, 'health' includes both physical and mental health, and 'development' includes physical, intellectual, emotional, social and behavioural development.

To assess whether health or development are being significantly impaired, s31(10) CA89 tells us to compare the health or development of the child in question 'with that which could reasonably be expected of a similar child'. What is a 'similar child'? Perhaps this was thought to be obvious – there are standard expectations for certain age groups and a developmental assessment will show whether a child is within the 'normal' range. But the Act does not tell us which similarities to import from our actual child into our hypothetical 'similar' child – there is no point comparing him with a child who is similar in all respects, including his neglectful or abusive upbringing. The question was considered in Re O which concerned significant harm caused by lack of education.[7] There the judge said 'in this context a "similar child" means a child of equivalent intellectual and social development, who has gone to school, and not merely an average child who may or may not be at school'. It seems, therefore, that we have to consider a hypothetical 'average' child of the same age and potential, but factor out elements of abuse or neglect.

The definition of significant harm includes 'impairment suffered from seeing or hearing the ill-treatment of another'. This was added with domestic violence in mind, but it could equally apply to a case where one child is abused while another is not, but suffers indirectly.

Significant

The word 'significant' is not defined in the Act. Is 'significant' the same as 'serious'?

9.1 – Not serious but significant?

Four-month-old Robert has bruises to his face. His father cannot see what all the fuss is about. He argues that bruises are not serious – no medical treatment is needed, and they leave no scars. This is true – Robert's injuries are not medically serious, but they can still be significant.

---

7   *Re O (A Minor) (Care Order: Education: Procedure)* [1992] 2FLR 7 High Court.

That is not to say that the degree of seriousness is irrelevant. To justify compulsory intervention in a family's life there must be, in the words of Hedley J, 'something unusual; at least something more than the commonplace human failure or inadequacy'.[8] In that case, the children were 'in need', had suffered and would continue to suffer harm – but it did not reach the level of 'significant' harm.

The degree of certainty

At the outset of a child protection investigation, only limited information is available but, if the case goes to care proceedings, by the final hearing the matter will have been investigated and assessed in minute detail. Not surprisingly, therefore, the law requires the existence of significant harm to be demonstrated with an increasing degree of certainty at each stage.

SUSPICION

To justify an initial child protection investigation, s47 CA89 requires 'reasonable cause to suspect' actual or likely significant harm. There must be 'reasonable cause' – the authority cannot descend on a family at random to see if there is a problem – but the information only has to be enough to warrant suspicion.

In one case the applicant complained to court because the local authority started an investigation to see if he posed a risk to children despite his acquittal for criminal charges of sexual abuse.[9] He argued that, as he had been found innocent by the criminal court, there could be no grounds for suspicion. The High Court disagreed. The fact that a criminal court had not found evidence 'beyond reasonable doubt' did not rule out 'reasonable cause to suspect', a much lower test.

BELIEF

A higher level of certainty is expected by the time it comes to a court application. To obtain an emergency protection order (EPO), the applicant must establish that 'there is reasonable cause to believe' that significant

---

8   *Re L (Care: Threshold Criteria)* [2007] 1FLR 2050 High Court, at paragraph 51. This case is discussed further in Chapter 11.

9   *R (ota S) v. Swindon Borough Council* [2001] 2FLR 776 High Court.

harm is likely.[10] 'Believe' is a stronger word than 'suspect', so a greater level of evidence is needed. For the next stage, an interim care order, the court must be satisfied that 'there are reasonable grounds for believing' not only that significant harm exists, but also that it is attributable to inadequate care or the child being beyond control.[11]

SATISFIED

To make a final care or supervision order, the court must be 'satisfied' on the balance of probabilities that threshold criteria exist. The House of Lords has explicitly said that suspicion is not enough to establish the grounds for a care order.[12] It is, however, all that is required to trigger the local authority's duty to investigate under s47 CA89.

---

s47(1) CA89 Where a local authority –

- (a) are informed that a child who lives, or is found, in their area –

  - (i) is the subject of an emergency protection order; or

  - (ii) is in police protection; or

  - (iii) has contravened a ban imposed by a curfew notice within the...Crime and Disorder Act 1998 or

- (b) have reasonable cause to suspect that a child who lives, or is found, in their area is suffering, or is likely to suffer, significant harm, the authority shall make, or cause to be made, such enquiries as they consider necessary to enable them to decide whether they should take any action to safeguard or promote the child's welfare.

The duty to investigate

Most cases fall in category (b), which includes referrals about a child's welfare from other agencies and from members of the public.

---

10   s44 CA89.
11   s38 CA89 – discussed further in Chapter 12.
12   *Re H & R (Child Sexual Abuse: Standard of Proof)* [1996] 1FLR 80 House of Lords. Affirmed by the House of Lords in *Re B (Children)* [2008] UKHL 35.

Enquiries are not just to decide whether child protection measures need to be taken – 'any action' to safeguard or promote the child's welfare could include:

- taking care proceedings

- providing services to the child and family (s17 CA89)

- helping the family resolve problems themselves

- taking no action at all.

If the authority decides that some action should be taken, then it must take it 'so far as it is both within their power and reasonably practicable to do so'.[13] If the authority decides not to make any court applications, it must consider whether to review the case at a later date.[14]

---

s47(4) CA89 Where enquiries are being made under subsection (1) with respect to a child, the local authority shall (with a view to enabling them to determine what action, if any, to take with respect to him) take such steps as are reasonably practicable –

(a)   to obtain access to him; or

(b)   to ensure that access to him is obtained, on their behalf, by a person authorised by them for the purpose,

unless they are satisfied that they already have sufficient information with respect to him.

The Act says that enquiries must be made but their nature and extent is left to the authority's judgment, informed by guidance. The one statutory requirement is that the child must normally be seen.

This section is backed up by the duty to apply for an EPO if access to the child is refused or information as to his whereabouts is denied.[15] So far as practicable and consistent with the child's welfare, the authority must ascertain and give due consideration to the child's wishes and feelings about any action to be taken.[16]

---

13   s47(8) CA89.

14   s47(7) CA89.

15   s47(6) and s44(1) CA89 – for more detail on emergency protection orders see Chapter 10.

16   s47(5A) CA89.

The importance of someone actually seeing the child cannot be over-stated. One of the many haunting aspects of the Victoria Climbié tragedy is that, in Lord Laming's words:[17]

> in the last few weeks before she died, a social worker called at her home several times. She got no reply when she knocked at the door and assumed that Victoria and Kouao had moved away. It is possible that at the time, Victoria was in fact lying just a few yards away, in the prison of the bath, desperately hoping that someone might find her and come to her rescue before her life ebbed away.

Other agencies

Other local authorities and education, housing and health authorities have a statutory duty to assist with s47 CA89 enquiries by providing relevant information and advice.[18] The concept of inter-agency working in child protection should be so deeply ingrained that a formal request for help should not be necessary – but it is useful to know the statutory basis for doing so if required. Partner agencies can also be reminded of their own statutory duty to have regard to the need to safeguard and promote children's welfare in discharging their functions.[19]

Time and again, enquiry reports highlight failures in inter-agency working and stress the need for close co-operation and information sharing. Statutory duties can only do so much; agencies must put procedures in place and foster links at ground level so the theory of co-operation becomes second nature in practice.

Guidance

Most of the detailed instruction on inter-agency working and assessment appears in guidance, particularly the *Framework for the Assessment of Children in Need and their Families* (the Framework)[20] and *Working Together to Safeguard*

---

17   Laming (2003), paragraph 1.11 (see note 2 above).
18   s47(9)–(11) CA89.
19   s11(2) CA04.
20   Department of Health (2000) *Framework for the Assessment of Children in Need and their Families*. London: Stationery Office, available at www.dh.gov.uk/en/Publicationsandstatistics/Publications/PublicationsPolicyAndGuidance/DH_4003256, accessed 11 August 2008.

Children – A Guide to Inter-agency Working to Safeguard and Promote the Welfare of Children (Working Together).[21]

The Framework and Part I of Working Together are issued under s7 Local Authority Social Services Act 1970 so must be followed unless there are exceptional reasons for not doing so. It is wise to be familiar with the full text of both documents, which give authoritative and detailed practical advice. If you find ever yourself responding to a complaint or explaining your actions in court you will be very glad to be able to refer to the statutory guidance you followed.

Working Together stresses the need for careful records to be kept at every stage. This cannot be overemphasised, especially from a legal point of view. Action can only be taken on a sound basis if information is noted carefully and accurately – otherwise misunderstanding and miscommunication can lead to mistakes. All decisions (including decisions not to take a particular step) and the reasons for them must be recorded. Legal challenges to action taken, or not taken, can arise long after everyone involved has left or forgotten the case; only the records remain to explain what was done and why.

Enquiries and assessments

The procedure laid out in detail in Working Together and the Framework is, briefly, as follows. An initial assessment is carried out in a maximum of seven days from receipt of a referral, but if the situation clearly falls within s47 CA89, especially if it is urgent, it can in reality be very brief indeed.[22] There should be a strategy discussion between the local authority, police and other relevant agencies, including the referring agency, to decide whether to carry out a s47 CA89 enquiry by undertaking a core assessment (following the Framework guidelines). Legal advice may be needed.

Enquiries might result in concerns being discounted leading to no further action, or reveal that the child is in need, not at risk, moving the case from s47 CA89 to s17 CA89. If, however, it appears that the child is at continuing risk of significant harm, a Child Protection Case Conference should be convened.

Throughout the assessment, including when seeking views and information from others, your objective may be to resolve problems informally

---

21   HM Government (2006) *Working Together to Safeguard Children*. London: Stationery Office, available at www.everychildmatters.gov.uk/workingtogether, accessed 12 August 2008.

22   Cases where emergency action is needed are discussed further in Chapter 10.

but it is best to assume that the case will end up in court. Every conversation and observation should be carefully recorded – it could become crucial evidence. Requests for information from other agencies should be made professionally with an eye to a possible future court application. If a doctor or other expert is asked to provide a report or carry out an assessment, it is good practice to send a formal letter of instructions in the same way as if proceedings were under way. Ryder J gave guidance on instructing medical experts including during pre-proceedings investigations.[23] They should be asked effectively to work through their differential diagnosis, highlighting any contradictory or inconsistent features, and to indicate the range of possible mainstream opinions including whether one answer might be that the cause of any injury is unknown. The Family Justice Council gives authoritative guidance on how to formulate a letter of instructions, a task best left to lawyers.[24]

Child Protection Case Conferences

The Case Conference mechanism is not statutory, but appears in Working Together.[25] The Conference's role is to:

- bring together information from people and agencies involved with the child and family

- analyse that information

- make a judgment about whether the child is at continuing risk of significant harm

- decide on future action.

The LSCB sets local procedures, including fixing the quorum, but Working Together states that at least two agencies as well as the local authority should be represented. The Chair must be independent from operational and line management responsibility for the case and is accountable to the Director of Children's Services. Parents should be invited unless there are exceptional reasons to the contrary. Even if they cannot attend, their views should be put to the meeting and they should be fully informed of discussions and given full minutes unless there are good reasons for part of the

---

23   *Oldham MBC* v. *GW and PW* [2007] EWHC 136 (Fam) [2007] 2FLR 597 High Court.
24   See Appendix E of *Family Justice Council Annual Report 2006*, available at www.family-justice-council.org.uk/docs/fjc_ra.pdf, accessed 12 August 2008.
25   Working Together, paragraphs 5.80–5.135 (see note 21 above).

minutes to remain confidential. Consideration also needs to be given to the attendance of the child and other family members and advocates, all in accordance with local policies determined by the LSCB.

The Case Conference's job is to determine whether the child is at continuing risk of significant harm, not whether he has already suffered harm – harm may have occurred but the risk may be over. Alternatively, he may not yet have suffered harm but there is a risk that he will do so if action is not taken.

If the Conference determines that a continuing risk exists, the child becomes a 'child subject to a child protection plan'. The Chair of the Conference decides the primary category of harm (physical, emotional, sexual abuse or neglect) which is noted on the child's record. The Conference then prepares an outline protection plan and establishes the core group to put it into practice. The child's case must be reviewed by a further conference within three months, and at least six monthly thereafter.

The Conference has no power to decide whether any legal proceedings should be taken. It may make recommendations but the decision whether or not to initiate care proceedings lies solely with the local authority.

The local authority must maintain a list of children subject to child protection plans, the replacement for the old Child Protection Register. Agencies must be able to access this list at all times; at 3am on Christmas Day if necessary.

CHALLENGING CASE CONFERENCE DECISIONS

The LSCB must devise a procedure for complaints about Case Conferences and disagreements should be resolved by internal procedures. The courts are rarely involved although, as a last resort, judicial review is potentially available. In one case, the court found that a Conference was wrong to enter the child's name on the Child Protection Register because it had heard no evidence about that individual child (information had centred on siblings).[26] It is an important reminder that children within the same family do not come as a 'job lot' – each child must be considered individually.

The process must be fair and the courts can intervene if it is not. In one such case, not only was the child registered but a particular individual was registered as the abuser without even giving him the opportunity to

---

26   R v. *Hampshire County Council ex parte H* [1999] 2FLR 359 High Court.

comment on the allegations.[27] Such a blatantly unfair procedure could not stand, even before the Human Rights Act 1998. Legal challenges to Case Conferences may be rare, but there is no excuse to abandon principles of fairness and justice.

Child assessment orders

Imagine the situation: you suspect that a child might be suffering or likely to suffer significant harm but cannot be sure without a particular assessment. The parents refuse and the child is not old enough to consent to the assessment for herself. What can you do? You cannot go ahead with the assessment without parental consent and you cannot apply for an EPO or care order because, without the assessment, you have insufficient evidence.

This is precisely the situation for which child assessment orders (CAOs) were designed.[28] On the local authority's application, the court can authorise a specific assessment to be carried out and require the child to be produced for that purpose, although the child can refuse to co-operate if he is of sufficient age and understanding.

These orders are rarely sought. Usually in practice either parental co-operation is secured, making a CAO unnecessary, or the case proceeds rapidly to the stage where, even without the assessment, evidence exists for an EPO or care proceedings.

A CAO can only order an assessment lasting a maximum of seven days, restricting the eligible type and scope of assessment – a single medical examination or initial psychiatric assessment could be covered but a core assessment is out of the question. An investigative interview with the child could be ordered, but applications for CAOs can only be made on notice to the child's parents, allowing the opportunity for the child to be coached on what to say during the interview.

In spite of their shortcomings, it is important to remember that CAOs exist and can sometimes be a useful weapon in your armoury.

---

27   *R v. Norfolk County Council ex p X* [1989] 2FLR 120 High Court.
28   s43 CA89.

Particular situations

Joint police and social work investigations

An allegation of physical or sexual abuse or domestic violence involving a child triggers a local authority investigation under s47 CA89 but it is also a report of a crime leading to a police investigation.[29] The two agencies must co-ordinate their responses and share information from the moment a referral comes in and LSCBs should devise local protocols to ensure this happens. Once proceedings start, the Court of Appeal has emphasised the need for close liaison between police and local authority children's services.[30] Wherever possible, criminal and care proceedings should be co-ordinated with linked directions hearings.

Interviewing alleged victims, perpetrators and potential witnesses is a key issue. Mistakes made even at the earliest stage of enquiries could taint evidence and jeopardise the prospects of successful action. For example, if an interview with an alleged perpetrator is not conducted under caution, any confession will be inadmissible in a criminal trial.

Interviewing children is a particularly sensitive task. Working Together says:

> It is important that even initial discussions with children are conducted in a way that minimises any distress caused to them, and maximises the likelihood that they will provide accurate and complete information. It is important, wherever possible, to have separate communication with a child. Leading or suggestive communication should always be avoided. Children may need time and more than one opportunity in order to develop sufficient trust to communicate any concerns they may have, especially if they have a communication impairment, learning disabilities, are very young or are experiencing mental health problems.[31]

Detailed guidance on conducting interviews with children is contained in the authoritative guideline *Achieving Best Evidence in Criminal Proceedings: Guidance for Vulnerable or Intimidated Witnesses, including Children.*[32] If they

---

29   For a thorough and clear exposition of legal considerations see Law Society (2007) 'Related Family and Criminal Proceedings', available at www.family-justice-council. org.uk/docs/RelatedFamCrimPro.pdf, accessed 12 August 2008.

30   *R* v. *Levey* [2006] EWCA Crim 1902 [2007] 1FLR 462 Court of Appeal.

31   Working Together, at paragraph 5.64 (see note 21 above).

32   Home Office (2006) *Guidance for Vulnerable or Intimidated Witnesses, including Children,* available at www.homeoffice.gov.uk/documents/achieving-best-evidence, accessed 12 August 2008.

are not followed, any video recorded interview with a child is likely to be ruled inadmissible in a criminal trial, so the child will have to attend court to give all his evidence in person.

In care proceedings, the rules of evidence are more flexible. If the guidelines are not followed to the letter, interviews may still be considered by the court but given diminished weight. As a judge said: 'where the guidelines have not been followed, evidence of young children can be dangerously suspect'.[33]

Even the most immaculate video interview can, however, be undermined if at an earlier stage the child has been questioned clumsily or carelessly. Any discussions with the child from the very first contact must be handled professionally and with an eye to later court proceedings. It is vital to keep a careful and accurate record of every contact with the child, recording not just the child's answers but also the questions asked.

9.2 – Recording questions

Sally said 'Daddy punched me', but what was the question? It could have been:

- 'What happened?' – a non-leading question enabling Sally freely to recall events, giving her answer considerable evidential value

- 'Did Mummy or Daddy hit you?' – a closed question, giving Sally two options, both presuming that a parent has hit her, greatly reducing the value of her answer

- 'Tell me how Daddy hurt you' – a wholly leading question just asking Sally to confirm the questioner's version of events, making her answer evidentially worthless.

If there is no record of the question asked, the court will treat the answer with caution and Sally's clear disclosure will be undermined.

In *Re B* a police officer and social worker conducted a preliminary interview with children without recording it and noting only the answers, not the questions.[34] The Court of Appeal, discussing the *Achieving Best Evidence* guidelines, noted that children can sometimes:

---

33   *G v. DPP* [1997] 2FLR 810 High Court, at 813F.

34   *Re B (Allegation of Sexual Abuse: Child's Evidence)* [2006] EWCA Civ 773 [2006] 2FLR 1071 Court of Appeal.

- be poor historians
- view adults as authority figures
- be suggestible
- want to please
- be unable to express themselves clearly
- be misunderstood
- fail to understand what is being said or done.

Hughes LJ stressed the importance of giving children the maximum possibility of recalling freely, uninhibited by questions, what they are able to say and of taking a careful note of questions as well as answers. He explained that the guidelines are intended to produce the most reliable evidence that can be obtained. The fact that a family case concentrates on a child's welfare does not mean that unsatisfactory evidence can be given greater weight than it can properly bear.

Key points to remember include the following:

- only people with specialist training and experience should conduct interviews
- interviewers should be appropriate to the case, including consideration of their gender
- the child should be able to communicate in his first language (spoken or signed) wherever possible
- any special needs must be taken into account, seeking specialist help or advice where necessary
- interviewers should have an understanding of relevant cultural or religious considerations
- no one but the interviewer(s) should be present with the child
- leading questions should be avoided
- children should not be coached or offered incentives
- technical equipment must work efficiently, the room must be adequately lit and the video recording must show the child and the room clearly

- the purpose of the interview must be clear with no confusion between forensic and therapeutic interviews (therapeutic interviews usually have little evidential value).

Is parental consent needed to interview a child? Usually parents decide who can speak to their child, but in child protection cases it may be essential to proceed without seeking prior parental consent. Examples in Working Together include situations where:

- the child may be threatened or otherwise coerced into silence

- important evidence will be destroyed

- a competent child does not wish the parent to be involved.[35]

The decision and the reasons for it should be clearly recorded on the file.

Protecting children with disabilities

Clearly, in principle, a child with disabilities should receive the same protection from abuse and neglect as any other child. In practice, Working Together reports that children with disabilities, especially those with multiple disabilities, are for a variety of reasons even more vulnerable to abuse than other children.[36]

Investigation of alleged abuse or neglect of a disabled child demands strong inter-agency co-operation, often requiring specialist help, such as assistance with communication. Interviews with disabled children require particularly careful planning. If a disabled child has to give evidence in the criminal court, special measures, including using communication aids, are available thanks to the Youth Justice and Criminal Evidence Act 1999.

Where concern turns on impairment of health or development, the definition of significant harm poses a particular challenge in the context of disability. What is a 'similar child'? Clearly the hypothetical similar child must have the same disability as the actual child, but the effect of even the same diagnosed disability can vary widely from one child to another. Precisely where on the spectrum does a 'similar child' lie? How can we establish whether our child's health or development is impaired by his innate difficulties or by inadequate, neglectful or abusive parenting? This can be very difficult in practice and depends on close observation, detailed

---

35   Working Together, at paragraph 5.65 (see note 21 above).
36   These issues are further discussed in Working Together, paragraphs 11.26–11.31 (see note 21 above).

evidence gathering and careful inter-agency co-operation, including seeking specialist advice.

How does the local authority's duty to support the child and family fit in with the duty to protect the child? Hedley J tackled this issue in a case involving a child with a major and life-long disability.[37] He expressed the view that the local authority cannot fail to put in support and then use that failure as grounds for compulsory intervention in the child's life. He said 'a parent cannot be said to be responsible for falling below the standard of "reasonable care" if the public authorities cannot or do not provide what would be reasonably necessary to support that parent'.[38] Cooperating with that advice and support is part of responsible parenting, and failure to do so can be taken into account in assessing whether to move to child protection measures.

Disability in itself, and the very idea of the abuse of disabled children, can raise extra levels of sensitivity and emotional response amongst those involved, perhaps particularly amongst professionals inexperienced in disability issues (possibly including lawyers and the courts). Those working with the family may have difficulty changing from a mindset of support and empathy to one of investigation and moving their focus from the parents to the child. These factors need to be acknowledged in the process.

Emotional abuse and neglect

Emotional abuse or neglect is an element of all types of ill-treatment, but can also cause significant harm on its own. Indeed, emotional abuse and neglect can cause profound and lasting damage and should not be underestimated or given less priority than other more visible or acute forms of abuse. Emotional ill-treatment can be 'inhuman' or 'degrading' within Article 3 of the European Convention on Human Rights.

Emotional ill-treatment can too easily be overlooked, simply because it usually takes place behind closed doors, is chronic, invisible and there is no straightforward evidence – it does not show up on an X-ray. However, with careful observation and close inter-agency working, it is possible to find evidence. Observations of interactions between parents and child, direct work with the child, school reports of a child's academic performance, behaviour and self-esteem and psychological assessments can all build up an evidential picture which is not apparent to any single agency.

---

37   *LBH (A Local Authority* v. *KJ and Others)* [2007] EWHC 2798 (Fam) High Court.
38   *LBH*, at paragraph 22 (see note 37 above).

Unborn babies

Sometimes concerns arise for a child even before birth because of the histories of older children in the family or because the parents' lifestyle or behaviour is likely to harm the baby. Court proceedings cannot be taken in respect of a child before birth, but child protection procedures can and should be. This can include holding a Case Conference and making an unborn child subject to a child protection plan. In extreme cases, a plan may be needed to take emergency action as soon as the baby is born.[39] All relevant agencies and professionals (obviously including midwives) must be fully briefed.

Fabricated or induced illness

This form of child abuse is a highly sensitive issue to be approached with care and clarity of analysis. In these cases, parents may report non-existent illness or symptoms (the illness is fabricated) or the symptoms may be real but caused or exacerbated by the actions of parents or carers (the illness is induced).

Ryder J confirmed that the old term 'Munchausen syndrome by proxy' should be abandoned and 'factitious and induced illness by proxy' only used to describe events, not as a substitute for factual analysis and risk assessment; the focus must be on establishing what has actually happened, not applying a label.[40] Co-operation is vital, and in complex cases there should be a formal inter-disciplinary meeting to co-ordinate and assess available information. Although medical and scientific evidence is often crucial, the wider context of social, emotional, ethical and moral factors is also relevant. If you come across such a case, refer to the comprehensive guidance in the Department of Health publication *Safeguarding Children in Whom Illness is Fabricated or Induced.*[41]

Diagnosing fabricated or induced illness does not fall within social work expertise. Obvious as this may seem, it was not apparent to the social workers in one case who obtained an EPO on the basis of their concerns

---

39 See Chapter 10 for more information on emergency procedures.
40 *A County Council* v. *A Mother, A Father* & *X, Y and Z* [2005] 2FLR 129 High Court.
41 Department of Health (2002) *Safeguarding Children in Whom Illness is Fabricated or Induced.* London: Department of Health, available at ww.dh.gov.uk/en/Publicationsandstatistics/Publications/PublicationsPolicyAndGuidance/DH_4008714, accessed 12 August 2008.

of factitious or fabricated illness, formed without taking medical advice or raising the issue at Case Conference.[42] Successful inter-agency working depends on each professional knowing his boundaries, understanding the limits of his own expertise, recognising when to call on others and respecting their contributions.

Dealing with parents

Child abuse and neglect is not limited to any social class, professional or educational background or level of ability. In practice many families involved in child protection investigations are already known to agencies and often come from a particular social sector. Articulate, affluent and able parents may be encountered less often, and can pose a particular challenge in a child protection investigation. It should not be so, but Case Conferences can feel very different when the parents are able and assertive. Such parents often instruct lawyers at an early stage and challenge the legitimacy of every action, making some professionals feel intimidated and uncertain of their ground. Consciously or not, some people, even professionals, feel that such people could not have harmed their children and bring an inherent scepticism to the investigation. Such cases demand a scrupulous regard to procedures, sound legal knowledge, a rigorous approach to investigation and a determination not to be deflected from protecting the child.

At the other end of the spectrum, disadvantaged parents and those with disabilities, learning difficulties or mental health problems can be vulnerable to the process exploiting their lack of knowledge, understanding or assertiveness. Steps must be taken to ensure that the process is fair and their full participation is not impeded,[43] including where appropriate helping them understand information, using interpreters or advocates and taking specialist advice, while never compromising the child's best interests. The record must show how any special needs have been taken into account, ready to answer any allegation that the process has been unfair.

Not surprisingly, families caught up in child protection procedures can be unco-operative. The High Court has stressed 'lack of co-operation by parents is never a reason to close a file or remove a child from the Child Protection Register. On the contrary it is a reason to investigate in greater

---

42   *Re X (Emergency Protection Orders)* [2006] EWHC 510 (Fam) [2006] 2FLR 701 High Court, discussed further in Chapter 10.

43   *Re G (Care: Challenge to Local Authority's Decision)* [2003] 2FLR 42 High Court.

depth.'[44] Difficult families can also be the most dangerous. Risks must be assessed and addressed when planning an investigation. If professionals feel concerned, intimidated or frustrated, imagine how a child feels living in that household.

As Wall LJ said, 'any system can deal with the compliant'.[45] The challenge to social work professionalism is working with those who are uncooperative, including young people themselves. Lack of co-operation never absolves a local authority from its statutory duties. Munby J commented about a young man who failed to co-operate in devising a pathway plan:

> The fact that a child is unco-operative and unwilling to engage, or even refuses to engage, is no reason for the local authority not to carry out its obligations under the Act and the Regulations. After all, a disturbed child's unwillingness to engage with those who are trying to help is often merely a part of the overall problems which justified the local authority's statutory intervention in the first place. The local authority must do its best.[46]

The same applies to families in the child protection process. Failure to co-operate should lead to redoubling efforts, rethinking strategies and harnessing inter-agency co-operation to the full, not abandoning children to their fate.

Complex investigations

Sometimes a case which starts with a single allegation grows beyond all expectations. Often, such cases turn on allegations of sexual abuse, with ever more potential victims and perpetrators coming to light, often linked to a particular institution. Allegations may relate to current or historical abuse, and are unlikely to respect local authority boundaries. Further complications arise if the media show interest in the case.

Such investigations demand careful co-ordination, strategic organisation and a rigorous attention to detail. It is important to remember that each child is an individual, whether or not he happens to be involved in a case of organised or multiple abuse. If a child is the subject of a Case Conference or court proceedings, evidence must be gathered relating to

---

44   *Re E (Care Proceedings: Social Work Practice)* [2000] 2FLR 254 High Court, at paragraphs 257–258.

45   *R (M) v. LB Hammersmith and Fulham* [2006] EWCA Civ 917 [2007] 1FLR 256 Court of Appeal, at paragraph 74.

46   *R (J) v. Caerphilly CBC* [2005] EWHC 586 (Admin) [2005] 2FLR 860 High Court, at paragraph 56.

the particular child, not merely as part of a wider group. The government issued guidance on handling such cases, *Complex Child Abuse Investigations: Inter-agency Issues*[47] – follow its strategic advice if one of your cases is in danger of expanding exponentially.

Points for practice

1. Child protection is built upon a detailed framework of statute, regulation and guidance. A sound knowledge of this framework is essential.

2. In difficult cases, go back to basics – remind yourself of the law and analyse the case applying those key principles.

3. Always assume every case will end up in court. Record everything promptly. Note every decision and reasons for it and always keep paperwork up to date.

4. Processes must be demonstrably fair to all involved.

5. Never allow emotions to cloud your judgment. Seek supervision and advice to remain objective. Keep your focus on the child.

6. Foster inter-agency relationships. Real inter-agency co-operation depends on individual workers building links. Knowing who to call and being able to trust their response is worth a multitude of written policies.

47 Home Office (2002) *Complex Child Abuse Investigations: Inter-agency Issues*, available at www.police.homeoffice.gov.uk/news-and-publications/publication/operational-policing/child_abuse_guidance.pdf, accessed 12 August 2008.

Chapter 10

Emergency Action

Child protection is an unpredictable business. In emergency situations, the stakes are high; failing to act swiftly and decisively could expose a child to serious harm, even death, but equally we must not forget that, as Munby J said in the case of *X Council* v. *B* (*X* v. *B*), 'summarily removing a child from his parents is a terrible and drastic remedy'.[1] Such situations demand robust legal provisions and procedure and sound professional practice.

Police protection and emergency protection orders

The two key provisions for the immediate protection of children are in Part V of the Children Act 1989 (CA89): police protection,[2] an administrative power exercised by the police, and emergency protection orders (EPOs)[3] made by a court. In both cases, we do not look back at what has happened but forward to see whether significant harm is likely if action is not taken, to remove a child if he is unsafe or prevent him from being removed from a safe place (such as hospital). The fact that these sections should be invoked only in a situation of true urgency is implied rather than explicitly stated in the Act.

Given the similarities between the two provisions, how do you decide which to use? Working Together says 'police powers should only be used in exceptional circumstances where there is insufficient time to seek an

---

1   *X Council* v. *B* [2004] EWHC 2015 (Fam) [2005] 1FLR 341 High Court.
2   s46 CA89.
3   s44 CA89.

EPO, or for reasons relating to the immediate safety of the child'.[4] Police protection 'should be used only when necessary, the principle being that wherever possible the decision to remove a child from a parent or carer should be made by a court'.[5]

Police protection

s46(1) CA89 Where a constable has reasonable cause to believe that a child would otherwise be likely to suffer significant harm, he may –

(a)   remove the child to suitable accommodation and keep him there; or

(b)   take such steps as are reasonable to ensure that the child's removal from any hospital, or other place, in which he is then being accommodated is prevented.

A Home Office Circular gives detailed guidance to the police on how to exercise their powers.[6] Proper procedures are particularly important given that police protection is a purely administrative matter; it is not an order and no court is involved. There is no independent scrutiny of the action taken or the grounds for it and no mechanism for parents or child to challenge or appeal against the decision. Human rights issues (Article 6, the right to a fair trial, and Article 8, the right to respect for private and family life) immediately spring to mind.

Police protection is purely a means of providing immediate safety for the child so the police do not obtain parental responsibility (PR). It is a short term measure, lasting a maximum of 72 hours, and must be terminated earlier than that if the danger has passed.

The police must take reasonable steps to inform:

---

4   Department of Health (2000) *Working Together to Safeguard Children – A Guide to Inter-agency Working to Safeguard and Promote the Welfare of Children.* London: Stationery Office, paragraph 5.51, available at www.everychildmatters.gov.uk/workingtogether, accessed 12 August 2008.
5   Working Together, paragraph 2.105 (see note 4 above).
6   Home Office (1989) 'The Duties and Powers of Police under the Children Act 1989', Home Office Circular 44/2003, available at www.crimereduction.homeoffice.gov.uk/victims/victims29.htm, accessed 13 August 2008.

- the child
- his parents
- anyone else with PR
- the person the child was living with

of the action taken, reasons for it and what might happen next. The officer should also try to ascertain the child's wishes and feelings. In theory, he should grant such contact as is both reasonable and in the child's best interests to people including the child's parents but in reality the case usually passes to the local authority before there is any realistic question of contact.

The police officer's first duties include informing the local authorities of the areas where the child was found and where the child normally lives (if different) and ensuring that he is moved to local authority accommodation. In practice the local authority usually takes over responsibility for the child and the future conduct of his case very quickly. Police protection immediately triggers the duty to carry out a s47 CA89 investigation, so the local authority must urgently consider if steps need to be taken to continue the child's protection. If not, the authority may decide to return the child home immediately.

It is always worth remembering that the police have other powers which may be of considerable assistance in an emergency. If it appears that a criminal offence has been or is being committed, or if there is a breach of the peace, the police may have power to arrest and remove from the scene the person who poses the immediate threat to the child. This may be preferable to removing the child and may make it possible to consider child protection measures in a more planned way.

Emergency protection orders
GROUNDS
One of the grounds for EPOs ties in with s47 CA89 and is available only to local authorities. If you are conducting a s47 CA89 investigation and you believe that you need urgent access to the child but the parent unreasonably refuses to allow you to see him, you can apply for an EPO.[7]

---

7   s44(1)(b) CA89.

The more commonly used ground for an EPO is available to anyone at all, although it is extremely rare for anyone other than the local authority to apply.[8]

---

s44(1) CA89 ...the court may make the order if, but only if, it is satisfied that –

    (a)   there is reasonable cause to believe that the child is likely to suffer significant harm if:

        (i)   he is not removed to accommodation provided by or on behalf of the applicant; or

        (ii)   he does not remain in the place in which he is then being accommodated...

Just as for police protection, therefore, the focus for an EPO is on what is likely to happen if action is not taken, rather than what has already happened. The objective can be to remove the child from an unsafe place or to keep him in a safe one.

Court application

An EPO can only be made by a court. Unlike police officers, social workers have no power to remove a child without such an order. Failure to appreciate this led Nottingham City Council into serious and much publicised difficulties when a baby was removed at birth without court authority.[9] Unless there is already a case about the same child under way in another court, the application goes to the Family Proceedings Court. An EPO can be made by a single magistrate and procedures are available for this to happen out of office hours where necessary.

Notice

How much advance warning – if any – should the parents be given of an EPO application? The court rules provide for parents with PR and the

---

8   s44(1)(a) CA89.
9   *R v. Nottingham City Council* [2008] EWHC 152 High Court.

child to have a minimum of one day's notice but, at the discretion of the Justices' Clerk, the court can proceed without any notice at all.[10]

Whether notice should be given is a separate question from whether an order should be made – the court could agree to proceed without notice, but then, on hearing the application, decide not to make an order. The decision about notice is an important one but no specific grounds are found in the Act or the court rules, nor is there any official guidance to advise Clerks on how to exercise their discretion. Not surprisingly, research reveals that practice varies enormously around the country and this has a knock-on effect on local authority practice.[11] In areas where courts are reluctant to hear EPOs without notice, the local authority is likely to seek assistance from the police, using police protection to bypass the court. This cannot have been the original intention of the Act.

Clearly there are cases in which it is essential to proceed without notice. The European Court of Human Rights has said:[12]

> the court accepts that when action has to be taken to protect a child in an emergency, it may not always be possible, because of the urgency of the situation, to associate in the decision-making process those having custody of the child. Nor may it even be desirable, even if possible, to do so if those having custody of the child are seen as the source of an immediate threat to the child, since giving them prior warning would be liable to deprive the measure of its effectiveness.

Proceeding without notice has profound implications. The court only hears one side of the story and the parents have no opportunity to have their say – indeed the first time they know anything has happened is when the knock comes on the door, they are presented with an order and the child is summarily removed. The human rights implications are obvious. For this reason, Munby J said, 'save in wholly exceptional cases, parents must be given adequate prior notice of…any application by a local authority for an EPO. They must also be given proper notice of the evidence the local authority is relying upon.'[13]

---

10   'Ex parte' in the old terminology.
11   J.M. Masson, M. Winn Oakley and K. Pick (2004) *Emergency Protection Orders: Court Orders for Child Protection Crises.* Warwick: School of Law, Warwick University (funded by the NSPCC and Nuffield Foundation). Summary available at www.nspcc.org.uk/ Inform/publications/Downloads/EPOsummary_wdf48088.pdf, accessed 13 August 2008.
12   *Hasse* v. *Germany* [2004] 1FLR 39 ECtHR, at paragraph 95.
13   *X Council* v. *B*, at paragraph 57 (vii) (see note 1 above).

If you are wondering how it is possible to give a day's notice in a true emergency, you are not alone. Arguably if parents can be given one day's notice, then they could be given three days (the notice period for an interim care order), or the court could be asked to abridge that period. Whether the situation truly is an emergency should be carefully considered in an immediate strategy discussion involving the police and other relevant agencies.[14] If instant action has already been taken by one agency, the strategy discussion should occur as soon as possible thereafter. Legal advice should always be taken. In an emergency, there is a greater need than ever for robust procedures, clear-sighted analysis, reasoned decisions and careful record-keeping.

WHAT IS – AND WHAT IS NOT – AN EMERGENCY?

Working Together suggests that an emergency involves a risk to life or the likelihood of immediate serious harm.[15] The European Court of Human Rights, cited by Munby J, said that a child's immediate removal is justified in a case of 'imminent danger' which must be 'actually established'.[16] It is a draconian measure requiring 'exceptional justification' and reasons which are 'extraordinarily compelling'. Emergency action is to be reserved for cases of real urgency, where there is an immediate threat or imminent danger which cannot be managed in any other way. As Munby J said: 'However compelling the case may be, both the local authority which seeks an EPO and the justices in the FPC who grant such an order assume a heavy burden of responsibility.'[17]

Cases of physical harm, where there is actual risk to life and limb, are the most likely to warrant emergency action. Cases of physical neglect can justify emergency action if they have reached the stage of imminent risk – for example a child neglected literally to the point of starvation. Many sexual abuse allegations, unless there is specific information of immediate risk, are more suited to care proceedings than emergency action. Cases of fabricated or induced illness often involve a long course of action and do not warrant instant removal unless the allegation is that the parent provokes a medical emergency (such as asphyxiation or poisoning). It

---

14   Working Together, paragraph 5.49 (see note 4 above).
15   Working Together, paragraph 5.49 (see note 4 above).
16   *P, C and S* v. *UK* [2002] 35 EHRR 31, [2002] 2FLR 631 European Court of Human Rights, at paragraphs 116, 131, 133.
17   *X Council* v. *B*, at paragraph 35 (see note 1 above).

is difficult to imagine a case of emotional abuse or neglect which justifies emergency action.

A chronic situation, however serious, does not become an emergency simply because professionals have just found out about it – it is the imminence of the danger which must be judged. Nor can simple lack of information or the need for assessment establish a genuine emergency unless there is other information to show imminent risk of serious harm.

EVIDENCE

An EPO application may be an unusual one, but it is still a court application and evidence must be produced and given on oath. If written evidence is available, it should be presented to the court, so if an emergency arises in a family where a core assessment has already been carried out or a Case Conference held, the court should receive copies of reports and minutes. Local authorities always have a duty to give full, frank and balanced information to the court, to present the case fairly and ensure that the court is objectively informed about both the facts and the relevant law. The responsibility to do this is even heavier when the local authority is the only party present in court.

Munby J said:

> The evidence in support of the application for an EPO must be full, detailed, precise and compelling. Unparticularised generalities will not suffice. The sources of hearsay evidence must be identified. Expressions of opinion must be supported by detailed evidence and properly articulated reasoning.[18]

Even if parents are not present during the application, they should be given a full account of the evidence presented to the court as soon as possible. Inevitably in truly urgent cases most evidence is presented orally rather than in writing, so the Clerk's note of the evidence is particularly important.

WHO GOES TO COURT?

In many local authorities, social workers apply for EPOs unaccompanied and unrepresented, especially when the application is made without notice. However, this is contrary to judicial guidance that the importance of a local authority lawyer on an EPO application should not be underestimated, even more so on an application without notice. The local authority's law-

---

18   *X Council* v. *B*, at paragraph 57 (vi) (see note 1 above).

yers should at least be consulted before an application is made and should ensure that parents are properly served with any order and with full information about the evidence presented to court.

REASONS

The court rules require the court to record not only its order but the reasons for its decisions both on the question of notice and on the substantive application. In an urgent case, the decision can be announced and the reasons put in writing later.

LENGTH OF ORDER

An EPO can be made for a maximum of eight days, with the possibility of one extension on further application to court for up to seven days.[19] These are maximum times and the order ought to be made for the shortest period appropriate to the case – the doctrines of proportionality and minimum intervention require nothing less. The court should certainly not automatically make an EPO to last until the next day listed for care proceedings, as often happens in practice. Munby J commented:

> I suspect that all too often EPOs are made unthinkingly or automatically for the maximum period of 8 days. That is simply not acceptable. No EPO should be made for any longer than is absolutely necessary to protect the child… If all this means that FPCs have to rearrange their sitting patterns, then so be it.[20]

Experience and research show us that EPOs usually lead on to care proceedings, which take months.[21] We are not, therefore, simply concerned with a week or two in a family's life: an EPO sets a case off on a particular track, from which it can be difficult later to deviate. This very earliest step on the path is therefore of even greater significance.

EFFECT OF EPOS

An EPO directs anyone who is in a position to do so to produce the

---

19   s45(4) CA89.
20   *X Council* v. *B*, at paragraph 49 (see note 1 above).
21   Masson, Winn Oakley and Pick (2004) (see note 11 above).

child to the local authority which holds the order.[22] The authority has the immediate power to remove the child, or, if he is in a safe place, prevent his removal. But should it exercise this power? According to Munby J, even after obtaining the order, the local authority must actively consider whether it still needs to act on it, or whether any less intrusive measure will suffice.[23] If this is not done, even with an EPO in its pocket, the local authority could conceivably be acting unlawfully in removing the child. Munby J said: 'the FPC decides whether to make an EPO. But the local authority decides whether to remove.' He advised: 'Though no procedure is specified, it will obviously be prudent for local authorities to have in place procedures to ensure both that the required decision making actually takes place and that it is appropriately documented.'

The EPO gives PR to the local authority, shared with the parent(s). However, as the EPO is only a short term order, clearly this PR can only be exercised in such a way as is reasonably required to safeguard or promote the child's welfare for the duration of the order.[24]

A child should not necessarily be kept away from home for the entire duration of the EPO; on the contrary, there is a specific statutory duty to return him home as soon as it is safe to do so.[25] The position should be subject to daily review, which should of course be duly recorded.

EXAMINATIONS AND ASSESSMENTS

The court can include in an EPO a direction for the child to be medically examined or psychiatrically assessed, subject to the child's right to refuse if he is of sufficient age and understanding.[26] The direction can forbid any such examination or assessment, for example, in a case of suspected sexual abuse where the child has already had repeated intimate medical examinations.

CONTACT

During an EPO the child should have 'reasonable contact' with:

---

22   s44(4) CA89.
23   X Council v. B, at paragraph 57 (xii) (see note 1 above).
24   s44(5) CA89.
25   s44(10) CA89.
26   s44(6), (7) and (8) CA89.

- his parents (including a father without PR)
- anyone else with PR
- the person he was living with immediately before the order
- anyone with a contact order.[27]

Rather than leave contact to the local authority's judgment as to what is 'reasonable', the court has power to direct what contact should or should not occur.[28]

EXCLUSION REQUIREMENTS

In a case in which only one person poses a risk to the child, it might be better to remove that person from the scene rather than disrupt the child. The court has a power to do just that by attaching an exclusion requirement to an EPO.[29] The conditions for this are:

- there is reasonable cause to believe that, if the relevant person is excluded from the child's home, the child will not be likely to suffer significant harm or the local authority's s47 enquiries will not be frustrated
- there is someone else living there who is able and willing to give the child the care he needs
- the person who will care for the child consents to the order being made.

If the conditions are met, the court can attach the exclusion requirement to the EPO, requiring the relevant person to leave and stay away from the home, and a power of arrest can be attached to the order. Alternatively, the court can accept a formal undertaking from the person concerned, but no power of arrest can be attached. A similar exclusion order or undertaking can later be attached to an interim care order[30] (but not a full care order). The local authority has a discretionary power to help the excluded person to find alternative accommodation.[31]

Although in principle the idea seems a good one, there are some

---

27 s44(13) CA89.
28 s44(6)(a) CA89.
29 s44A CA89.
30 s38A CA89.
31 s17 and Schedule 2, paragraph 5 CA89.

problems. The first lies in the way the section is drafted. The requirement has to be added to an EPO. To get an EPO you must show that the child is likely to suffer significant harm if he is not removed. But to get the exclusion requirement added to the EPO, you have to show that the child will not suffer harm and will not need to be removed if the excluded person leaves. Both cannot be true at the same time: logically, if you establish the grounds for the exclusion order, the grounds for the EPO itself disappear. In practice this technical problem is simply ignored.

Second, there are often practical problems. You have to show that the risk to the child comes from only one identified person but that there is another competent carer in the home. Even if this is so, you are effectively entirely dependent on the other person not only to care for the child but also to co-operate fully in keeping the other person out. Can you completely rely on that person? How can you police the arrangement?

Third, the exclusion requirement can only ever be a short term solution. Even if the case continues into care proceedings, a similar order can be attached to an interim care order, but not a full care order, so ultimately another solution must be found.[32] The result of these difficulties is that exclusion requirements are used less in practice than was originally hoped, but it is still important to remember that they exist as an option in an appropriate case.

WARRANTS

Not surprisingly, people whose children are being removed are not always fully co-operative. As a social worker, you do not have automatic powers to compel co-operation. It is always wise, therefore, to consider whether you need to ask the court to add further provisions to the EPO, for example:

- You do not know where the child is, but someone else does: the court can direct that person to give you information about where the child is.[33]

- You need to enter and search premises to find the child: the court can authorise you to do so,[34] although you do not have the power to force entry.

---

32   Such as an injunction under the Family Law Act 1996.
33   s48(1) CA89.
34   s48(3) CA89.

- The court has reasonable cause to believe there might also be another child or children on the same premises who should be subject to an EPO (for example you obtain an EPO on one child trafficked for use in child prostitution. Other children in the same situation are also likely to be on the premises): it can authorise you to search the premises for the other child/ren too, and, when you find them, if you are satisfied the grounds for an EPO exist for them too, the court's order authorising the search has the effect as if it were an EPO.[35] You can therefore remove all the children on the premises at the same time without having to go back to court.

- You are refused entry to the premises or access to the child when you try to execute the EPO, or it is likely that this will happen: the court can issue a warrant authorising the police to help you, using reasonable force if necessary.[36]

PARENTS' RIGHT TO APPLY TO DISCHARGE THE EPO

An application to apply to discharge the EPO can be made by:

- the child

- his parents

- anyone else with PR

- anyone he was living with at the time of the EPO

but this right does not arise until 72 hours after the order was made.[37] So, a child can be summarily removed from home and the parents can do nothing about it for three days. Even that limited right is removed if the parents were given notice and were present at the hearing, even if they had no time to find a lawyer or to mount an effective opposition to the application.

APPEALS

Given the high stakes involved in emergency action, either party might want to appeal if they believe the court got it wrong. The local authority might want to appeal against the refusal to proceed without notice to the

---

35   s48(4) and (5) CA89.
36   s48(9) CA89.
37   s45(8) and (9) CA89.

parents, or against the refusal of an EPO. Parents might want to appeal against the making of an EPO.

The position is quite simple: there is no appeal.[38] Even if the court clearly made an unreasonable decision or got the law wrong there is no appeal available to the local authority, parents or child. You might justifiably ask how this fits with the Human Rights Act 1998; indeed Munby J commented when looking at a number of aspects of EPOs:

> Whether the matter be viewed from the perspective of the child or the parent, it is not immediately obvious how some of this is altogether compatible with the increasingly rigorous approach to Article 8 of the European Convention now being adopted by the Strasbourg Court.[39]

It would be no surprise to find the provisions for police protection and emergency protection orders being reformed in the foreseeable future.[40]

A CAUTIONARY TALE – LESSONS FROM RE X

If you wanted to invent a case study illustrating all the errors it is possible to make in an EPO application, you would struggle to improve on the true case of Re X.[41]

X was a nine-year-old girl, who had been the subject of two Child Protection Case Conferences, and whose name was on the Child Protection Register under the category emotional harm. The child protection plan involved a relatively low level of intervention. A legal planning meeting concluded that there were no grounds for care proceedings. A further Case Conference took place at which no reference was made to any suggestion of factitious or induced illness. The Conference decided to continue the previous plan, and recommended a further legal planning meeting.

That same afternoon, a hospital nurse contacted the social worker to give her updated information, not to make a child protection referral. She reported that the mother had taken X to hospital with a stomach pain and was asking for X to be seen by a doctor, although a nurse had thought there was no problem. The doctor was seeing X at the time and would telephone the social worker with the result later.

---

38   s45(10) CA89.

39   X Council v. B, at paragraph 38 (see note 1 above).

40   For further discussion of EPOs see L. Davis (2007) 'Protecting Children in an Emergency – Getting the Balance Right.' Family Law Journal 37, 727.

41   Re X (Emergency Protection Orders) [2006] EWHC 510 (Fam) [2006] 2FLR 701 High Court.

Within two hours of the end of the Case Conference, and without waiting to hear from the doctor, the social worker and her manager had obtained an EPO. Why? Clearly uppermost in the social workers' minds was their suspicion of fabricated or induced illness, a suspicion never raised by any doctor, on which the social workers had never taken any medical advice and which had never been raised at Case Conference. McFarlane J must have felt he was stating the obvious when he said that this 'is not a diagnosis that can be made by social workers acting alone, it is matter that requires skilled medical appraisal'.[42]

The social worker took legal advice. The lawyer was 'not sure' that the grounds existed for an EPO, but the application went ahead regardless. McFarlane J deprecated the practice that allowed the social worker to override legal advice – any such decision should be made by someone above team manager level.

The team manager totally misunderstood the legal grounds for an EPO. She said, 'I could not say that X was 100% safe in that household.' As McFarlane J said, 'that assertion is nothing like the test needed to justify an EPO application'.[43] When in the final care hearing witnesses were asked to explain the imminent danger to X that afternoon, 'none of them could give a satisfactory reply'.[44] The judge concluded:

> The reality is that X was not in imminent danger of harm that in any way justified her removal from parental care that afternoon. There was, even on the evidence available to the social workers and the justices, no grounds for applying for, let alone making, an EPO... This was a long way from being an emergency protection order case.[45]

The lawyer attended court with the social work manager, but merely tendered the social work evidence without doing anything to ensure that the evidence was accurate or balanced or that the court was properly informed of the relevant law.

The court heard the application without any notice to the parents. It gave no reasons for this decision; indeed it did not seem to give the question of notice any separate consideration at all. The court was keen to proceed quickly, conscious of a busy list of cases to follow. Instead of

42   *Re X*, at paragraph 67 (see note 40 above).
43   *Re X*, at paragraph 77 (see note 40 above).
44   *Re X*, at paragraph 72 (see note 40 above).
45   *Re X*, at paragraph 79 (see note 40 above).

waiting for the social worker to arrive with the files, it proceeded on the oral evidence of the team manager who had only a broad knowledge of the case. McFarlane J listed 13 assertions made by the manager in evidence,[46] and described 'every single one' of them as 'misleading or incomplete or wrong'; 'the picture given to the magistrates by the team manager was, in my view, so seriously distorted that it is likely to have led the bench to have a totally erroneous view of the issues of the case'.[47] The magistrates had no written information and were not even told that there had been a Case Conference that very day.

The magistrates' reasons for their decision were 'that the child would suffer imminent harm unless an EPO is made'. The judge described this as 'wholly inadequate and...in effect no more than a statement that the bench found the case proved'.[48] 'The emergency nature of the application, whilst requiring prompt determination, does not absolve the court of its duty to give a reasoned explanation for its decision.'

The parents and their representatives did not receive the details of the evidence presented at the EPO until the final hearing of the care proceedings 14 months later – 14 months in which the child had been placed away from home. The final painful twist in the case was that, at the end of the care proceedings, the judge found that there were insufficient grounds for a care order. There had never been a good reason to separate parents and child.

The judge did not doubt that the social workers acted in good faith for the best of motives, but their actions fell 'disastrously short of what was required'.[49] As well as the incalculable damage caused to the child and family, the local authority was ordered to pay £200,000 towards the parents' legal costs. No case could illustrate more clearly what can go wrong where social workers and their advisers act precipitately and without a sound knowledge of legal principles and procedures.

Points for practice

1. In a true emergency, there is no time to look up the law and procedures. You need to know them – or where to find them.

---

46   *Re X*, at paragraphs 47–48 (see note 40 above).
47   *Re X*, at paragraph 50 (see note 40 above).
48   *Re X*, at paragraph 54 (see note 40 above).
49   *Re X*, at paragraph 60 (see note 40 above).

2. Keep in mind the key considerations at all times (see the *aide-mémoire* in Appendix 6).

3. Keep a cool head – clear thinking is vital in an emergency.

4. Only take emergency action if it is truly justified. Carefully record everything including reasons. Keep all decisions under constant review.

5. Always take legal advice and insist on legal representation if you go to court.

6. Keep all parties' human rights in the forefront of your considerations, especially the child's rights to life (Article 2) and protection from ill-treatment (Article 3), the parents' right to a fair trial (Article 6) and everyone's right to respect for their family life (Article 8).

Part 5

Care Proceedings

Chapter 11

The Threshold Criteria

When can the state step in?

The philosophy underlying the Children Act 1989 (CA89) and the Human Rights Act 1998 (HRA) was explained by Hedley J like this:[1]

> Basically it is the tradition of the UK, recognised in law, that children are best brought up within natural families... It follows inexorably that society must be willing to tolerate very diverse standards of parenting, including the eccentric, the barely adequate and the inconsistent. It follows too that children will inevitably have both very different experiences of parenting and very unequal consequences flowing from it. It means that some children will experience disadvantage and harm, while others flourish in atmospheres of loving security and emotional stability. These are the consequences of our fallible humanity and it is not the provenance of the state to spare children all the consequences of defective parenting. In any event, it simply could not be done... Only exceptionally should the state intervene with compulsive powers and then only when a court is satisfied that the significant harm criteria in s31(2) is made out.

---

1   *Re L (Care: Threshold Criteria)* [2007] 1FLR 2050 High Court, at paragraphs 50–51.

The concept of the threshold

The grounds to be made out before the court can even consider making a care or supervision order are the same and are commonly known as the 'threshold criteria'. The court cannot make these orders of its own initiative even if it would be in the child's best interests to do so; there must be an application and the threshold must be crossed – if not, they are not an option.

Two-stage process

In a final care hearing, the court has to answer two questions:

1. Are the threshold criteria met? If the answer is 'no', the matter ends there.

2. If 'yes', which order (if any) is in the child's best interests?

Even if the threshold is crossed, care or supervision orders are not inevitable: they are choices among a range of options to meet the child's needs. The court applies the s1 CA89 principles,[2] the child's welfare being paramount, and uses the welfare checklist to analyse his best interests.

Care proceedings, even if the threshold is crossed, might result in:

• a care order

• a supervision order

• a package of s8 orders (such as residence to grandmother, contact to mother, no contact to father and prohibited steps preventing contact), possibly coupled with a supervision order

• no order.

Threshold criteria

Harm

As we saw in Chapter 9, 'harm' includes physical, emotional and sexual abuse as well as neglect causing impairment to health or development. Hedley J said:

---

2   Discussed in more detail in Chapter 2.

it would be unwise to attempt an all embracing definition of significant harm. One never ceases to be surprised at the extent of complication and difficulty that human beings manage to introduce into family life. Significant harm is fact specific and must retain the breadth of meaning that human fallibility may require of it.[3]

---

s31(2) CA89 A court may only make a care order or a supervision order if it is satisfied

  (a)   that the child is suffering, or is likely to suffer, significant harm; and

  (b)   that the harm, or likelihood of harm, is attributable to –

    (i)   the care given to the child, or likely to be given to him if the order were not made, not being what it would be reasonable to expect a parent to give to him; or

    (ii)   the child's being beyond parental control.

Significant

State intervention in family life can only be justified if the harm reaches a certain level of severity reflected in the word 'significant' or, as Hedley J put it, 'the exceptional rather than the commonplace'. This was in a case in which he found that the harm the children were suffering and would continue to suffer was not serious enough to be 'significant', so the threshold was not crossed.

'Is suffering' or 'is likely to suffer'

11.1 – 'Is' suffering

Ann is suffering significant harm. Care proceedings are started and Ann goes into foster care. At the final hearing 40 weeks later, is Ann suffering significant harm?

---

3   In *Re L*, at paragraph 51 (see note 1 above).

The court must be satisfied that the child 'is' suffering significant harm. In normal English usage, 'is suffering' signals something happening at the present moment. But during the months before a case reaches a final hearing, the child should be protected, so that he is not suffering significant harm when the judge comes to decide whether the threshold criteria exist. If we use the normal meaning of the word 'is', it looks like the threshold criteria are not met precisely because the system has worked to protect the child. That cannot make sense.

This very issue came to the House of Lords in the case of *Re M*.[4] Their Lordships decided that, when considering whether the threshold criteria are satisfied, the court must cast its mind back to the situation in existence at the 'relevant date' when protective measures started. So a child who was suffering significant harm at the start of the case, even though he is safe by the time of the final hearing, can still fall within the words 'is suffering significant harm'. For the sake of common sense, their Lordships had to change the rules of English grammar so that 'is' can mean 'was'.

Logically, the same problem applies to the words 'is likely to suffer' and the same solution applies – the court looks at what was likely at the relevant date.[5]

What is the relevant date?

11.2 – The relevant date

> Bella's care proceedings start on 27 December. The final hearing is held the following September. Which is the relevant date for deciding if the threshold criteria are met?

The key question is: when did protective measures start? Often, as here, this is the start of the care proceedings. So, in Bella's case the court looks not at the situation in September, but at what was happening the previous December.

---

4   *Re M (A Minor) (Care Order: Threshold Criteria)* [1994] 2FLR 557 House of Lords.
5   *Southwark LBC v. B* [1998] 2FLR 1095 High Court.

11.2.1

Care proceedings started on 27 December after Bella was taken into police protection on Christmas Day and continue until the following September. Which is the relevant date?

This time, the protective measures started before the care proceedings, when the police took Bella into their protection. So the court looks at the situation on Christmas Day, not when the care proceedings started, by which time Bella was already safe.

11.2.2

Bella's story started when she was voluntarily accommodated in November. Contrary to agreement, her parents arrived drunk at the foster home on Christmas Day demanding to take Bella home. The foster carer called the police, who took Bella into police protection, keeping her at the foster home. Care proceedings started on 27 December and continued until September.

This time, Bella has been under the protection of the authorities since she first went into foster care, even though that was initially a voluntary arrangement. At the final hearing in September, the court looks back to the previous November to see if the threshold criteria existed then. Measures do not have to be compulsory to be protective.

When must the evidence be available?

11.3 – Information obtained during proceedings

In five care cases, further information comes to light during the proceedings. Can you present the new evidence to court?

11.3.1

Carl has been sexually abused. During the proceedings, he discloses the abuser's name.

11.3.2

David's case is based on physical and emotional abuse. During the proceedings, his mother is diagnosed with a bipolar affective disorder.

11.3.3

Ellie's case is one of physical abuse. After she is taken into care, it transpires that she has also been sexually abused.

11.3.4

Fiona is in foster care. On contact visits, the superviser observes little attachment between Fiona and her parents.

11.3.5

George was failing to thrive at home, but blossoms in foster care.

At the start of a case you rarely have all of the evidence the court will need to decide the threshold question – it often comes to light as enquiries and assessments are carried out during the proceedings. Can you use evidence to prove the threshold if the information was not available or even did not exist at the relevant date? The Court of Appeal confirmed that you can – it does not matter when the information becomes available as long as it relates to the situation in existence at the relevant date.[6]

In our examples, Carl's disclosure (*11.3.1*) relates to the abuse he was suffering at home and David's mother's diagnosis (*11.3.2*) helps us to understand the situation when protective measures began. Both relate to the relevant date.

In Ellie's case (*11.3.3*) we now know about a type of harm about which we previously knew nothing – but as long as evidence shows the abuse happened when she was at home, it still relates to the relevant date so can be used to satisfy the threshold criteria. If the local authority obtains mate-

---

6   *Re G (Care Proceedings: Threshold Conditions)* [2001] EWCA Civ 968 [2001] 2FLR 1111 Court of Appeal.

rial relevant to the threshold it has a duty to put it before court even if it was not the original basis for proceedings.[7]

Observations of Fiona's contact with her parents (*11.3.4*) indicate what their relationship might have been like at home – although we must take into account the artificiality of supervised contact and the changed circumstances before drawing too many conclusions.

The fact that George (*11.3.5*) thrives when he receives good care implies that there is nothing organically wrong and his previous failure to thrive was due to the care he was receiving. We must be careful here, though – as Hedley J said, if children are removed from low-functioning parents and placed with competent foster carers 'it would be really very surprising indeed if some changes, particularly on the educational front, were not to be apparent'.[8] The fact that children do better with excellent foster carers does not of itself prove that their parents' care was not good enough – the level of George's failure to thrive at home must in itself constitute significant harm.

11.4 – New events

Medical opinion says that baby Harry's fractures are non-accidental, so care proceedings are started. There are no other concerns for him. The strain of the proceedings causes Harry's mother to have a nervous breakdown and the parents' marriage to break up.

What if something completely new and different happens during the proceedings? Can you use evidence of the mother's mental health problems and the instability of the parental relationship to establish the threshold criteria? These matters did not exist at the relevant time (indeed they have been caused by the proceedings themselves) so they cannot count towards establishing the threshold. They may be relevant in the court's decision as to what order, if any, to make if – and only if – the threshold criteria are made out.

If the parents' medical experts show that Harry's fractures were due to a rare medical condition, not ill-treatment, the case falls apart and the threshold criteria are not met – regardless of the fact that Harry now has a mentally unstable mother and separated parents.

---

7   *Re A (Children: Split Hearing)* [2006] EWCA Civ 714 [2007] 1FLR 905 Court of Appeal.
8   *Re L*, at paragraph 19 (see note 1 above).

How 'satisfied' does the court have to be?

As we saw in Chapter 9, suspicion is enough for a s47 CA89 enquiry and belief justifies an EPO, but neither is enough for a care or supervision order. The court must be 'satisfied' on the evidence that the threshold criteria are proven. As Baroness Hale explained in the important case of *Re B*,[9] 'the threshold is there to protect both the children and their parents from unjustified intervention in their lives. It would provide no protection at all if it could be established on the basis of unsubstantiated suspicions.

As care proceedings are civil proceedings, the case must be proven 'on the balance of probabilities'. This is a lower level than civil proceedings, where the case must be proven 'beyond reasonable doubt'. In *Re B* Lord Hoffman explained that the standard of proof is 'the degree of persuasion which the tribunal must feel before it decides that the fact in issue did happen' and in care proceedings, the court 'must be satisfied that the occurrence of the fact in question was more likely than not'.[10]

Before *Re B* was decided, there was a series of cases (starting with another House of Lords case, *Re H & R*[11]), which suggested that stronger evidence was needed to satisfy a court about a serious allegation than a less serious one. The House of Lords in *Re B* clearly declared that this was a misunderstanding; as Baroness Hale explained,[12] 'there is no logical or necessary connection between seriousness and probability'.

Their Lordships eagerly grasped the opportunity to clarify the law. Baroness Hale was emphatic saying[13] that wanted to:

> announce loud and clear that the standard of proof in finding the facts necessary to establish the threshold under s31(2) or the welfare considerations in s1 of the 1989 Act is the simple balance of probabilities, neither more nor less. Neither the seriousness of the allegations nor the seriousness of the consequences should make any difference to the standard of proof to be applied in determining the facts.

We are now clear. To make a care order, the court must be satisfied that the facts which add up to show the threshold criteria are crossed are more likely than not to be true. That in itself may not be easy; as Baroness Hale

---

9   *Re B (Children)* [2008] UKHL 35, House of Lords at paragraph 54.
10   *Re B* at paragraph 4.
11   *Re H & R (Child Sexual Abuse: Standard of Proof)* [1996] 1FLR 80, House of Lords.
12   *Re B* at paragraph 72.
13   *Re B* at paragraph 70.

said,[14] 'I do not under-estimate the difficulty of deciding where the truth lies but that is what the courts are for'.

It is the local authority's job to produce the evidence to satisfy the statutory criteria, building up the whole picture. An apparently minor piece of information might be the piece of the puzzle which makes everything else fall into place. Lord Nicholls said:

> the range of facts which may be taken into account is infinite. The facts include the history of members of the family; the state of relationships within a family; proposed changes within the membership of a family; parental attitudes and omissions which might not reasonably have been expected, just as much as actual physical assaults. They include threats and abnormal behaviour by a child and unsatisfactory parental responses to complaints or allegations and facts which are minor or even trivial if considered in isolation, when taken together may suffice to satisfy the court of the likelihood of future harm.[15]

How likely is 'likely'?

The threshold criteria can be satisfied on the basis of 'likely' significant harm. The House of Lords[16] has decided that 'likelihood' means 'a real possibility, a possibility that cannot sensibly be ignored having regard to the nature and gravity of the feared harm in the particular case.'

The difficulty with the 'likelihood' part of the threshold criteria is that you are trying to establish something which, by definition, has not happened yet and which you hope never will happen. But this is not an exercise in speculation. Suspicion and belief cannot establish likely harm any more than they can show actual harm. A court can only be satisfied that a child is likely to suffer significant harm on the basis of facts which are themselves proven to be more likely than not to be true. As Baroness Hale explained,[17] judging likelihood is 'a prediction from existing facts, often from a multitude of such facts, about what has happened in the past, about the characters and personalities of the people involved, about the things which they have said and done, and so on.'

---

14 *Re B* at paragraph 59.
15 *Re H & R*, page 101B–C (see note 9 above)
16 *Re H & R*, page 101 B–C, affirmed by *Re B*.
17 *Re B* at paragraph 22.

But it is important to remember that these facts must still be proven, not simply that they might possibly have happened. Lord Hoffman[18] described our law as operating on a binary system – the only values are 0 and 1, so if a fact is not proven to the appropriate standard, it did not happen.

11.5 – Likely harm

> Kate is 16. She alleges sexual abuse by her stepfather. It is her word against his; there is no other evidence. Her mother and stepfather have two younger daughters, Linda and Laura. Are they likely to be sexually abused?

Linda and Laura's case depends entirely on Kate – they are only likely to suffer significant harm if the evidence shows that it is more likely than not that Kate has been abused, not just that it is possible that she might have been. If there is insufficient evidence to prove Kate's allegations on the balance of probabilities there is also insufficient evidence to show that the younger girls are 'likely' to be abused.

In some cases, the evidence may not prove that something has already happened but still show it is likely in the future. For example, a child exposed to persistent domestic violence might not yet have suffered emotional harm but nevertheless be likely to do so if the situation continues. The whole point of the 'likelihood' element of the threshold criteria is that we do not have to wait for children to be harmed first before we can protect them.

Attributable

Significant harm on its own does not satisfy the threshold criteria. A child with the best parents in the world might suffer significant harm – he could have a serious accident – but it does not justify care proceedings because the state only needs to step in if there is a link between the harm and parental failure. The threshold criteria are therefore only met if the significant harm is attributable either to inadequate care or lack of control.

An objective standard

When cases concern allegations of inadequate care, CA89 sets an objective standard, comparing the care the child is actually receiving to what

---

18   *Re B* at paragraph 2.

could reasonably be expected. It is not concerned with blame. Some cases involve deliberate harm but more frequently parents are doing their incompetent best, their mental ill-health, drug use, learning disability or their own abusive childhoods impairing their ability to care for their child. Their inadequate care may not be morally blameworthy – indeed, it may arouse considerable sympathy – but it can still satisfy the statutory criteria.

Wilson LJ said:

> one of the most difficult categories is that in which the case against the parents is not that they have actively mistreated their child but simply that, by reason of their learning difficulties or other such deficits, they lack the mental and other resources with which to provide him with adequate emotional or physical care.[19]

Wall LJ emphasised:

> the family courts do not remove children from their parents into care because the parents in question are not intelligent enough to care for them or have low intelligence quotas. Children are only removed into care: (1) if they are suffering or likely to suffer significant harm in the care of their parents; and (2) if it is in their interests that a care order is made. Anything else is social engineering and wholly impermissible.[20]

Whose standards?

The care it would be 'reasonable to expect a parent to give' sounds at first blush like a clear, objective standard; but it is value-laden and, at least to a degree, culturally determined. Courts increasingly find themselves having to apply the standard to families from very different backgrounds with varying cultural norms. How do they impose an objective standard in a diverse society?

One case involved ritual harm to a child associated with a traditional Congolese belief in witchcraft, although the court heard that physically harming a child is not part of the traditional belief.[21] Ryder J said 'this court has no hesitation in condemning ritual practices that cause physical or emotional harm to children'. Thus, there is a bottom line below which the court will not go whatever the claimed cultural justifications.

---

19   *Re L (Children) (Care Proceedings: Significant Harm)* [2006] EWCA Civ 1282 [2007]
     1FLR 1068 Court of Appeal, at paragraph 2(a).
20   *Re L*, paragraph 49 (see note 13 above).
21   *Haringey LBC* v. *S* [2006] EWHC 2001 (Fam) [2007] 1FLR 387, High Courts paragraph 3.

However, that is not to say that no variation can be allowed. Munby J had to deal with a case of an alleged forced marriage.[22] He said:

> the task of the court considering threshold for the purposes of s31 of the 1989 Act may be to evaluate parental performance by reference to the objective standard of the hypothetical 'reasonable' parent, but this does not mean that the court can simply ignore the underlying cultural, social or religious realities. On the contrary, the court must always be sensitive to the cultural, social and religious circumstances of the particular child and family. And the court should, I think, be slow to find that parents only recently or comparatively recently arrived from a foreign country – particularly a country where standards and expectations may be more or less different, sometimes very different indeed, from those with which we are familiar – have fallen short of an acceptable standard of parenting if in truth they have done nothing wrong by the standards of their own community.

He was nevertheless quite clear that in any cultural setting forced (as opposed to arranged) marriage is a gross abuse of human rights and a form of domestic violence: 'no social or cultural imperative can extenuate and no pretended recourse to religious beliefs can possibly justify a forced marriage'.[23]

A delicate but clear balance needs to be struck. Cultural, social and religious considerations must be taken into account but ultimately child abuse is child abuse and we must not shy away from protecting children whatever the family context.

Who must the harm be attributable to?

Sometimes, it is clear who abused a child. In other cases, there is more than one potential perpetrator but investigations clarify matters; medical evidence reveals the timing of injuries, a confession is made or eye witness evidence comes to light. But what if, after investigations are complete, the perpetrator is still uncertain? A criminal prosecution is probably ruled out – the CPS cannot prosecute several defendants on an either/or basis. But care proceedings are different. As a matter of policy, we cannot deny a child protection because we cannot identify the perpetrator – but how does this fit with the wording of the Act?

---

22 *Re K (A Local Authority v. N and Others)* [2005] EWHC 2956 (Fam) [2007] 1FLR 399 High Court, paragraph 26.

23 *Re K*, paragraph 85 (see note 16 above).

11.7 – Uncertain perpetrator

Two couples, A and B, both have babies of about the same age. Mrs B is a childminder and looks after baby A. So baby A spends time in both households; baby B does not. Baby A suffers serious shaking injuries. It is unclear from the evidence whether the injuries occurred when baby A was with the As or Mrs B.

If you were the social worker, would you take care proceedings on baby A, baby B or both? When a similar situation arose in Lancashire, care proceedings were commenced on both children – baby A for actual harm and baby B for likely harm.[24]

The judge who originally heard the case, unable to determine who had injured baby A, expressed his dilemma:

If the criteria are met and orders are made, I am exposing one child to the possibility of removal from parents who are no risk and have done no wrong... If the applications are dismissed then I will undoubtedly be causing one child to be returned to a parent, or parents, one or both of whom are an obvious and serious unassessed risk.

The case was appealed. On analysis, baby B's case depended on baby A – there was only a likelihood of significant harm if Mrs B harmed baby A – if Mr or Mrs A was the perpetrator, baby B was at no risk. There was suspicion about Mrs B but no more: the facts did not prove that she injured baby A so they could not establish a real possibility of future harm to baby B. The threshold criteria were not met for baby B, so the court could not make a care order, even if it wanted to, and B's case was over.

Baby A's parents appealed to the House of Lords. They argued that, although A had clearly suffered significant harm, it was not 'attributable' to their care so the threshold criteria were not met.

Their Lordships looked at the precise words of CA89. It says that the care *given to the child* must be not what it was reasonable to expect a parent to give – it does not say *by whom* that care must be given. Lord Nicholls said it primarily refers to parental care but, where there is shared care, it can include the care given by any of the carers if the court cannot determine which part of the care network has failed. Otherwise, it would be impossible to protect a child in any case with an unidentified perpetrator and such a conclusion would, Lord Nicholls said, be 'dangerously irresponsible'. The

---

24   *Lancashire County Council* v. *B* [2001] 1FLR 583 House of Lords.

police may be unable to prosecute anyone but social workers are still able to protect the child.

As always, there is a downside. This conclusion means that the threshold criteria can be satisfied when there is only a possibility that the parents caused the injuries. Wholly innocent parents may face losing their children – and children may be permanently separated from parents who have done nothing. But no system is perfect and this ruling at least errs on the side of caution.

Findings and concessions

The threshold findings are often agreed between the parties, subject to the court's approval. Obviously, reaching a sensible agreement is to be encouraged but the local authority must always consider carefully whether concessions offered on the threshold criteria are appropriate. If not, the authority should ask the court to hear the case and make findings. In every case it is vital to be clear as to what is, and what is not, negotiable.

For example in one case a man was acquitted of charges of sexual abuse of his three adopted children.[25] Care proceedings followed. The parents accepted a care order, conceding they had rejected the children, inappropriately chastised them and failed to meet their emotional needs. The local authority wanted the court to hear evidence and make findings on the sexual abuse allegations. The Court of Appeal confirmed that the local authority was right. Although there should be no unnecessary litigation, concessions must be examined to see whether they meet the justice of the case and the children's interests; here, they did not. The findings made would affect issues such as therapy, the care plan and contact. We could also add criminal injuries compensation – available to victims of sexual abuse, but not emotional rejection.

Which order?

Crossing the threshold is only the first step; the right order (if any) depends on the child's welfare. How do you approach assessments for the welfare stage when harm is established but the perpetrator is unknown? Normally

---

25   *Re M (Threshold Criteria: Parental Concessions)* [1999] 2FLR 728 Court of Appeal.

in court cases, facts which are not proven are discounted, but applying that principle to unknown perpetrator cases would cause difficulties, explored by Lord Nicholls in *Re O & N*:[26]

> it would be grotesque if such a case had to proceed at the welfare stage on the footing that, because neither parent, considered individually, has been proved to be the perpetrator, therefore the child is not at risk from either of them. This would be grotesque because it would mean the court would proceed on the footing that neither parent represents a risk even though one or other of them was the perpetrator of the harm in question. That would be a self-defeating interpretation of the legislation... The preferable interpretation of the legislation is that in such cases the court is able to proceed at the welfare stage on the footing that each of the possible perpetrators is, indeed, just that; a possible perpetrator.

In that case a six-month-old baby had a fractured skull and numerous other injuries. The father admitted punching her, causing the skull fracture, but the evidence was not clear on whether he or the mother caused the other injuries. Mother denied everything and had separated from the father. It might not be possible to prove who did it – but being honest, who would you suspect? Lord Nicholls said a judge can indicate that, although he cannot make a finding either way, he considers one candidate to be the more probable perpetrator although the other remains a possibility.

In practical terms it is extremely useful. As a social worker, you can then work on the basis of the judge's indication in your assessments to reach your recommendations, aiming to prevent the child from being unnecessarily separated from the parent who did not harm her, while protecting her from the one who did.

Points for practice

1. Never lose sight of the threshold criteria amidst all the issues, agendas and distractions raised in care proceedings.

2. Evidence every case carefully. Be especially mindful of the need to overcome the court's inherent scepticism where you are making serious allegations.

---

26 *Re O & N (Minors)* and *Re B (Minors)*, at paragraphs 27–28 (see note 12 above).

3. You can take care proceedings even if you cannot prove who the abuser was.

4. Be prepared for negotiations. Be clear what is and is not negotiable – always know your bottom line.

Chapter 12

Care Proceedings – Interim Stages

Care proceedings application

Only a local authority can take care proceedings.[1] However strident partner agencies or a Case Conference may be in their opinions, they cannot compel the local authority to act.

Even the court cannot make a local authority take proceedings – it can issue a direction for a report under s37 Children Act 1989 (CA89)[2] and couple it with an interim (not a full) care order, but if the local authority then decides not to apply for a care order, the court can do nothing. The Court of Appeal was very frustrated with one authority which resolutely refused to take care proceedings, seeking instead to use a prohibited steps order to protect a child against a sex offender.[3] Although this approach was misconceived, even the Court of Appeal could not force the council to start care proceedings. The boundary between the roles of courts and local authorities is clear, but can cause tension.

Which court?

Care proceedings start in the Family Proceedings Court (FPC) unless there is already a case concerning the child in another court. From the FPC, the case can be transferred up to the County Court or the High Court on grounds of:

---

1   Or the NSPCC, but this book concentrates on local authorities.
2   See Chapter 4 for more details.
3   *Nottinghamshire County Council* v. *P* [1993] 2FLR 134 Court of Appeal.

- gravity
- complexity
- the likely length of proceedings.

The idea is that all cases are dealt with in a court of the appropriate level. For example, cases of general neglect – failure to feed or clothe children properly – can stay in the FPC, whereas cases involving complex or conflicting medical evidence cannot. Cases should be transferred up as soon as possible – a late transfer will cause delay.

Parties

Anyone with parental responsibility (PR) is automatically a party to care proceedings. Party status brings with it the right to:

- attend all court hearings
- be represented by a lawyer
- see all the evidence
- contribute evidence.

A married father has PR and is entitled to be a party to care proceedings. In one case, the mother did not want her husband to be involved in proceedings, saying he was unaware of the existence of the baby, who was the product of rape.[4] The Court of Appeal referred to the strong presumption that a child born in a marriage is legitimate and found there was insufficient evidence that this husband was not the father. Rules about service and party status should only be relaxed in exceptional circumstances.

A father without PR is not automatically a respondent but he is entitled to be notified of proceedings so that he can apply for party status. If there is any doubt about paternity it can be resolved by the court, using DNA testing if necessary. It is best not to make assumptions. In one case, although both mother and putative father confirmed paternity, the local authority and Guardian thought they knew better, and did not notify him or include him in assessments.[5] This serious error and injustice led to the care order

---

4   *Re AB (Care Proceedings: Service on Husband Ignorant of Child's Existence)* [2004] 1FLR 527 Court of Appeal.

5   *Re B (Care Proceedings: Notification of Father without Parental Responsibility)* [1999] 2FLR 409 High Court.

being set aside and the whole case being re-heard. The court should have been asked to decide whether the alleged father should be involved.

Anyone with whom the child was living at the time the proceedings were commenced is also entitled to notification, whether or not they have PR. This might include a step-parent, a parent's civil partner or cohabitant, or any other carer, related or not.

The court can add people as parties to the proceedings but only if they have a separate case from others already involved. So a grandmother will not be made a party merely to support the mother – she can just be a witness – but if she puts herself forward as a carer for the child in opposition to the parents, she has an independent case and may be made a party in her own right.

The child's role

In care proceedings, the child is automatically a party and is represented by both a Children's Guardian (provided by CAFCASS) and a solicitor. The Guardian gives instructions to the solicitor and they work as a team unless the child is competent to instruct the solicitor himself. If so, and if his wishes are different from the Guardian's view of his best interests, the solicitor represents the child and the Guardian puts her own case.

Although the child is a full party, in practice his involvement in the case is different from other participants. It is very rare for a child to file a statement or to attend court. Magistrates and judges rarely meet the person whose future they are deciding and at present, despite anxious discussion about the issue, there is no expectation that they should do so.[6]

Sometimes a child's disclosures are vital evidence in a case. Normally in family courts (unlike criminal courts) the child does not give evidence in person but the court watches any video-recorded interview and hears from adults who witnessed what the child said. This is hearsay, but the flexible rules of evidence in the family court mean it can be taken into account.

What if the parents want the child to give evidence in person and be cross-examined like any other witness? Smith LJ summed up the court's approach:[7]

---

6   For a more detailed discussion, see L. Davis (2007) 'Children in Court' and 'Children in Court – A Postscript.' *Family Law Journal 37*, 65 and 434 respectively.

7   *LM v. Medway Council and RM and YM* [2007] EWCA Civ 9 [2007] 1FLR 1698 Court of Appeal.

the correct starting point in my view (in accordance with past Court of Appeal guidance) is that it is undesirable that a child should have to give evidence in care proceedings and that particular justification will be required before that course is taken. There will be some cases in which it will be right to make an order. In my view, they will be rare.

Wilson LJ said that a child should only have to attend court if her live evidence is necessary to decide the case fairly and provided it would not be 'oppressive' to the child.

Those judgments were given in one of the rare cases when the child's attendance was required. The case concerned allegations of sexual abuse of L by her father, allegations first made not by L but by her mother. L then made the same allegations herself. Later, the mother not only retracted her allegations but said that she had coached L into making false disclosures. No one in court knew whether, if asked, L would persist in her allegations or follow her mother in withdrawing them. This key gap in the evidence could only be filled by asking L herself what she now wanted to say. Wilson LJ emphasised how unusual the situation was, saying 'the present case does not reflect the straightforward situation in which a parent who has been accused by a child denies the accusation and aspires to cross-examine her or him'. Normally children should not have to go to court. Be prepared to resist any attempt to insist that they should and to advise the court on the likely impact on the child of such an experience.

In an exceptional case when a child does have to attend, she should give her evidence by live TV link and have all the same protections as a child witness in the criminal court.

Procedure

A detailed exposition of procedure is beyond the scope of this book.[8] Full details are set out in the Public Law Outline (which replaced the Care Proceedings Protocol from 1 April 2008).[9] Documentation is standardised, consistent procedures are set out and all cases must be actively managed by the court.

---

8   For detailed guidance on procedure, case preparation and giving evidence see L. Davis (2007) *See You in Court – A Social Worker's Guide to Presenting Evidence in Care Proceedings.* London: Jessica Kingsley Publishers.

9   Public Law Outline (2008), available at www.judiciary.gov.uk/docs/public_law_outline.pdf, accessed 13 August 2008.

The local authority is expected to carry out a lot of work and prepare a considerable bundle of documents before even issuing proceedings (except, of course, in an emergency or other case where swift action is required). The child's parents must be informed in writing that care proceedings are contemplated (a 'Letter before Proceedings') and then invited to a meeting along with their representative to discuss the matter.

A core assessment should be carried out before proceedings and filed with the court at the very start of the case. All previous reports (such as s7 or s37 reports), assessments of relatives and friends, minutes of meetings, records of discussions with the family and all other relevant documentation must be submitted to the court at the outset. The authority must also prepare documentation for the case itself including a social work chronology, a schedule of proposed findings (setting out exactly what the court is being asked to conclude), an initial social work statement, a care plan and a timetable for the child, which sets out not only the steps to be taken in the legal process but also important steps in the child's life such as the dates of reviews or medical assessments or significant educational changes like a change of school.

The court sets a timetable for hearings and gives directions for each party to 'file' (send to the court) and 'serve' (copy to the other parties) statements of evidence and reports. All local authority evidence must be submitted on time. Close teamwork between social workers and legal advisers is vital to prepare and present the case as clearly as possible.

In care proceedings, all evidence is put in writing and disclosed to all parties before any hearing. Uncontested applications often proceed just on written evidence and legal submission without any live evidence.

Interim orders

Care proceedings take several months from beginning to end. Obviously the question arises as to what happens to the child in the meantime. The court has the option of making an interim care order (ICO) or interim supervision order (ISO) but this is by no means inevitable – it is quite possible for the child to remain at home with no order throughout the case.

There must be a good reason for any interim order to be made, so the local authority must consider as separate issues:

- whether care proceedings should be started at all; if so,

- whether an interim order should be sought; and if an ICO is made,
- whether the child should be removed from home.

None of these decisions should be made lightly. An interim order does not in any way pre-judge the final hearing but a child could be away from home for nine months or more under interim orders. The implications for the child, family and for the assessments to be undertaken are enormous. For this reason the Court of Appeal stressed that the standard required to justify the interim removal of a child is 'very high' and cannot be founded on speculative evidence.[10]

s38(2) CA89 A court shall not make an interim care order or interim supervision order...unless it is satisfied that there are reasonable grounds for believing that the circumstances with respect to the child are as mentioned in s31(2).

The reference to s31(2) CA89 means that the court must look to the threshold criteria (both the significant harm and attributability elements) and have reasonable grounds to believe that they exist. Even then, an interim order does not automatically follow – the court must exercise its discretion. The Court of Appeal has stressed that a child's removal from parents is not to be sanctioned unless the child's safety requires interim protection.[11]

The importance of interim orders must not be underestimated and, not surprisingly, many ICO applications are contested. The Court of Appeal gave the following guidance about contested interim hearings:[12]

- an interim hearing is circumscribed in ambit
- findings of disputed fact should be rare
- oral evidence and cross-examination should be restricted to issues essential to establish a holding position
- it is not a dress rehearsal for the final hearing
- the court has power to determine its own procedure.

---

10   *Re M (Interim Care Order: Removal)* [2005] EWCA Civ 1594 [2006] 1FLR 1043 Court of Appeal.
11   *Re K and H* [2006] EWCA Civ 1898 [2007] 1FLR 2043 Court of Appeal.
12   *Re B (ICOs: Renewal)* [2001] 2FLR 1217 Court of Appeal.

The first ICO or ISO can be made for up to eight weeks. If the first is shorter than eight weeks, the second can be made for the balance of the eight weeks. Thereafter, orders can last up to four weeks at a time.

Although we sometimes talk about 'renewing' interim orders, in theory the court reconsiders the case and makes a fresh order every time. In practice, however, once the first interim order is made, further orders are often made by an administrative process with nobody attending court. But if the parents want to contest every time, they are entitled to do so. In one such case there were four successive contested interim hearings.[13] The Court of Appeal confirmed that the judge was entitled on the fourth occasion to limit the evidence to changes since the last hearing and did not have to go through the whole case again.

THE EFFECT OF AN ICO

An ICO gives the local authority PR which lasts as long as the order. PR is shared with the parent(s), but not equally as, just as under a full care order, the local authority can restrict the parents' exercise of their PR where necessary to safeguard and promote the child's welfare. So, the local authority decides on contact arrangements (subject to any interim contact order made by the court) and, most importantly, it decides where the child lives during the ICO. This could be in foster care, a children's home, in an extended family placement, or at home.

If the child stays at home under an ICO, the authority can remove him at any time during the ICO without returning to court. The judge in one such case tried to control the authority's use of its power.[14] He did not want the children to be removed without the parents having time to apply to court first, so he added a recital to the ICOs requiring the authority to give the parents 48 hours' notice if it decided to remove the children.

The Court of Appeal found that the judge was wrong; a court must decide to make an order or not, rather than to try to invent a half-way house, and it should not make an order unless it is necessary and proportionate, no lesser interference being able to achieve the objective. ICOs give the local authority power to remove the children without a return to court. If the judge did not want this to happen, he should not have made ICOs. Instead, he should have adjourned the ICO application, putting the onus on the

---

13   *Re B (ICOs: Renewal)* (see note 12 above).
14   *Re B (Care: Interference with Family Life)* [2003] 2FLR 813 Court of Appeal.

authority to go back to court to justify the children's removal, rather than on the parents to stop it. Local authorities should never accept any attempt to fetter their powers under an ICO.

---

s38(6) CA89 Where the court makes an interim care order, or an interim supervision order, it may give such directions (if any) as it considers appropriate with regard to the medical or psychiatric examination or other assessment of the child; but if the child is of sufficient understanding to make an informed decision he may refuse to submit to the examination or other assessment.

(7) A direction under subsection (6) may be to the effect that there is to be –

    (a)   no such examination or assessment; or

    (b)   no such examination or assessment unless the court directs otherwise.

Interim assessments

During the interim phase of proceedings, s38(6) CA89 gives the court control of assessments of the child, although it cannot force a competent child to co-operate against his will. Assessments of the adults involved do not come within s38(6) CA89 although they form an important part of the evidence in care proceedings. No one can compel an adult to co-operate, but if they do not, it has obvious implications for their case.

Residential assessments

One way to conduct an intensive assessment of a family's functioning is through a residential assessment. Can the court insist on such an assessment even if the local authority does not agree? The answer depends on whether the assessment proposed falls within the wording of s38(6) CA89. If not, the court has no power to order it, even if it would be in the child's best interests: s1 CA89 does not apply to this subsection as it concerns an interim evidential issue, not the child's upbringing. There have been several important cases on the subject.

In the first key case, *Re C*, the social worker (supported by a psychologist and the Guardian) recommended a residential assessment but the local authority managers refused, partly on financial grounds.[15] Could the court insist on a residential assessment? The question went all the way to the House of Lords.

Their Lordships found that s38(6) CA89 deals with the tension between the local authority's power to make decisions in the interim and the court's need to have information for the final hearing. Lord Browne-Wilkinson said: 'The purpose of subsection (6) is to enable the court to obtain the information necessary for its own decision, notwithstanding the control over the child which in all other respects rests with the local authority.' If the court could not order interim assessments, the local authority would control the information before the court. As Lord Browne-Wilkinson said: 'To allow the local authority to decide what evidence is to go before the court at the final hearing would be in many cases…to allow the local authority by administrative decision to pre-empt the court's judicial decision.'

But subsection (6) refers to an 'assessment of the child'. Does this stretch to an assessment of the whole family, where the focus might be more on the parents' behaviour than on the child? Lord Browne-Wilkinson reasoned that it is impossible to assess a young child divorced from his environment, especially for issues such as the relationship between parents and child. He said:

> subsections (6) and (7) of section 38 of the Act are to be broadly construed. They confer jurisdiction on the court to order or prohibit any assessment which involves the participation of the child and is directed to providing the court with the material which, in the view of the court, is required to enable it to reach a proper decision at the final hearing…[16]

So, the statutory words 'assessment of the child' were stretched to become 'assessment which involves the participation of the child'. As a result, the court has power to order residential assessments.

Thereafter, residential assessments became increasingly common and specialist services were developed, offering treatment and therapy to overcome parents' difficulties while assessing the family. But can providing treatment for parents really come within a subsection concerned with assessing a child? The subsection again came before the House of Lords in *Re G*, a case in which the stakes were high, the mother's previous baby (by

---

15   *Re C (Interim Care Order: Residential Assessment)* [1997] 1FLR 1 House of Lords, at page 7G–H.

16   *Re C*, at page 9 (see note 15 above).

a different father) having died.[17] The family was placed at a hospital providing a family assessment and specialist psychiatric therapy. Their Lordships decided that, once an assessment had been carried out, the local authority could not be ordered to continue the placement so that the mother's therapy could continue: the statutory words 'assessment of the child' could not be stretched to mean therapy for a parent.

Baroness Hale said:

> what is directed under s38(6) must clearly be an examination or assessment of the child, including where appropriate her relationship with her parents, the risk that her parents may present to her, and the ways in which those risks may be avoided or managed all with a view to enabling the court to make the decisions which it has to make under the Act with the minimum of delay. Any services which are provided for the child and his family must be ancillary to that end. They must not be an end in themselves.[18]

So s38(6) CA89 does cover assessment of the attachment between parents and child but not assessment of the parent's ability to change or programmes aimed at rehabilitation, such as treatment, therapy or improving parenting skills. In practice, however, it is difficult to draw the line: all assessment involves an element of training or treatment, and vice versa.

The House of Lords also stressed that s38(6) CA89 assessments must be time-limited – a few months at most rather than the year proposed in *Re G*.

In spite of *Re G*, residential assessments have been given fresh impetus by the Court of Appeal,[19] which has placed a strong emphasis on fairness to parents and the need for full evidence to be available to the court in a case where refusing a residential assessment would effectively make the final outcome a foregone conclusion.

Wall LJ said:

> it is manifestly in the interests of [the child] to see if his parents are able to care for him, and it is the responsibility of the court to ensure that it has the best evidence on which to reach a conclusion about his welfare. It is also procedurally fair for his parents to be given the opportunity to

---

17   *Re G (A Minor) (Interim Care Order: Residential Assessment)* [2005] UKHL 68 [2006] 1FLR 601 House of Lords.

18   *Re G*, paragraph 69 (see note 18 above).

19   *Re L and H (Residential Assessment)* [2007] EWCA Civ 213 [2007] 1FLR 1370 Court of Appeal.

demonstrate that they can overcome their manifest difficulties and care for him, and it would, in my judgment, be unfair were they to be denied that opportunity.[20]

Similarly in *Re K* the Court of Appeal ordered a two-day assessment of the parents, even though it could not address important issues like their reluctance to address problems of drugs, alcohol and violence and their long term capacity to sustain change, because it was their last chance and it was only fair to give them that chance.[21]

WHO PAYS?

The parents' and child's Legal Aid does not cover the cost of residential assessments. This means that, if the court decides that such an assessment is necessary, the local authority must bear the full cost, which can be enormous. The court can take budgetary arguments into account but financial considerations are unlikely to outweigh other factors in the court's decision. Bodey J described as 'unsatisfactory if not invidious' the situation where the court is asked to choose between overwhelming an already overstretched local authority or denying a residential assessment to a parent for whom it may be the last chance to avoid losing his or her child. He urged further consideration of the funding issue.[22]

12.1 – Residential assessments in practice

Janet is 18 and spent her teenage years in care. She was promiscuous, used drugs and alcohol and was involved in crime. She gave birth to baby Kylie but, when told that care proceedings would be commenced, abandoned her in hospital, went on a drinking spree and refused to attend contact for some weeks. However, she is now attending contact, is affectionate towards Kylie and competent at practical tasks. Janet's solicitor asks for a residential assessment. The local authority budget holder wants to resist the application.

---

20   *Re L and H*, paragraph 91 (see note 19 above).
21   *Re K (Care Order)* [2007] EWCA Civ 697 [2007] 2FLR 1066 Court of Appeal.
22   *A Local Authority v. M (Funding of Residential Assessments)* [2008] EWHC 162 (Fam) High Court.

1. Can the local authority argue that the court has no power to order the assessment?

   - Is it really an assessment which 'involves Kylie's participation'? This can include assessing:
     - the attachment between Janet and Kylie
     - the risks posed by Janet to Kylie and how to manage them
     - Janet's parenting skills
   - Is it time-limited (no more than a couple of months)?
   - Will it provide material which is relevant and necessary to the court for its final decision?

   If the answers to the above questions are 'yes' the court has discretion to order the assessment. But if:

   - it is really a programme for Janet and Kylie's participation is not essential, for example to:
     - provide treatment or therapy for Janet
     - improve Janet's skills
     - assess Janet's ability to change
   - the timescale for the assessment is more than a couple of months

   the court has no power to order the assessment even if it would like to.

2. Even if the court has power to order the assessment, can the local authority persuade the court not to do so? Ask:

   - Would it be unfair to Janet to refuse the assessment, making the final outcome a foregone conclusion?
   - Can the information to be provided by the assessment be provided in any other way? (Resisting one type of assessment is very difficult without an alternative proposal to provide information of equal value.)
   - Does the specific assessment proposed really address the issues essential for the court?
     - Does the unit have the necessary expertise to carry out the work?
     - Exactly what is proposed? Is it likely to produce a useful assessment?

o   How will findings of the residential assessment translate into life in the community – does the artificiality of the setting make the assessment invalid?

o   What level of supervision is proposed?

o   Will Kylie be safe?

o   Are expectations clear and unambiguous and are measures of success/progress/failure explicit?

3.   How much will the assessment cost and can a financial argument be raised? (Your budget holder will thank you for being notified of the issue at an early stage.)

Expert assessments

Assessments are often needed from experts such as paediatricians, radiologists, psychiatrists and psychologists. Anyone involved in actually treating a family member is likely to become a witness in the proceedings. Other experts may be called in to undertake assessments and give opinions specifically for the purposes of the court case, although this should happen only where an expert opinion is truly necessary for the court to decide the case.

The court must give permission before the child can be examined or assessed. Detailed procedures for selecting and instructing experts are set out in the Practice Direction 'Experts in Family Proceedings Relating to Children' which came into force on 1 April 2008.[23] Clear instructions must be sent setting out the expert's task and the precise questions they are to consider. Letters of instruction should be drafted by a lawyer following the guidance in the Practice Direction.

However eminent the expert and however forceful his findings, it is the court, not the expert, that makes the final decision. The court is not bound to agree with an expert, although before a judge can reject expert evidence, it must be analysed under cross-examination,[24] and the judge must give reasons for departing from the expert view. In one case the Court of Appeal found that the judge had given too much weight to personality testing showing the mother scored highly on 'lie scales'.[25] Expert evidence

23   Available at www.hmcourts-service.gov.uk/cms/files/Experts-PD-flagB-final-version-14-01-08.pdf, accessed 14 August 2008.
24   *Re W (A Child: Care Order)* [2005] EWCA Civ 649 Court of Appeal.
25   *Re S (Care: Parenting Skills: Personality Tests)* [2005] 2FLR 658 Court of Appeal.

must also be seen in context of the whole case. As Ryder J explained, a court makes findings of fact on all the available evidence, not just scientific or medical materials – the wider context of social, emotional, ethical and moral factors must also be considered.[26]

Local authorities and courts have to be able to rely on the experts instructed. Being an expert witness is an important task and court is not the place for anyone to expound his personal theory or a controversial point of view. Experts must be honest and declare whether the conclusions they propose would be accepted by the majority of their profession.

Scientific understanding progresses so experts instructed in care proceedings must be up to date with latest developments. For example, as the court discovered, the current thinking is that subdural haematomas are caused by a lesser degree of force than was previously thought, albeit still a level of force which is unacceptable.[27] In another case the court discovered the dangers of relying on colposcopy photographs in diagnosing sexual abuse, when experts indicated that the photographs did not reflect what they had actually seen.[28] The judge said that, although it is important to avoid repeated examinations, it may nevertheless be preferable to causing grave and irreparable injustice and harm to the family. In that case, the experts finally agreed there was no evidence of abuse. Holmes J pointed out that there is a considerable subjective element in the medical assessment of the physical signs of sexual abuse (in the absence of clearly diagnostic evidence) and therefore 'purely medical assessments and opinions should not be allowed to predominate'.[29] Medical assessments of sexual abuse should be in line with the latest guidelines from the Royal College of Paediatrics and Child health.'[30]

Confidence in the medical profession was shaken by a series of criminal cases in which mothers were convicted of killing their babies on medical evidence later found to be unreliable. In Angela Cannings's criminal appeal, the Court of Appeal said:

26 *A County Council* v. *A Mother, A Father & X, Y and Z* [2005] 2FLR 129 High Court.

27 *Re A & D (Non-accidental Injuries: Subdural Haematomas)* [2002] 1FLR 337 High Court.

28 *Re Y (Evidence of Abuse: Use of Photographs)* [2003] EWHC 3090; [2004] 1FLR 855 High Court.

29 *Leeds City Council* v. *YX and ZX (Assessment) of Sexual Abuse)* [2008] EWHC 802 (Fam) High Court.

30 *The Physical Signs of Child Sexual Abuse: An Evidence-based Review and Guidance for Best Practice.* For more information see www.rcpch.ac.uk/Research/Research-Activity/Child-Protection-Research, accessed 13 August 2008.

a great deal about death in infancy is as yet unknown… We cannot avoid the thought that some of the honest views expressed with reasonable confidence in the present case will have to be revised in years to come… What may be unexplained today may be perfectly well understood tomorrow. Until then any tendency to dogmatise should be met with answering challenge. Further research is necessary.[31]

These criminal cases led to reconsideration of some care cases including two in which care orders had been made because mothers had harmed their babies. The Court of Appeal confirmed that the Cannings case does not change the local authority's responsibility to prepare cases on the civil standard.[32] In the criminal arena a divergence of medical opinion might mean that the case cannot be pursued but this is not so in care proceedings. The family court does not consider incidents in isolation but looks at their sequence and pattern, and takes into account the whole picture, including non-medical evidence. It also operates under less restrictive rules of evidence, applying a less demanding standard of proof than a criminal court. So, the fact that a parent might be acquitted (or not even charged) in a criminal case does not mean that findings cannot be made in a family case. Interestingly, the reverse is also true. Although the judge in one care proceedings case could not decide who was responsible for a baby's death, the father was nonetheless prosecuted and convicted of manslaughter. He objected, arguing that the care proceedings had already dealt with the issue. The Court of Appeal rejected his argument: the decision in care proceedings did not and could not determine the criminal case.[33]

Split hearings

Medical evidence is often crucial to the court's first question in care proceedings, namely whether the threshold criteria are met. Only if they are does the court proceed to the second question of what order, if any, should be made.

Often all the evidence on both questions is given in the same hearing and the court gives a single judgment passing seamlessly from the first question to the second. However, sometimes it is impossible to carry

---

31   *R v. Angela Cannings* [2004] EWCA Crim 1, paragraph 22.
32   *Re U (Serious Injury: Standard of Proof); Re B* [2004] EWCA Civ 567 [2004] 2FLR 263 Court of Appeal.
33   *R v. Levey* [2006] EWCA Crim 1902 [2007] 1FLR 462 Court of Appeal.

out welfare assessments to advise the court on the appropriate outcome without factual issues being decided first. In such cases, a 'split hearing' might take place; the first hearing (a 'fact-finding' or 'causation' hearing) deals with factual matters and the second, some time later, decides the final outcome. As Wall J explained, the essence of a split hearing is to identify a factual issue critical to the threshold which must be tried first.[34] Psychiatric or psychological assessments are unlikely to assist in this fact-finding task; assessments of the parents should be carried out at the second stage on the basis of the facts found by the court.

12.2 – Split hearing

Baby Alexander has numerous bruises. The court needs to decide whether these are:

- caused deliberately and if so by whom
- the result of carelessly rough handling
- due to a rare medical condition.

The court holds a fact-finding hearing first, concentrating on medical evidence and the parents' explanations for the injuries. As a social worker, you have little relevant evidence to give at this stage.

If the judge decides the bruises are due to a medical disorder and there are no other allegations, the threshold is not crossed and the case is over. If he finds that the injuries are deliberate and are caused by one parent, the couple may separate and the other put him/herself forward as a sole carer, so you will be assessing a very different situation. If the judge finds Alexander was handled roughly because the parents knew no better, your assessment for the welfare stage might concentrate on parenting skills and the prospects for improvement. Everyone can move forward on the basis of the judge's findings.

At the second hearing the judge hears professional evidence, of which your social work assessment is an important part, to decide on what order, if any, should be made in Alexander's best interests.

If a split hearing is to be held, the issues and the exact purpose of the fact-finding hearing must be clear:[35] either it is to determine whether the threshold criteria are met (in which case, if the answer is 'no', the whole case ends) or to determine a particular question of fact to inform subsequent

---

34   *In Re CB & JB (Care Proceedings: Guidelines)* [1998] 2FLR 211 High Court.
35   *Re A (Children: Split Hearing)* [2006] EWCA Civ 714 [2007] 1FLR 905 Court of Appeal.

assessments (so the case continues whatever findings of fact are made). The findings must be sufficiently precise to be useful in subsequent assessments, unlike in one case where the parties agreed findings at a causation hearing which were so vague and inadequate that the issues had to be re-examined at the final hearing.[36]

If a case is suitable for a split hearing, early directions should be given for evidence and hearings listed without delay. Both hearings should be heard by the same judge. This may sound obvious, but in one case, not only did different judges hear the first and second stages, but the second judge did not even have a transcript of the fact-finding judgment.[37] There is also the possibility that things might change between the two hearings, as happened when the mother in one case changed her story between the two stages of proceedings.[38] The Court of Appeal said that the court should treat the preliminary findings as a foundation, then make the necessary adjustments to reflect subsequent developments, which should be rigorously tested through examination and cross-examination.

Once findings are made, everyone must respect them. Great Ormond Street Hospital (GOSH) had expressed the opinion in one case that sexual abuse had probably occurred and mother was not responsible for the children's allegations.[39] The judge, however, disagreed and rejected every allegation of abuse, disbelieved the mother on every issue and found her to be the originator of the false allegations. GOSH nonetheless continued to work with the children on the basis that they had been sexually abused. The judge said that agencies or experts whose assistance is sought by the court to resolve contact problems should 'proceed on the basis of findings of fact by the court' and 'be even handed, fair and transparent as between parents'. They must not lose sight of the court's ultimate authority and responsibility for decision making.'

Points for practice

1. Have a sound knowledge of procedure. Obey all court directions and work closely with your legal team.

---

36 *Re D (Child: Threshold Criteria)* [2001] 1FLR 274 Court of Appeal.

37 *Re G (Care Proceedings: Split Trials)* [2001] 1FLR 872 Court of Appeal.

38 *Re M (Children: Determination of Responsibility for Injuries)* [2002] EWCA Civ 499, [2003] 1FLR 461 Court of Appeal.

39 *Re N (Sexual Abuse Allegations: Professionals Not Abiding by Findings of Fact)* [2005] 2FLR 340 High Court, at paragraph 18.

2.   Consider carefully any application for interim orders and be able to justify any application to remove a child from home.

3.   Always assume court cases will be fully contested and prepare accordingly.

4.   Be prepared to resist applications to make a child attend court.

5.   Be prepared for applications for residential assessments.

6.   Consider carefully whether an expert's opinion is needed, but remember that the court, not the expert, decides the case.

7.   If a case is suitable for a split hearing, raise the issue as soon as possible. Ensure you are clear about the purpose of the hearing. Always respect the findings of the court.

Chapter 13

Care Proceedings – Care Orders and Care Plans

Recommendations to the court

The argument in many cases centres not on the threshold criteria, but on the child's future – should an order be made? If so, what should it be? This is inextricably linked with the plans for the child – the court cannot and will not grant a care order without a proper care plan.

Care planning

The starting point is always that the child should remain at home if possible or, if removed, should be returned as soon as possible. The European Court of Human Rights said:

> the taking of a child into care should normally be regarded as a temporary measure to be discontinued as soon as circumstances permit and any measures of implementation of temporary care should be consistent with the aim of reuniting the natural parent and child.[1]

Always keep under review whether a return home is possible.

In care planning, put simply, the questions are:

- Can the child live with either or both of his parents?

- If not, can a member of the extended family care for him?

- If not, is there a carer available in the child's social network?

---

1   *Johanssen v. Norway* [1997] 23 EHRR 33 [2003] 2FLR 1166 ECtHR.

Only if the answer to all of the above is 'no' should you consider placement with 'strangers', through fostering or adoption.[2]

These options have to be considered, assessments carried out and procedural requirements complied with all within the timescale of the care proceedings. It is a tall order and there is simply not enough time to work through the questions one by one. This gave rise to the concept of twin track (or, often, multiple track) planning, a practice given judicial approval by Bracewell J who said that it should be clearly explained to the family that two options are being considered: rehabilitation within a strictly limited timescale or adoption outside the family.[3] Considering all options at the same time does not pre-empt the final decision. Twin track planning should be raised early in the proceedings and any necessary directions sought.

Do not confuse twin tracking with 'concurrent planning' schemes when a child is placed from the start with a family who foster him with a view to rehabilitation but, if this is unsuccessful, will adopt him.

Parents first

The presumption is that a child should normally be with a natural parent if available. This can lead to particular tensions in reconstituted families where children are half-siblings, as in one case involving three children.[4] The care plan was for the eldest two to be placed with their grandmother, and the youngest with his father. The grandmother argued all three siblings should stay together, living with her. The Court of Appeal said that the question was whether there were any compelling factors to override the child's right to be brought up by a natural parent; it was not appropriate to balance the two households to see which would provide a better home. There may be cases where the value of the sibling relationship overrides the natural parent's presumption, but this was not one. This case illustrates the dilemma for the court when the welfare of each of the children is paramount, but their needs conflict.

---

2   For an illustration, see the care planning scenario in Appendix 8.
3   *Re D & K (Care Plan: Twin Track Planning)* [1999] 2FLR 872 High Court.
4   *Re D (Care: Natural Parent Presumption)* [1999] 1FLR 134 Court of Appeal.

Family placement

Placing a child within his extended family can have the advantage of pre-serving at least an element of his identity and heritage. In human rights terms, it is a less drastic interference with the right to respect for family life than removal to strangers, so is more likely to be a proportionate interven-tion, subject always to the overriding need to secure the child's welfare which is paramount.

'Family' in this context is not limited to blood relationships, confirmed by the Court of Appeal in a case where the proposed 'family' member was the mother's foster sister, rather than a birth relative – that was not a prob-lem, but delay was, as the potential carer only came forward at the final care hearing.[5] Wall LJ said the local authority 'plainly should have called a family group conference', adding 'it is equally plain that KB should have put herself forward at a much earlier stage'. As he put it:

> The moral of the case, yet again, is that the available options for a child should be teased out as early as possible, and if a family member wishes to be considered to care for a child, he or she should come forward at the earliest possible opportunity.[6]

In some families there may be several potential carers and it can be im-practicable to carry out a full assessment on every one, so the practice has grown up of a 'viability assessment' to see whether proceeding to a full assessment is justified. Any such preliminary assessment could eliminate a potential in-family carer from any further consideration so must be under-taken professionally and fairly. The court found one such viability assess-ment flawed and inadequate.[7] The child's interests required an exhaustive investigation of the options open to fulfil his welfare needs, so the court ordered a thorough independent viability assessment. Courts depend on an amalgam of expertise from different disciplines, and competent social work assessments are essential.

Confidentiality issues

Involving the extended family in planning for the child inevitably requires disclosing information about the child's situation and the family's problems

---

5   *G & B (Children)* [2007] EWCA Civ 358 [2007] 2FLR 140 Court of Appeal.
6   *G & B*, paragraph 42 (see note 5 above).
7   *Re M-H (Assessment: Father of Half Brother)* [2006] EWCA Civ 1864 [2007] 2FLR 1715 Court of Appeal.

– information which would normally be confidential. If court proceedings are ongoing any information included in evidence filed at court can only be disclosed with court permission.

If the parents and child (if old enough) agree to matters being discussed within the extended family, there is no difficulty. But what if there is no agreement – or if it is a situation where the wider family do not even know of the child's existence? This is a delicate issue, also encountered in some adoption cases. Great care must be taken and no decision should be taken lightly. Once information is disclosed it cannot be undisclosed – you cannot put the genie back into the bottle – but a decision not to contact someone may equally have life-long consequences. There are human rights issues on all sides, most obviously Article 8 (right to respect for private and family life). If anyone's rights are to be breached the question is whether the breach is justified.

13.1 – Disclosing information: Human rights

Julie gives birth to Kelly and wants to place her for adoption. Julie has not told Liam (Kelly's father) of the pregnancy or birth and does not want him to know. If Liam is told against her wishes, it is a breach of Julie's right to have her privacy respected. If Liam is not told, his (and possibly his parents') possible right to a family life with Kelly is breached.

Kelly has a right to a life with her family. If Liam is not told, she may miss out on a relationship with or even placement in her birth family.

One person's rights must be balanced against another's.

Each case depends on its own facts and legal advice is essential. Skilled social work may resolve the problem through discussion and persuasion but, if not, it is important to tease out the issues. What exactly is the reason for the refusal – is there a reasonable justification? Is there any evidence to support any allegations – for example if a mother claims her parents abused her as a child, are there any records to support that claim? Or if she does not want the birth father to be informed because he is violent, has she ever reported domestic violence? On the other hand, is there any information to indicate that wider family members might be able to offer the child a home?

If necessary, the court can either direct that people should be contacted, or confirm that they should not. If proceedings are neither under way nor contemplated, the High Court could be asked to exercise its inherent jurisdiction – a marvellously flexible jurisdiction enabling the High Court to do almost anything necessary to fill a gap in family legislation.

Cases turn so much on their individual circumstances that it is difficult to draw out general guidance, but they can illustrate the issues considered by the courts. A cautionary tale appeared in a case where the mother relinquished her baby for adoption at birth, alleging that the putative father had been violent and insisting that he should not be contacted.[8] The baby was placed for adoption with experienced adopters and settled beautifully. Only when the adoption application was made did the court insist that the father be informed. He turned out to be 'unimpeachable' and engaged to be married to a nursery nurse. The mother admitted that her allegations of violence were untrue. The father wanted to care for the baby, who was by then settled and bonded with the adoptive family. The failure to tackle the issue earlier meant the court was faced with an impossible choice (in the end the baby stayed with the adopters).

The Court of Appeal said that in such cases the question was where a particular father lay on the spectrum of unmarried fathers (from a rapist at one extreme to a fully involved father at the other).[9] In Re H; Re G the court came to different conclusions in two such cases.[10] One father had a right to a family life with the new baby because the parents had previously lived together and had an older child for whom the father paid maintenance and had some contact. He had to be informed of the baby's existence. The other father had no Article 8 right because the couple had never lived together and had lost touch.

In another adoption case, the issue was whether the possibility of an extended family placement should be considered, when the family knew nothing of the baby's existence.[11] The judge found there was no reason to doubt the mother's views that the relatives could not care for the baby. Revealing the information would not be in the child's best interests – it would disrupt the family, jeopardise the co-operation between mother and adoption agency, and would be an unjustified breach of the mother's right to confidentiality.

However, in another case a child was subject to care proceedings with a likely adoption care plan.[12] The father had had a close two-year relationship with mother, was willing to pay maintenance and maintain contact

8   Re O (Adoption: Withholding Agreement) [1999] 1FLR 451 Court of Appeal, a case under the old adoption law, but still a striking illustration of the dilemma.

9   Re R (Adoption: Father's Involvement) [2001] 1FLR 302 Court of Appeal.

10   Re H; Re G (Adoption: Consultation of Unmarried Fathers) [2001] 1FLR 646 Court of Appeal.

11   Z County Council v. R [2001] 1FLR 365 High Court.

12   Birmingham City Council v. S, R and A [2006] EWHC 3065 [2007] 1FLR 1223 High Court.

but did not want his devout Muslim family to know about the child, fearing ostracism. The court had to decide whether his family had to be told. The court found evidence of a possibility that someone from the extended family might come forward as a carer, so gave the father a limited time to tell the family himself before the local authority and Guardian contacted them. Sumner J said:

> adoption is a last resort for any child. It is only to be considered when neither of the parents nor the wider family and friends can reasonably be considered as potential carers for the child. To deprive a significant member of the wider family of the information that the child exists who might otherwise be adopted is a fundamental step that can only be justified on cogent and compelling grounds.[13]

He continued:

> what is at the heart of this case are the rights of 8 month old A who may be placed for adoption if her mother is held unable to care for her. They include her right to be brought up by her own family.[14]

The Court of Appeal stressed that the child's welfare is the overriding issue.[15] Where the mother requests confidentiality, enquiries should only be made of the father and wider family if there is a prospect of finding a long term carer for the child. In that case, the local authority should not have informed the maternal grandparents and should not contact the putative father.

Kinship care

The term 'kinship care', often used in practice, is not a legal term and does not connote a particular legal status. A child can be placed with extended family members:

- as local authority foster carers
- under a residence order
- under a special guardianship order
- as adopters.[16]

---

13   *Birmingham City Council* v. *S, R and A*, paragraph 73 (see note 12 above).
14   *Birmingham City Council* v. *S, R and A*, paragraph 76 (see note 12 above).
15   *Re C (A Child)* [2007] EWCA Civ 1206 Court of Appeal.
16   For a summary of the differences between residence, special guardianship and adoption orders see the 'at a glance' chart in Appendix 2.

Having decided to recommend placement with a family member, analyse the needs of the case to decide which order fits best, rather than picking an order first and making the placement fit.

Which order?

Making a recommendation to the court requires a clear understanding of the nature and effect of each of the available orders. Private law orders as well as public law orders need to be considered.[17]

Care orders and supervision orders

The grounds, standard of proof and degree of evidence required are exactly the same for care and supervision orders, but the characteristics of the two orders could hardly be more different.[18] This is most clearly seen where the plan is for the child to remain at home, when the options are:

- a care order (CO) (subject to complying with regulations)[19]
- a supervision order (SO)
- no order.

Which should it be?

Does the local authority need parental responsibility?

Only a CO confers parental responsibility (PR) on the local authority. The parents do not lose their PR but the authority can overrule them where necessary to safeguard or promote the child's welfare.[20] The local authority does not acquire PR under a SO; its role is to 'advise, assist and befriend' the child.[21]

---

17   See Chapters 4–6 for details on private law.
18   See the 'at a glance' chart in Appendix 7.
19   Set out in the Placement of Children with Parents etc. Regulations 1991 SI
      1991/893. London: Stationery Office, available at www.opsi.gov.uk/si/si1991/
      uksi_19910893_en_1.htm, accessed 7 August 2008.
20   s33(3) and (4) CA89.
21   s35(1)(a) CA89.

Does the local authority need power to remove the child without notice?

Under a CO the local authority decides where the child lives. Even if it places the child at home it can change its mind and remove him at any time without returning to court. This raises issues of the right to respect for family life (Article 8) and the right to a fair trial (Article 6). The court must be convinced that such a power truly is proportionate to the needs of the case.

Under a SO, the parent(s) decide where the child lives and the local authority has no power to remove him. If removal becomes necessary, the local authority is back to square one and must seek an EPO, ask the police to take the child into police protection or start fresh care proceedings. The court cannot simply 'scale up' a SO to a CO, although it can vary a CO down to a SO.[22]

How long should the order last?

A CO lasts until the child turns 18 unless the court discharges the CO,[23] or makes another order (such as residence or adoption) which automatically brings the CO to an end.

In contrast, a SO lasts for up to one year, with a possibility of extension on application to the court for up to three years in total. In practice, applications to extend SOs are uncommon. Usually, either the situation improves so a further order is unnecessary, or the SO is not working so a different response – perhaps a CO – is needed.

Who decides when protection ends?

Once a CO is made, it only comes to an early end if someone applies to court and the court decides on the evidence that it is no longer needed. If a SO is made, it simply fades away unless the local authority actively brings the matter back to court to seek an extension. A CO continues unless the court ends it; a SO ends unless the court extends it.

---

22   s39(4) CA89.
23   s39(1) CA89.

What is the local authority's position?

Under a CO, the local authority is legally responsible for the child, but if the child is at home, in reality the parents have practical care and control, subject to periodical social work visits. The authority is arguably in a position of responsibility without power. Under a SO, the parents are legally responsible for the child, and the authority's role is to assist.

Which is the right order?

The court can make whichever order it thinks fit; it can impose a CO on a local authority which seeks a SO or vice versa. How does it decide?

In one case, the local authority sought a SO but, as a previous child had died, the court did not think this sufficient to protect the new baby.[24] The maximum duration of three years was inadequate for a young baby and the judge thought that safeguards should be lifted, if at all, by the court, not by the local authority simply allowing a SO to expire. Similarly, on another occasion, parents and local authority agreed on a SO but the court agreed with the Guardian that the continued protection of a CO was needed for the eighth child of a family where the seven older children had all been removed on COs just the previous year.[25]

However, there must be clear reasons to impose a stronger order than the one sought.[26] The starting point should be the less interventionist order unless there are cogent reasons to the contrary. A desire to encourage the authority to take action by imposing duties on it is not a good reason.

Since the Human Rights Act, there is a greater emphasis on proportionality. The court has said that, where a child is placed at home, Parliament intended that the very serious step of removing him should normally occur as a result of independent judicial authority, not administrative action.[27]

Although a SO is significantly less powerful, it is still a court order and should not be taken lightly – as Hale LJ stressed:

> nobody should be in any doubt that a supervision order is compulsory. The parents' failure to cooperate is very cogent evidence indeed that something more stringent may be needed, or, at the very least, that there is a continuing risk of harm to the child.[28]

---

24   *Re D (Minor) (Care or Supervision Order)* [1993] 2FLR 423 High Court.
25   *Re D (Care Order or Supervision Order)* [1999] 2FLR 621 High Court.
26   *Re O (Care or Supervision Order)* [1996] 2FLR 755 High Court.
27   *Oxfordshire CC* v. *L (Care or Supervision Order)* [1998] 1FLR 70 High Court.
28   *Re O (A Child) (Supervision Order: Future Harm)* [2001] 1FLR 923 Court of Appeal, at paragraph 23.

In that case, the risk was at the lower end of the spectrum and the slowness of deterioration and protection from other sources meant there was no need for the power of instant removal without going to court first. Proportionality is the key: where a SO is proportionate to the risk, there is a duty to ensure that it is made to work, including ensuring that partner agencies co-operate in the support and protection plan.

Do SOs add anything to the option of the child staying at home under no order but subject to a child protection plan? In one case, the court confirmed that a SO should only be made if it was better than no order and not just to encourage the local authority to perform its duties.[29] In that case, the mother was more likely to co-operate under an order which placed obligations on her and the local authority would allocate greater resources to monitoring the children's welfare, so an order was justified.

Care plan

Under a CO the court entrusts the local authority with a child's whole future. Not surprisingly, the court must know what the authority plans to do and to be assured that those plans are realistic.

The court cannot grant a care order without first considering the care plan,[30] which the local authority has a statutory duty to prepare and keep under review.[31] Each child must have a separate care plan and, while for siblings plans are often similar, they must not be unthinkingly duplicated – children do not come as a 'job lot' and each needs individual consideration.

The required contents of a care plan are set out in the Local Authority Circular LAC (99)29.[32] As well as stating what the plan is, it must also give reasons, realistic timescales and specific outcomes. The manager's countersignature confirms the backing of the authority as a whole, implying that the necessary resources will be allocated to put it into effect.

---

29   *Re K (Supervision Orders)* [1999] 2FLR 303 High Court.
30   s31(3A) CA89.
31   s31A CA89.
32   Department of Health (1999) 'LAC (99)29: Care plans and care proceedings under the Children Act 1989', available at www.dh.gov.uk/en/Publicationsandstatistics/ LetterandCirculars/LocalAuthorityCirculars/AllLocalAuthority/DH_4004535, accessed 14 August 2008.

Summary of care plan contents

1.   Overall aim, including timescale.

2.   Child's needs, including:

   • considerations arising from race, culture, religion, language, special educational needs, health or disability

   • the child's wishes and views, how far these have been followed and reasons for departing from them

   • a summary of how the child's needs might be met

   • contact arrangements, including the purpose of contact.

3.   Views of the child's parents and relevant others, including reasons for departing from their wishes.

4.   Placement details and timetable, including:

   • placement type and details

   • timescale for making the placement

   • likely duration of placement

   • health and education arrangements

   • rehabilitation plans

   • services to the child, family members and carers

   • parents' role.

5.   Management and support by the local authority, including:

   • responsibility for implementing the overall plan and specific tasks within it

   • review dates

   • contingency plan

   • arrangements for the child and family to have input into the planning process

   • arrangements for notifying of disagreements and making representations or complaints.

Roles of the court and local authority

The court must consider the local authority's care plan, but it cannot dictate its contents. The court's job is to decide whether or not a care order should be made, but thereafter it is the local authority's job to exercise PR and the court cannot tell it what to do. If the court and local authority agree as to what should happen to the child, there is no problem, but what if they disagree?

CAN THE COURT MAKE INTERIM ORDERS INSTEAD OF A FINAL ORDER, TO KEEP CONTROL?

In appropriate cases, if a care plan is uncertain, the House of Lords has said that the court should defer a final order until 'the way ahead is no longer obscured by an uncertainty that is neither inevitable nor chronic'.[33] In that case, the plan was so uncertain that, as Hale LJ said, 'although there was a real need for the children to be in care, there was also a real risk of a disproportionate response to those needs'.

The court should be given a care plan which is sufficiently firm and particularised for everyone to have a reasonably clear picture of the likely way forward in the foreseeable future. If uncertainties need to be resolved before the court can decide whether there should be a CO at all, then it should only make a final order when the material facts are as clearly known as can be hoped.

13.2 – Interim order

Michael's parents have long-standing drug problems. They are now co-operating with services to manage and reduce their habit. Michael goes home under an interim care order (ICO). At the final hearing, the placement is still in its early days.

If the final hearing goes ahead, the authority has no choice but to seek a full CO, planning to keep Michael at home with a contingency plan of removal if the problems recur. Instead, it is better for the court to adjourn the final hearing, making further ICOs until things become clearer. If all goes well, the authority may not need to seek a CO at all – a SO or even no order might be more proportionate. However, if the placement collapses, at the final hearing the local authority

---

33   *Re S (Minors) (Care Order: Implementation of Care Plan); Re W (Minors) (Care Order: Adequacy of Care Plan)* [2002] 1FLR 815 House of Lords.

will seek a CO with a care plan of permanent placement elsewhere. Everyone, including the court, will have a much clearer idea of the way forward.

However, sometimes uncertainties can only be worked out after the order is made: cases cannot continue for ever. As Wall J said:

> there are cases…in which the action which requires to be taken in the interests of children necessarily involves steps into the unknown. Provided the court is satisfied that the local authority is alert to the difficulties which may arise in the execution of the care plan, the function of the court is not to seek to oversee the plan but to entrust its execution to the local authority.[34]

So, ICOs are not there to continue the court's supervisory role. Wall J's comment was later approved by the House of Lords: 'a proper balance needs to be struck between the need to satisfy the court of the appropriateness of the care plan and the avoidance of over-zealous investigations into matters which are properly the responsibility of the local authority'.[35]

WHAT IF THE COURT DISAGREES WITH THE LOCAL AUTHORITY'S CARE PLAN?

The court cannot dictate a care plan. Its powers are limited to granting or refusing orders within its repertoire.

The local authority seeks COs in three cases.

13.3 – Foster care or grandmother?

In Nigella's case the care plan is for long term fostering. The court thinks she should live with her grandmother.

13.4 – Contact

For Oliver, the authority proposes a permanent placement with no direct contact with his mother. The judge thinks contact should continue.

---

34   *Re J (Minors) (Care: Care Plan)* [1994] 1FLR 253 High Court, page 256B.
35   *Re J*, page 262 (see note 34 above).

13.5 – To rehabilitate or not?

The plan for Peter is to rehabilitate him to his parents. The judge's view is that Peter should never go home.

In the first two cases, the court can achieve the outcome it considers to be in the child's best interests by making orders of its own motion. In Nigella's case the court can refuse to make a CO and instead make a residence order or special guardianship order to the grandmother. For Oliver, the judge can add to the CO a contact order under s34 Children Act 1989 (CA89) imposing the nature and level of contact he thinks appropriate. But in Peter's case, the judge has a problem. If he refuses to make the CO, Peter will go home – precisely the outcome the judge wishes to avoid. But if he makes the CO, he entrusts Peter's care to the local authority – knowing it proposes to implement a plan under which Peter will go home.

Balcombe LJ expressed the problem like this:

> the judge is therefore faced with the dilemma…that, if he makes a care order, the local authority may implement a care plan which he or she may take the view is not in the child or children's best interests. On the other hand, if he makes no order, he may be leaving the child in the care of an irresponsible, and indeed wholly inappropriate, parent. It seems to me that, regrettable though it may seem, the only course he may take is to choose what he considers to be the lesser of two evils… I have to say that this is not a position to which judges who exercise jurisdiction in the family courts are unaccustomed. There is very rarely a right answer in relation to children – it is usually a case of trying to decide which is the less wrong one.[36]

Before reaching that stage, however, the court can ask the local authority to reconsider the care plan. In one such case, when the local authority changed its care plan at the last minute, the judge adjourned the matter for further consideration.[37] The Court of Appeal said he was right to do so – he had not yet reached the 'lesser of two evils' stage, indeed he was trying to avoid it by asking the local authority to reconsider. The Court of Appeal was unhappy about the local authority's belligerent attitude. Wall LJ said:

---

36   In *Re S and D (Children: Powers of Court)* [1995] 2FLR 456 Court of Appeal, pages 634G–635C.

37   *Re S & W* [2007] EWCA Civ 232 [2007] 2 FLR 275 Court of Appeal.

Care proceedings are only quasi-adversarial. There is a powerful inquisitorial element. But above all, they are proceedings in which the court and the local authority should both be striving to achieve an order which is in the best interests of the child. There needs to be mutual respect and understanding for the different role and perspective which each has in the process. We repeat: the shared objective should be to achieve a result which is in the best interests of the child... In the overwhelming majority of cases in which there is a disagreement between the local authority and the court over a child's care plan, that disagreement is resolved by careful reconsideration on both sides. In our experience, as a consequence, such disagreements are extremely rare. That is as it should be. It is patently not in the interests of the already disadvantaged children involved in care proceedings for there to be a stand-off between the court and the local authority, the result of which, as here, is still further delay in resolving the children's future placements.[38]

Points for practice

1.   Carrying out all necessary steps in time requires strong organisation and clear thinking.

2.   Twin tracking does not mean that all options are treated equally – always start with the presumption that placement at home is best if possible.

3.   Use family group conferences where appropriate, remembering confidentiality issues.

4.   Have a clear understanding of the nature and effect of the different orders available. Fit the order to the case; never try to make the case fit the order.

5.   If a child is to remain at home, start with a presumption of a SO and only seek a CO if you have clear reasons to justify it.

6.   If you ask the court to entrust a child to your authority's care, you owe it to the court and the child to present a carefully drawn up, realistic care plan.

---

38   *Re S & W*, paragraphs 35 and 38 (see note 37 above).

Chapter 14

Contact and Enforcing Care Plans

Contact

Contact is a key element in a care plan. Under the Children Act 1989 (CA89) the court must consider contact arrangements and invite the parties to comment on them before making a care order.[1]

Contact should be an integral part of the plan, not (as it sometimes appears to be) added as an afterthought. The reasons for and purpose of contact should be analysed to inform recommendations as to the nature and level of contact between the child and each relevant person, remembering that a child may need contact with each parent, grandparents, siblings, extended family members, former foster carers or any number of other people. Each relationship needs to be considered separately but without forgetting the whole picture – it is hardly in the child's interests to be passed around like a parcel from one contact visit to the next.

Contact must also be seen in the context of the child's placement. Sometimes contact needs have to be sacrificed to meet more important placement needs, although this should never be lightly done; restrictions on contact may constitute a breach of the right to respect for family life, so must always be justifiable and proportionate.

Although the legal basis for contact with a child in care is different from private law contact, many of the considerations are the same and the aide-mémoire in Appendix 3 applies equally to both.[2]

---

1   s34(11) CA89.
2   s34 CA89, contact with a child in care; s8 CA89, private law contact.

The statutory presumption

The local authority has a statutory duty to allow a child in care 'reasonable contact' with his parents (including a father without parental responsibility (PR)), guardians and anyone who had a residence order which was discharged by the making of the care order.[3]

What is 'reasonable' depends on all the circumstances of the case. The local authority must exercise its discretion properly, taking relevant considerations into account and ignoring irrelevant factors, consulting appropriate people (including the parents and child) and taking their views into account. The child's best interests are the key consideration – contact should not be dictated by the availability of premises, supervisors or other resource issues. Nor should a formulaic response be adopted – a particular level of contact should not be suggested simply because that is the authority's usual practice for children of that age. The rationale for and reasonableness of the decision should be clearly demonstrable and documented on the file. If not, the authority will be unable to resist an argument for more contact.

It would be stretching the word 'reasonable' too far to argue that it includes no contact at all. If contact is to be severely restricted or denied, the local authority should consider seeking an order giving it permission to refuse contact.[4]

Contact with others

As a child in care is a 'looked after' child, the authority has a statutory duty 'unless it is not practicable or consistent with his welfare' to 'endeavour to promote' contact between the child and his parents, anyone else with PR and, in a phrase striking for its breadth, 'any relative, friend or other person connected with him'.[5] Contact with the child's parents is often such a difficult and pressing issue that it can be easy to overlook other relationships that may be just as important for the child, including contact with siblings.

---

3   s34(1) CA89.
4   s34(4) CA89, discussed further below.
5   Schedule 2 CA89, paragraph 15.

Contact orders

Rather than leaving contact to the local authority's discretion, the court has power to make a defined contact order. An application for such an order can be made by the local authority or child,[6] by anyone with a statutory presumption of reasonable contact,[7] or anyone else with the court's permission.[8] The court also has power to make such an order of its own motion even if no one has made an application.[9] The court can include such conditions as it thinks appropriate in any contact order, if necessary prescribing the precise details of when, where and how contact should take place.

The court is not bound by the local authority's care plan and can make a contact order of its own motion, even one which is incompatible with the plan if it is in the child's best interests.[10] If a contact order causes difficulty, the authority can apply to court to vary the order.[11]

Refusing contact

The local authority can refuse contact to anyone who has neither a statutory presumption nor a court order in his favour, provided that it is a reasonable exercise of its discretion.

However, the local authority cannot simply refuse contact to someone who has a statutory right to reasonable contact; it needs court permission to do so. The court can, on application by the local authority or the child or of its own motion, make an order under s34(4) CA89 which authorises the local authority to refuse contact between the child and a named person.

Such an order does not compel the authority to refuse contact – it is not an order forbidding contact (which is possible, albeit highly exceptional).[12] Instead, it gives the authority power to refuse contact, a power which must be exercised properly and reasonably. The authority must actually turn its mind to the question of whether, when and how to use that power – obtaining a s34(4) CA89 order should not lead to an automatic and unthinking refusal of contact. As always, the decision and the reasons for it should be clearly recorded on the file.

---

6   s34(2) CA89.
7   s34(3)(a) CA89.
8   s34(3)(b) CA89.
9   s34(5) CA89.
10   *Berkshire CC* v. *B* [1997] 1FLR 171 High Court.
11   s34(9) CA89.
12   Under s34(2) or (3) CA89.

It is not acceptable practice to seek a s34(4) CA89 order just in case it might be needed one day. Such an order should not be made while there is a realistic possibility of rehabilitation or 'merely against the possibility that circumstances may change in such a way as to make termination of contact desirable. For an order to be justified, a probable need to terminate contact must be foreseeable and not too remote.'[13]

This was confirmed by the Court of Appeal which said that a judge, having formed the view that the mother should have contact four times a year, should have made a positive order for such contact, not (as he did) grant the local authority a s34(4) CA89 order in case the mother failed to exercise the contact.[14]

If the authority is clear from the outset that an individual should not have contact, it should seek a s34(4) CA89 order at the same time as the care order; if a problem arises later, it must make a separate application to court.

If an emergency arises, the local authority can suspend contact which it is otherwise bound to grant (either under the statutory presumption or an order) for up to seven days where it is necessary to do so to safeguard or promote the child's welfare.[15] The procedural requirements of the Contact with Children Regulations 1991 must be followed,[16] including serving written notice as appropriate on:

- the child (if he is of sufficient understanding)
- parents
- guardians
- anyone who had a residence order discharged by the care order
- anyone else the authority considers relevant.

The notice specifies the decision, its date and duration and the reasons for it and outlines the remedies available in case of dissatisfaction. If the suspension does not resolve problems, it buys time to apply to court for an order.

---

13 *Re T (Termination of Contact: Discharge of Order)* [1997] 1FLR 517 Court of Appeal, page 525C.
14 *Re S (Care: Parental Contact)* [2005] 1FLR 469 Court of Appeal.
15 s34(6) CA89.
16 Contact with Children Regulations 1991 SI 1991/891, available at www.opsi.gov.uk/si/si1991/uksi_19910891_en_1.htm, accessed 14 August 2008.

Contact where the plan is adoption

If the care plan is adoption, the local authority must seek a placement order under the Adoption and Children Act 2002, wherever possible at the same time as the care order. The court must consider contact within the placement order application.[17]

Implementing care plans

The court must consider the care plan before it makes a care order, but once the order is made it is up to the local authority to implement the plan. The court has no monitoring role and only discovers whether the authority does what it promised if another application (for discharge of the care order or a contact order) later comes to court.

Obtaining a care order is just the start of a child's life in care. Implementing a care plan should be given as much priority as care proceedings themselves, but too often children have been left to drift in care while child protection cases take priority. However beautifully constructed the care plans presented to court, the reality is that many children in care experience multiple moves, do poorly in education and experience ongoing problems in adult life.

One such case, arousing righteous judicial fury, was *Re F*.[18] Care orders were made on two boys in 1992. The following year, the local authority decided not to rehabilitate, but did nothing else. By 1999 the boys were in residential care with no care plan and no social worker. In 2000 a new social worker finally started looking for permanent substitute carers. The case came to court when the parents applied for unsupervised contact. Munby J said the state had failed the parents and children gravely and repeatedly and (using the terminology of the threshold criteria) had itself caused significant educational, emotional, psychological, social and behavioural harm with enduring consequences to the boys. He said 'It is difficult to speak with moderation and without indignation at Lambeth's conduct', the handling of certain aspects of the case was 'scandalous' and 'Lambeth's dereliction of duty is shaming'. He stressed:

> The State assumes a heavy burden when it takes a child into care... If the State is to justify removing children from their parents, it can only be on

---

17   For more on placement orders see Chapter 16.
18   *Re F; F v. Lambeth LBC* [2002] 1FLR 217 High Court.

the basis that the State is going to provide a better quality of care than that from which the child has been rescued.[19]

We can anticipate this argument being used on behalf of parents resisting care orders – effectively they could argue 'we may not be very good parents, but the local authority is even worse'.

Expressing frustration at care plans which are not implemented is one thing, but can the court do anything about it? Another case of local authority failure went all the way to the House of Lords.[20] The care plan presented to the court on the making of the care order promised a programme leading to rehabilitation in six to nine months including:

- family therapy (not started)

- therapy for mother (cancelled)

- an adult social worker for mother (none allocated as she was not eligible – no one had checked before this was put in the plan)

- a family centre programme (only just started).

A frustrated Court of Appeal wanted to find a way to bring implementation of care plans under judicial control, so used this case to invent the idea of 'starred milestones' within care plans. The objective was to highlight those elements of a plan so crucial that failure to implement them would constitute a breach of human rights and to compel a return to court if those elements of the plan failed. Hale LJ acknowledged that there was nothing in CA89 to authorise this invention, but said there was nothing to prevent it.

However, the House of Lords found that the Court of Appeal had taken judicial creativity too far. Lord Nicholls 'respectfully but emphatically' could not agree that it was a legitimate exercise in statutory interpretation. Going back to first principles, he reminded us: 'Interpretation of statute is a matter for the courts; the enactment of statutes and amendment of statutes are matters for Parliament.' The scheme of the CA89 is that, once a care order is made, the responsibility for the child lies with the authority, not the court. The introduction of a supervisory role for the court constituted an amendment of the legislation, something only Parliament could do.

---

19   *Re F*, at paragraph 43 (see note 18 above).
20   *Re S (Minors) (Care Order: Implementation of Care Plan); Re W (Minors) (Care Order: Adequacy of Care Plan)* [2002] 1FLR 815 House of Lords.

Lord Nicholls took the view that the court is not the ideal forum to monitor a care plan in any event – it does not have a close, personal and continuing knowledge of the child and cannot respond with immediacy and informality to practical problems and changed circumstances. Supervision by the court would foster, rather than prevent, drift. The court is also divorced from the local authority's task of managing financial and human resources for all children in need in its area.

If parents are aggrieved by failure to implement a plan, they can apply for contact or the discharge of the care order or sue for breach of their human rights. A child of sufficient age and understanding can do the same, but the real gap in the law is where a care plan fails but the child is not competent to take a case to court on his own behalf. Their Lordships laid this problem firmly at the door of Parliament.

Independent Reviewing Officers

The government's solution to the problem was to create the role of the Independent Reviewing Officer (IRO) by amending s26 CA89. The details of the role were fleshed out in regulations,[21] and guidance,[22] which must be followed save in exceptional circumstances as it is issued under s7 Local Authority Social Services Act 1970.

An IRO is a qualified and experienced social worker, independent of line management or budgetary responsibility, whose job is to keep the case of every looked after child under review.

In summary, the IRO's job is to:

- chair the statutory review meetings for a looked after child (these must be held within four weeks of the child first becoming looked after, then within three months, and thereafter at no more than six monthly intervals)

- ensure reviews are held within the prescribed timescales and brought forward where appropriate

- review pathway plans of young people who remain looked after beyond 16

---

21   The Review of Children's Cases (Amendment) (England) Regulations 2004 SI 2004/1419 (with separate regulations for Wales), available at www.opsi.gov.uk/si/si2004/20041419.htm, accessed 14 August 2008.

22   'Independent Reviewing Officers Guidance', available at www.everychildmatters.gov. uk/resources-and-practice/IG00007, accessed 14 August 2008.

- ensure that:
    - the child's views are heard (this may include meeting the child)
    - reviews remain child and family centred
    - appropriate people contribute to the review
    - appropriate people attend the review
    - the care plan is carried out
    - people responsible for implementing decisions are identified
- monitor outcomes
- complete Part 2 of the child's Review Record, evaluating the plan, how far it is meeting the child's needs and whether any changes are needed
- address any problems with a child's care plan (see below)
- notify senior managers of any failure to review a child's case or to implement review decisions
- present periodical reports to the local authority for audit, quality assurance and individual performance management
- identify and report on good and poor practice.

The local authority must inform the IRO of any failure to make arrangements to implement a review decision or any significant changes in circumstances after a review.

As part of the strategic role, the IRO service manager should deliver an annual report to the lead member for Children's Services identifying good practice and areas for improvement, highlighting any matters needing urgent attention.

Addressing problems

The IRO must first to try resolve problems in a child's care plan by taking the matter up within the local authority – all the way to chief executive level if necessary.

If the IRO cannot resolve the problem and considers that the child's human rights may be being breached he should:

232 The Social Worker's Guide to Children and Families Law

- if the child is competent and wants to take the case to court himself, help him get advice from a suitably qualified and experienced solicitor

- if the child cannot take a case himself, see if a suitable adult (possibly, but not necessarily, one of the child's parents) is willing to pursue a case on the child's behalf

- if no one else is available, refer the matter to CAFCASS.

CAFCASS in turn considers whether the case should be taken to court on the child's behalf. A court application could be:

- under CA89

- a free-standing application under the Human Rights Act 1998

- an application for judicial review.

No local authority will want the ignominy of having a case referred to CAFCASS, let alone taken to court. This alone should be a good incentive to proper care planning.

14.1 – Discharge application

Jackie is in care. The care plan was for services to be provided to re-habilitate her to her mother's care. This has not happened and Jackie wants to go home. Jackie, or someone on her behalf, could apply under s39 CA89 for the care order to be discharged. (Jackie's mother could also apply; indeed she might be the more appropriate applicant.)

14.2 – Contact application

Keith is in care, placed separately from his sister Lily. He wants to see her more often. The local authority fails to increase contact. Keith, or someone on his behalf, could apply for a contact order. In such an application, Lily's welfare is the court's paramount concern – if there is a conflict, her interests supersede Keith's.

14.3 – Human rights claim

Michael is a teenager in care. He can be threatening, rude and un-co-operative. He is not invited to reviews because of his disruptive behaviour. A review decides to change his placement and reduce contact to his parents. Michael could argue that his human rights were breached by failing to involve and consult him about plans and seek an injunction to stop the changes and/or damages.

14.4 – Judicial review

Nicola has multiple disabilities and challenging behaviour. An expert devises a care plan for her, including a specialist residential placement requiring joint health, social and educational funding. The funding cannot be agreed, so instead the authority proposes to place her in a less specialist unit, with piecemeal health and education services. Nicola's representative might seek a judicial review of the decision, arguing it is unreasonable, and asking the court to quash the decision and order a rethink.

Lessons from case law

CHANGING CARE PLANS – DISCHARGE OF CARE ORDER

In *Re O*, the care plan was for the children to remain at home, therapy to be provided to mother and children and shared care with a foster family to be arranged.[23] Instead, there was no social work contact for five months and long periods of minimal professional input, no shared care and no therapy provided for the children. The care plan was then changed on the advice of a psychiatrist who mistakenly believed that the mother was the perpetrator of sexual abuse. The decision was made to remove the children and place them in long term residential care with limited contact. Not surprisingly, on the mother's application, the care order was discharged and replaced by a residence order with a supervision order. The main factor in the breakdown of the care plan was the local authority's failure to provide the support agreed.

CHANGING CARE PLANS – BREACH OF HUMAN RIGHTS

Parents retain their PR even when a child is under a care order. They have a right to be informed and consulted, especially about significant changes. In

---

23 *Re O (Care: Discharge of Care Order)* [1999] 2FLR 119 High Court.

Re G, children were rehabilitated to their parents' care in accordance with the care plan.[24] Two years later the social workers became concerned about the children's care. A meeting, which did not involve the parents, decided to remove the children from home. Unsurprisingly, the parents took the matter to court which found that the parents' rights under Article 8 (the right to respect for family life) had been breached. Human rights are not limited to the care proceedings process, but extend to all decision-making including the implementation of the care order.

Where significant changes to a care plan are proposed, the local authority has a duty to inform parents of the proposed change, setting out precisely the facts relied upon, and give them an opportunity to answer allegations and make representations. Parents and their representatives should normally be invited to attend any meeting where critical decisions are to be taken. The local authority must also make full and frank disclosure of all key documents including attendance notes of meetings and minutes of conferences. Where parents have a limited capacity to understand written communication the local authority must make sure that this does not impede their full participation in the process.

The case of *Re C* illustrates the lengths to which the courts expect local authorities to go even in the face of parental hostility.[25] The mother herself was only 14 and had been in care since she was six. The care plan for her baby was rehabilitation under specialist supervision, with a contingency of removal if there was an emergency or failure to progress. She was to be informed of any removal plan and given the opportunity to mount a legal challenge.

Things went wrong very quickly and the mother made serious threats to the foster mother. The local authority met in the mother's absence and decided to remove the baby for adoption. As the mother was threatening to harm people it was considered dangerous to involve her in the plan or give her notice, but the authority did keep her lawyer informed. When told of the removal, the mother assaulted the social worker and police officer and refused to discuss the future with the local authority.

The mother sought a Human Rights Act injunction to force the authority to place the baby back with her under the care plan. The case went up to the Court of Appeal which found that the baby's removal was lawful,

---

24   *Re G (Care: Challenge to Local Authority's Decision)* [2003] 2FLR 42 High Court.
25   *Re C (Breach of Human Rights: Damages)* [2007] EWCA Civ 2 [2007] 1FLR 1957 Court of Appeal.

and every opportunity had been given to the mother's lawyer to challenge decisions. However, the failure to consult the mother before moving from one track to the other in the plan was still a procedural breach of the mother's human rights, albeit one which was not significant enough to justify damages.

COURT PERMISSION TO REFUSE INFORMATION

Does this mean that even the most abusive and undeserving parents must always be fully informed and involved? The presumption is that they must, unless, in an extreme case, the court says otherwise. In *Re C*, a 13-year-old girl was desperate that her father (who was serving a long sentence for raping her) should not be informed or consulted about her future.[26] His PR had already been discharged on the girl's application. The High Court made a declaration absolving the local authority from any obligation to consult him. This might be a breach of his human rights, but he had forfeited consideration of his rights; the child's rights prevailed. The local authority was to provide him with limited annual information on the child's general well-being and progress and to inform him only of very significant events such as life-threatening illness or proposed adoption.

It is worth bearing this possibility in mind. If you have a case extreme enough to justify such an order, raise the issue during the care proceedings, rather than having to return to court later.

THE CHILD'S ROLE

In *Re X* a troubled teenager from London was placed under an ICO in a children's home in Devon, where she was doing well.[27] A psychiatrist recommended she should remain there until she was 16. The local authority's placement panel decided instead to return her to London. This decision was reached without reading reports or consulting the girl's mother, Children's Guardian or the children's home. Munby J found the process was fundamentally defective. Such a significant decision should not be taken without reading the papers and consulting relevant people. The mother's human rights had been breached, and the care plan would expose the child to further harm.

---

26   *Re C (Care: Consultation with Parents Not in Child's Best Interests)* [2005] EWHC 3390 [2006] 2FLR 787 High Court.

27   *Re X, London Borough of Barnet* v. *Y and X* [2006] 2FLR 998, High Court.

Munby J observed that the authority had placed too much weight on the wishes of an out of control and wayward teenager set on self-destruction and had too much regard for 'government inspired targets and expressions of ministerial view'. The authority maintained it was in the right, but graciously backed down to move things forward – if it had not done so, judicial review was likely.

Points for practice

1. Contact is a vital part of a care plan. Ensure you can justify your plans, and that your file shows your reasoning.

2. Care plans presented to court should be realistic and properly researched, then implemented.

3. Regularly reflect on whether the child's best interests are being met and everyone's human rights are being respected. Proper consultation, fair procedures and careful record keeping are essential.

4. Cases which drift or in which plans are not implemented are likely to end up back in court.

Part 6

Adoption

Chapter 15

Adoption Fundamentals and Adoption by Consent

What is adoption?

Adoption is the most far-reaching order a court can make in respect of a child. Some children are adopted as a result of their parents' choice, others via care proceedings – it is often the preferred care plan for young children where rehabilitation is ruled out.

Legally, adoption represents a complete transfer of a child from one family to another. It made perfect sense in an era when illegitimacy was socially unacceptable; an unmarried mother permanently relinquished her baby and a childless couple took him on as their own. Although society has changed and many older children now come to adoption, the basic legal model remains the same.

Adoption is governed by the Adoption and Children Act 2002 (ACA), which is still in its early days; some key elements are as yet untested in case law.[1]

Adoption is unique. It:

- terminates birth parents' parental responsibility (PR)[2]
- transfers exclusive PR to the adopter(s) – the child is treated in law as if born to them[3]

---

1   Adoption and Children Act 2002. London: Stationery Office, in force since 30 December 2005, replacing the Adoption Act 1976, available at www.opsi.gov.uk/acts/acts2002/ukpga_20020038_en_1, accessed 14 August 2008.
2   s46(2)(a) ACA.
3   s67(1) ACA.

- has life-long effect
- is irrevocable
- ends the child's relationship with the entire birth family
- creates new relationships with the whole adoptive family.

15.1 – Effect of adoption

Chardonnay's mother is Debbie, who has an older son, Chandler. Chardonnay is made subject to a care and placement order and is placed for adoption with Angela and Adam Smith, who already have an adopted son, Alexander. The moment the judge makes the adoption order:

- all court orders and rights under the Children Act 1989 (CA89) disappear
- Debbie loses her PR – she is no longer Chardonnay's mother
- Chandler is no longer her brother
- Angela and Adam become Chardonnay's parents with exclusive PR
- Alexander becomes Chardonnay's brother
- Angela and Adam can choose Chardonnay's name. She becomes Charlotte Smith
- Charlotte is now part of the Smith family for the rest of her life.

Debbie's and Adam's mothers both die. Each leaves all her money 'to my grandchildren'. Chardonnay/Charlotte inherits nothing from Debbie's mother, as she is no longer her granddaughter, but takes her share of Adam's mother's fortune.

The twin characteristics of permanence (adoption lasts a lifetime) and security (adoption orders are irrevocable) often make adoption a more attractive option for many young children in care than any of the orders available under the CA89, even special guardianship.[4] They also make adoption the most draconian order in human rights terms – there can be no greater interference with family life than terminating family relationships for ever.

---

4   For a summary of the differences between a residence order, special guardianship and adoption see the 'at a glance' chart in Appendix 2.

Where an adoption order is made against the birth parents' wishes, clear justification is required to show that it is proportionate to the need of the case.

Adoption agencies

Adoption is of such significance that, in most cases, it can only be arranged by an adoption agency. It is illegal to make a private arrangement,[5] or for money to change hands.[6] Non-agency adoptions are permitted in limited cases like step-parent adoptions and placements which start otherwise (e.g. private fostering or residence orders) and evolve into adoption.

Local authorities and registered adoption societies are 'adoption agencies', governed by the Adoption Agencies Regulations 2005 (AAR05).[7] Agencies must have written policies and procedures and have duties to all three sides of the 'adoption triangle':

- the child – including:
  - ° setting up a case record
  - ° explaining adoption to him
  - ° providing counselling
  - ° ascertaining his wishes and feelings
- birth parents – including:
  - ° explaining adoption
  - ° explaining the implications of giving consent to placement or adoption
  - ° ascertaining their wishes and feelings
  - ° providing counselling
  - ° providing written information
- prospective adopters – including:
  - ° providing counselling

---

5   ss92 and 93 ACA.
6   s95 ACA.
7   Adoption Agencies Regulations 2005 SI 2005/389, available at www.opsi.gov.uk/si/si2005/20050389.htm, accessed 14 August 2008.

      °   explaining the legal implications of placement and adoption

      °   giving written information.

Basic principles

The fundamental principles set out in s1 ACA closely resemble those of CA89, which is helpful in practice as most children reach adoption via CA89. However, there are two key differences. First, the s1 ACA principles apply to the adoption agency's decisions as well as the court's (s1 CA89 applies to the court alone), and second, the terms of s1 ACA are adapted to reflect the specific characteristics of adoption, particularly its life-long nature and the termination of birth family relationships.

Paramountcy principle

> s1(2) ACA The paramount consideration of the court and of adoption agency must be the child's welfare throughout his life.

The last three words of the subsection remind us that in adoption we must take a very long term view when judging a child's best interests.

Delay

As in CA89, there is a presumption that, 'in general, any delay in coming to the decision is likely to prejudice the child's welfare'.[8] This is always subject to the child's welfare; the 'no delay' principle does not justify coming to the wrong decision just because you can do so quickly.

Welfare checklist

When determining the child's best interests, the court and agency must consider the matters set out in the checklist which mirrors the CA89 list, adapted to the context of adoption. Just as in CA89 the list is not exhaustive – other relevant factors must be considered – and it does not dictate

---

8   s1(3) ACA.

the relative importance of each item; that depends on the circumstances of each case.

---

s1(4) ACA The court or adoption agency must have regard to the following matters (among others) –

(a) the child's ascertainable wishes and feelings regarding the decision (considered in the light of the child's age and understanding),

(b) the child's particular needs,

(c) the likely effect on the child (throughout his life) of having ceased to be a member of the original family and become an adopted person,

(d) the child's age, sex, background and any of the child's characteristics which the court or agency considers relevant,

(e) any harm (within the meaning of the Children Act 1989) which the child has suffered or is at risk of suffering,

(f) the relationship which the child has with relatives, and with any other person in relation to whom the court or agency considers the relationship to be relevant, including:

    (i) the likelihood of any such relationship continuing and the value to the child of its doing so,

    (ii) the ability and willingness of any of the child's relatives, or of any such person, to provide the child with a secure environment in which the child can develop, and otherwise to meet the child's needs,

    (iii) the wishes and feelings of any of the child's relatives, or of any such person, regarding the child.

(The word 'relative' includes parents, and 'relationships' are not restricted to legal relationships.)

Religion and culture

Although matters such as racial origins, religion and culture are already covered by heading (d) of the checklist, their significance in adoption warrants a separate subsection.

---

s1(5) ACA In placing the child for adoption, the adoption agency must give due consideration to the child's religious persuasion, racial origin and cultural and linguistic background.

When placing a child in a new family for life, the child's origins and identity are obviously important and must be given 'due consideration' but they do not override other factors, and are only part of the child's welfare overall. s1(5) ACA does not justify a child drifting in care waiting for a perfect match that never comes.

Range of powers and no order

The court and agency must consider the whole range of options available,[9] including orders under CA89,[10] which the court can make of its own motion without application. Another option is no order at all.

15.2 – Range of orders

Linda is subject to care proceedings. Rehabilitation is ruled out but Linda's aunt and uncle are suitable carers and want to adopt her.

The agency and the court must weigh up all the options – long term fostering, residence order, special guardianship or adoption. Adoption brings more security and permanence than the other options but at the price of the distortion of family relationships (aunt and uncle become parents; parents become aunt and uncle).[11]

---

9   s1(6) ACA.
10   For a summary of differences between residence, special guardianship and adoption orders see the 'at a glance' chart in Appendix 2.
11   See Chapter 5 for more discussion on the choice between adoption and special guardianship in family placements.

Who can be adopted?

Any child can be adopted provided he is:

- under the age of 18 at the date of the application[12]
- under 19 at the date of the order[13]
- not married.[14]

Who can adopt?

A single person or a couple can adopt. The usual minimum age is 21 but there is no statutory maximum. In practice adoption agencies operate policies as to adopters' ages but like all policies these must leave room for discretion in exceptional cases or they could be subject to judicial review.

A single adopter must be unmarried or, if married, the court must be satisfied that:

- the spouse cannot be found, or
- they are permanently separated, or
- the spouse is incapable of applying for adoption through mental or physical ill-health.[15]

What is a couple?

Previously, only married people could adopt as a couple. Now under the ACA, the word 'couple' includes unmarried couples, gay or straight.

---

s144(4) ACA In this Act a couple means –

(a) a married couple, or

(b) two people (whether of different sexes or the same sex) living as partners in an enduring family relationship.

---

12   s49(4) ACA.
13   s47(9) ACA.
14   s47(8) ACA.
15   s51(3) ACA.

Same sex couples are eligible to become adopters like any other couple and from 31 December 2008 adoption agencies may not discriminate against potential adopters on the basis of their sexuality.[16]

The idea of unmarried cohabitants, especially same sex couples, being able to adopt caused some controversy. In reality under the old legislation, unmarried couples used to adopt: one of them would adopt as a single person and both would obtain a joint residence order, giving shared PR (this did not give the partners equal status but it was the best solution then available). The courts had no difficulty in practice with the marital status or sexuality of the proposed adopter(s), focusing instead on the child's welfare. Courts rejected birth parents' opposition to adoption if it was based on the adopters' sexuality. It is a fiction to suppose that gay adoption is a revolutionary development.

However, until now children adopted by same sex couples have often been those who were hard to place – put bluntly gay adopters were a last resort. We wait to see whether in practice agencies will treat all couples equally when selecting a family for a particular child. If there comes a point where some couples are approved as adopters but never selected as a placement, legal challenges under the Human Rights Act 1998 are likely on the basis of the right to found a family (Article 12) being denied because of unlawful discrimination (Article 14).

Agency decisions

A local authority making adoption decisions does so as an adoption agency and must follow a prescribed procedure. Three main types of decision can only be made after considering the Adoption Panel's recommendation:

- Is adoption in the child's best interests?

- Should an applicant (individual or couple) be approved to adopt?

- Is the selected person/couple suitable to adopt the identified child/ren (the 'match')?

All three decisions can be made on the same occasion, but the first two questions must be answered positively before the agency can move onto the third. Usually, however, the three questions are considered separately and there are children approved for adoption waiting for a match, and

---

16   Equality Act (Sexual Orientation) Regulations 2007 SI 2007/1263, available at
     www.opsi.gov.uk/si/si2007/uksi_20071263_en_1, accessed 14 August 2008.

approved adopters waiting for a placement. If one agency cannot match a child with its own adopters, it can look for adopters approved by any other agency.

The Adoption Panel

Every agency must set up (or share with another agency) at least one Panel which must be chaired by a suitably qualified and experienced person.[17] There must be no more than ten members including:

- two social workers with at least three years' experience
- a local authority councillor
- the agency's medical adviser
- at least three independent people (not employees, recent employees, or councillors) including (wherever practicable) at least two people with personal experience of adoption.

The agency must appoint as its adviser a social worker with at least five years' experience (including management experience) to:

- assist in recruiting Panel members
- take responsibility for their induction and training
- liaise between Panel and agency
- monitor Panel performance
- advise the Panel generally and on particular cases.

The Panel must also obtain legal advice on each case.[18] The Panel must keep minutes of all meetings and a written record of all recommendations and reasons.

Approving a child for adoption

An agency can only place a child for adoption 'if it is satisfied that the child ought to be placed for adoption',[19] a conclusion which necessarily involves

---

17   Detailed provisions as to the Panel's composition and functioning are in the Adoption Agencies Regulations 2005 (see note 7 above).
18   AAR05 r18(2)(c).
19   s18(2) ACA.

considering and rejecting other options. However, deciding that adoption is the outcome for a child does not mean the agency must only seek an adoptive family. Particularly where a child may be difficult to place, the agency can widen the pool of potential carers for the child by considering long term foster carers as well as adopters.[20] The agency and the court can still be satisfied that a child 'ought' to be placed for adoption even if in relaity adopters may never be found.

The agency must obtain detailed information about all aspects of the child's history, characteristics, background and personality, the report of a medical examination and full information about the birth parents including details of their health history, background, religion and culture.[21] A detailed report known as the 'child's permanence report' must be prepared for the Panel.[22]

Information from care proceedings can be disclosed to the Panel without the need for court leave.[23] The child's birth parents' views form part of the social worker's report to the Panel, and the Children's Guardian's views should also be considered, but neither parents nor Guardian have the right to attend the meeting or make representations to it.

The Panel must consider all the reports submitted and request any further information it needs. The Panel's role is to:

- make a recommendation to the agency on whether adoption is in the child's best interests
- advise on contact arrangements
- advise on whether a placement order should be sought.

Crucially, the Panel does not make any decisions; it makes recommendations which then pass to the agency decision-maker who must not be a Panel member. The decision-maker must take the recommendation into account but does not have to follow it.

Approving potential adopters

The agency must set up a case record for any potential adopters. They must

---

20   *P (A Child)* [2008] EWCA Civ 535 Court of Appeal.
21   Full details of the information required appear in the Adoption Agencies Regulations 2005 Schedule 1 (see note 7 above).
22   AAR05 r17.
23   Family Proceedings Rules 1991, as amended.

be thoroughly assessed,[24] undergo medicals, provide references and have full police checks. Anyone convicted of or cautioned for certain offences against children is not eligible to adopt.[25] Prospective adopters must also be thoroughly prepared for the task of adoption.[26]

The prospective adopter receives a copy of the report at least ten days before it goes to the Panel, and his comments on it are put before the Panel.[27] He must also be invited to a Panel meeting. The Panel's job, after considering all the material before it, is to recommend whether the prospective adopter is suitable to adopt a child and it can advise about the age, sex and number of children for whom s/he is suitable. The agency decision-maker must consider the Panel's recommendation.

If the agency considers a person not suitable to adopt, it must notify him of this view and the reasons for it. He then has 40 days to make representations to the agency or to apply for an independent review panel to consider his case.

Once adopters are approved, their cases must be reviewed annually.

Matching

Matching is a delicate exercise, aiming to find the adopter(s) with the qualities and capacities to meet the child's needs. As was said in the European Court of Human Rights adoption is about 'giving a family to a child and not the child to a family'.[28]

Prospective adopters must receive appropriate information about the child, including a copy of the child's permanence report, to enable them to make an informed decision. However, their preparation and training should make them aware that no child comes with guarantees; some behaviours only manifest themselves and some secrets are only disclosed once a child feels secure. Being open with adopters is important: in one case, adopters successfully sued the local authority for failing to inform them of the severity of a child's behavioural difficulties which caused the adoptive mother to suffer a psychiatric illness.[29] They would not have gone ahead with placement had they known the truth.

---

24 Details of the matters for assessment appear in AAR05 Schedule 4.
25 Listed in AAR05 r23(2) and Schedule 3.
26 AAR05 r23.
27 AAR05 r25.
28 *Fretté* v. *France* [2003] 2FLR 9 ECtHR, at paragraph 42.
29 *A & B* v. *Essex County Council* [2003] 1FLR 615 High Court.

Before recommending a match, the Panel must consider the child's permanence report, the adopter's report and the agency's placement report which includes the reasons for proposing the placement and details of support services required. Again, the Panel recommends, but the agency decides. When a matching decision is made, the child's birth parent(s) must be notified in writing of the decision to place the child for adoption, but without providing identifying details of the prospective adopter(s).

Authority to place for adoption

Even when the agency has decided that adoption is in a child's best interests, it cannot place him for adoption without statutory authority to do so. The agency is authorised to place a child for adoption if either:

- the placement is a voluntary one with full parental consent (s19 ACA)
- a court makes a placement order (made with or without parental consent) (s21 ACA).

The consent route is appropriate where parents relinquish their child; a placement order is appropriate for children coming to adoption via care proceedings.

Parental consent

> s52(5) ACA 'Consent' means consent given unconditionally and with full understanding of what is involved; but a person may consent to adoption without knowing the identity of the persons in whose favour the order will be made.

Conditional agreement ('I agree as long as I can have contact') or without full understanding (due to learning difficulties, mental health problems or emotional distress) is not consent, so the case proceeds as if there is no agreement.

The ACA requires the consent of each 'parent', but in ACA (unlike CA89) the word 'parent' only means a parent with PR. Thus a father without PR is not required to give consent or have it dispensed with. Under

ACA unmarried partners have equal rights if they are adopters but not if they are the birth family.

Placement by consent

s19 ACA applies when the birth parents unconditionally agree to their child being placed for adoption. Although not limited to any particular situation, the classic scenario is the relinquishment at birth of an unplanned baby. In one such case the mother was clear from the outset that she wanted her baby adopted.[30] The local authority quite unnecessarily started care proceedings, meaning they had to allege likely significant harm. There was absolutely no need for this – it was exactly the situation for which s19 ACA was intended.

15.3 – A relinquished baby

Mary is an unmarried student expecting a baby conceived on a one-night stand. She asks the adoption agency to place the baby for adoption at birth.

The adoption agency must counsel Mary, giving her full information, including written information, about adoption and the implications of consent.

CONTACTING THE BIRTH FATHER

Mary will be the only person with PR for the baby, so only her consent is required to place him for adoption. Can the father just be ignored?

The first question is whether Mary will name him. If she refuses to do so in spite of sensitive social work, in practice little can be done. In a case where this arose, Munby J directed that beyond asking the mother once more for the father's name, no further steps should be taken to give the father without PR notice of intention to place the child for adoption.[31] Sadly this means that the child will know nothing about one half of his identity and heritage and have no chance of a relationship with his father.

If Mary names the father, if appropriate the agency should:

---

30 *Re C (A Child)* [2007] EWCA Civ 1206 Court of Appeal.
31 *Re L: X County Council* v. *C* [2007] EWHC 1771 (Fam) High Court.

- give him counselling
- obtain information from him
- ascertain his views
- find out if he intends to apply for PR, residence or contact.[32]

If Mary agrees to him being contacted, there is no problem. If, however, she objects, the dilemmas of conflicting human rights are raised.[33] Is it 'appropriate' to contact the father? In one such case the Court of Appeal decided that the putative father and the mother's wider family should only be contacted if there was a prospect of one of them providing the child with a home.[34] If in doubt, seek court guidance – the court rules allow an application to be made to the High Court for directions on whether to give a birth father notice of the intention to place a child for adoption.[35]

<hr>

15.3.1

Mary gives birth to baby Charlie. She confirms she wants him to be adopted and consents to him being placed for adoption.

Consent to placement

If a parent consents to placement for adoption under s19 ACA, a prescribed consent form must be witnessed by a CAFCASS officer as an independent safeguard. The adoption agency contacts CAFCASS, informing them in writing that Mary is prepared to consent, providing a copy of Charlie's birth certificate, Mary's name and address, a chronology of the agency's actions and confirmation that the legal position has been explained to Mary including giving her written information.

Once consent is given the local authority is authorised to place Charlie for adoption. He immediately becomes a 'looked after' child, even before he is actually placed.[36] Mary can consent either to Charlie being placed with particular adopters or any adopters identified by the agency.[37]

<hr>

32   AAR05 r14.
33   Discussed further in Chapter 13.
34   *Re C (A Child)* [2007] EWCA Civ 1206 Court of Appeal.
35   Rule 108, Family Procedure (Adoption) Rules 2005. See note 46.
36   s18(3) ACA.
37   s19(1)(a) and (b) ACA.

Consent given only for an identified placement is no longer valid if that placement cannot proceed, so from the agency's viewpoint it is best to ensure that there is at least a contingency of consent to placement with other adopters chosen by the agency should the identified placement not proceed.

In a planned relinquishment case, as much paperwork as possible should be completed before the birth, so the case can be brought to the Panel without delay. The authority should easily find a suitable match for Charlie in its pool of approved adopters and Mary should be involved in the choice, on the basis of anonymised information. It may be possible to make the 'best interests' recommendation for Charlie and to recommend the match with identified prospective adopters at the same Panel meeting.

ADVANCE CONSENT TO ADOPTION

15.3.2

Ann and Andrew are selected as adopters for Charlie. Mary is happy and wants to get the whole process over as quickly as possible.

Mary's consent to Charlie being placed for adoption is not the same as consenting to the adoption order itself.[38] A parent's consent is required at two stages: first consent to placement, then consent to adoption.

Consent to the order itself is usually given during the adoption proceedings, some time after the placement. However, for a parent in Mary's position there is the option under s20 ACA of giving advance consent to the adoption order itself at the same time as agreeing to placement or at any time thereafter. The consent can be limited to an adoption order in favour of the identified adopters or to adoption by any adopters chosen by the agency.[39] She can also declare that she does not wish to be informed of any adoption application being made, thus choosing to have no further involvement in the process, although she can later withdraw that statement if she changes her mind.[40]

---

38   Under s19 ACA.
39   s20(2) ACA.
40   s20(4) ACA.

Mary's consent to Charlie's adoption is not valid until he is at least six weeks old.[41] There is a prescribed form to record her consent to adoption which again must be witnessed by a CAFCASS officer. This form is sufficient to satisfy the court of Mary's consent when the time comes to make the adoption order.

The consent form Mary proposes to sign is of profound significance; she is agreeing in advance to lose all PR for and all legal relationship with Charlie for life. Clearly the greatest care must be taken to ensure that Mary truly understands the implications of her actions.

Parental responsibility

As soon as the agency is authorised to place a child (through parental consent or a placement order), the agency acquires PR.[42] Thus, as soon as Mary consents to Charlie's placement, her PR is shared with the agency.

When the agency places Charlie with Ann and Andrew, before they even apply for an adoption order they also acquire PR which is now shared four ways.[43] However, it is an unequal relationship as the agency can restrict the exercise of PR by Mary and/or Ann and Andrew. The agency should be clear from the outset exactly what role Mary will continue to play in Charlie's life and how much autonomy Ann and Andrew have before the adoption order is made.

Once the agency is authorised to place Charlie, contact is no longer governed by CA89. Deciding who Charlie should have contact with is an exercise of PR, so effectively is decided by the agency, subject to any contact order made by the court under s26 ACA.

Minimum placement period

In normal agency cases such as Charlie's, the child must be in placement for at least ten weeks before the adopters can apply to court.[44] This minimum period is usually sufficient in straightforward cases, but where children have more complex needs it often takes much longer for the prospective adopters to feel ready to launch their application. Even

---

41   s52(3) ACA.
42   s25(2) ACA.
43   s25(3) ACA.
44   s42(2) ACA.

if the statutory minimum period has elapsed, the court cannot make an adoption order unless it is satisfied that the agency has had sufficient opportunity to see the child at home with the adopter(s).[45]

Local authority foster carers who are not put forward as adopters by the agency cannot apply to adopt a foster child unless he has been in placement for at least a year or they obtain court leave to do so.

Adoption application

Adoption applications can be made to the Family Proceedings Court, County Court or High Court and are governed by the enormously detailed Family Procedure (Adoption) Rules 2005 (FP(A)R),[46] supplemented by Practice Directions.

The application is made by filing at court the prescribed form, the child's birth certificate, the applicants' marriage/civil partnership certificate (if any) and a fee. In a contested case, there must also be a Statement of Facts setting out the reasons for asking the court to dispense with parental consent.

Confidentiality

Adoptions are commonly arranged on a confidential basis. Even where parents actively request adoption, the adopters' identity and address usually remain confidential. In cases where parents are hostile or even dangerous, revealing the adopters' identity could actually put them and the child at risk.

If a placement is confidential, everyone involved – including office support staff – must be acutely aware of the need to maintain confidentiality and files must be clearly marked to highlight the issue. There are a thousand ways for information to slip out – a parent catching sight of a file's label, an unguarded comment, or documents being sent out by mistake. In one case the local authority promised adopters confidentiality yet their name was mentioned to the mother and grandmother and they were telephoned from the grandmother's home with no attempt to conceal their

---

45   s42(7) ACA.

46   Family Procedure (Adoption) Rules 2005 SI 2005/2795, London: Stationery Office, available at www.opsi.gov.uk/si/si2005/20052795.htm, accessed 14 August 2008.

number.[47] The adopters then suffered a campaign of harassment which they believed was from the birth family. The court said the local authority owed the adopters a duty of care. But for a lack of evidence about the harassment the authority would have been liable for damages.

Never guarantee confidentiality – nothing is ever 100 per cent secure; all you can promise is that everyone will do their best, following the agency's clear procedures. If maintaining confidentiality is not practical – perhaps because the child might reveal information during contact – discuss this with the prospective adopters in advance so they can consider their position before committing themselves.

In confidential cases, the court allocates a serial number to the case and the proceedings are conducted in a way so as not to reveal the adopters' identity.[48]

Court

When the application is issued, the court appoints a CAFCASS officer, fixes a first directions hearing or issues directions and asks the adoption agency to provide a copy of the consent form and a report. The case timetable is fixed, including the date of the final hearing. The court must manage the case actively including, where appropriate, encouraging co-operation and narrowing the issues in dispute.[49] Generally, reports filed in the proceedings are confidential and are not disclosed even to the parties except that individuals have the right to see anything written about them.

Agency report

The agency must file a comprehensive report.[50] As well as anything directed by the court, this must include:

- details of the report writer and the agency

---

47   *B and B* v. *A County Council* [2006] EWCA Civ 1388 [2007] 1FLR 1189 Court of Appeal.
48   FP(A)R r20.
49   FP(A)R r4.
50   The details to be included in the report are set out in the Practice Direction, available at www.justice.gov.uk/family/procrules/practice_directions/pd_part05c.htm, accessed 14 August 2008.

- procedural matters (such as who should be made a party, whether anyone is under 18 or needs the Official Solicitor)
- detailed information about the child, including a photograph
- detailed information about both birth parents
- relationships and contact, from the perspective of the child and the birth parents
- a summary of the agency's actions
- detailed information about the prospective adopters, including photographs and an assessment of their suitability to adopt
- the prospective adopters' views on religious upbringing, understanding of adoption and views on contact
- the agency's actions in respect of the prospective adopters
- details and assessment of the placement
- recommendations.

CAFCASS

The CAFCASS officer is to safeguard the child's interests and to file a thorough report. As well as witnessing any consent, she must investigate all relevant circumstances and provide the court with any assistance it requires.

Adoption with consent

Even where consent is clear, the court does not simply rubber stamp the arrangement; it must carefully consider all the elements of s1 ACA and consider the reports filed before deciding whether an adoption order is appropriate.

Contact

Before making an adoption order the court must look at existing or proposed contact arrangements, obtain the views of the parties and consider whether there should be any arrangements for contact post-adoption.[51]

---

51   s46(6) ACA.

The court can make a s8 CA89 contact order alongside the adoption order if that is in the child's best interests. Even if direct contact is inappropriate, indirect contact should always be considered.

The adoption order

The adopters and the child attend court for making of the final adoption order.[52] Although this is legally a momentous occasion, in practice the 'hearing' is short and relatively informal, even celebratory.

Withdrawal of consent

In our scenario, Mary has the right to withdraw her consent to the placement and her advance consent to the adoption order. However, the effect of her change of heart depends on its timing. Before Mary signs her consent she must understand that she cannot simply change her mind later and undo everything.

15.3.3

> Mary changes her mind and withdraws consent before Charlie is placed with Ann and Andrew.

The agency is no longer authorised to place Charlie for adoption. In the absence of consent, only a placement order can authorise placement for adoption and the agency is unlikely to be able to establish the grounds for such an order.[53] Even so, Mary cannot simply go to the foster home and take Charlie – only the authority can move him.[54] It must return Charlie to Mary within seven days of her withdrawal of consent (unless it applies for a placement order, when his return is suspended until the outcome of the application).[55]

---

52   FP(A)R r32(6).
53   See Chapter 16 for more details on placement orders.
54   s30(2) ACA.
55   s31(1) ACA.

15.3.4

Charlie is already placed with Ann and Andrew before Mary changes her mind.

The agency notify Ann and Andrew of Mary's change of heart and they have 14 days to return him to the agency (seven days if he is under six weeks old) – failure to do so is an offence. The agency must then return Charlie to Mary – again unless the agency applies for a placement order.

15.3.5

Ann and Andrew have made their court application to adopt Charlie before Mary changes her mind.

Once the application is under way, it is too late for Mary simply to change her mind and have Charlie back.

> s52(4) ACA The withdrawal of any consent to the placement of a child for adoption, or of any consent given under s20, is ineffective if it is given after an application for an adoption order is made.

Ann and Andrew do not have to return Charlie unless the court says so.[56] Effectively the court goes on to decide the adoption application.

If the withdrawal of consent is 'ineffective', logically the consent must still stand. Mary may not now oppose the adoption order being made unless she obtains court leave to do so,[57] which will only happen if the court is satisfied that there has been a change in circumstances since she gave her consent.

The consequences of Mary's advance consent are therefore far-reaching. Once the adoption application has been launched, possibly as little as ten weeks after Mary gave consent, her chances of resisting the adoption are extremely limited.

---

56   s32(5) ACA.
57   s47(3) ACA.

The putative father

15.3.6

Darren contacts the adoption agency saying he is Charlie's father and wants to care for him.

Darren does not have PR. Unless and until he acquires it, he is not a 'parent' whose consent is required to Charlie's adoption. Mary is unlikely to sign a PR agreement so his only option is to apply to court for a PR order under s4 CA89, which is bound to take time.

If Charlie is already placed with Mary's consent before Darren acquires PR, under s52(10) ACA Darren is treated as having consented in the same terms as Mary, so he is bound by a decision Mary took before he even knew of Charlie's existence. It is hard to see how that is the unconditional consent given with full understanding usually required of parents in adoption.

If Darren objects to adoption, he is in the same position as Mary in the previous examples, so it depends at what stage in the process he tries to 'withdraw' his deemed consent. If the adoption application is already under way, he must show a change in circumstances to get court leave to oppose the adoption order. We await a test case to decide whether belatedly discovering a child's existence counts as a sufficient change in circumstances. Challenges under the Human Rights Act seem likely.

Points for practice

1. Never forget the unique and far-reaching characteristics of adoption.

2. Regularly refer to the basic principles set out in s1 ACA.

3. Ensure birth parents are in no doubt about the enormity of giving consent under s19 or s20 ACA.

4. Adoption involves a lot of paperwork. A very organised approach is needed to get it all done in time.

5. Never guarantee confidentiality, but ensure all possible measures are taken to try to preserve it.

Chapter 16

Placement Orders, Contested Cases and Contact

Placement orders

> s21 ACA A placement order is an order made by the court authoris-
> ing a local authority to place a child for adoption with any prospective
> adopters who may be chosen by the authority.

In the absence of parental consent, obtaining a placement order is the only
way an adoption agency can be authorised to place a child for adoption.
Generally speaking, care proceedings and a placement order go together;
indeed, there is a statutory duty to apply for a placement order if adoption
is the care plan proposed to the court.[1]

Consent to placement under s19 Adoption and Children Act 2002
(ACA) is almost incompatible with care proceedings: it cannot be validly
given during care proceedings,[2] and consent previously given is invalidated
if a care order is made.[3] After a care order, although valid s19 consent can
be given, the agency has the option of seeking a placement order anyway
and is often best advised to do so.[4]

---

1   s22(2) ACA.
2   s19(3)(a) ACA.
3   s19(3)(b) ACA.
4   s22(3) ACA.

If possible, the placement order should be sought at the same time as the care order, otherwise there has to be another set of proceedings and more delay for the child. Logically, the court must decide on the care order application first and then consider the placement order application, but it can hear all the evidence and arguments in the same hearing and deliver one judgment covering both applications.

s21 ACA refers to the 'local authority', but the Court of Appeal confirmed that, in applying for a placement order, the authority acts as an adoption agency.[5] It cannot make the application until it is satisfied that the child ought to be placed for adoption,[6] a decision to be made by the appointed officer after considering the Panel's recommendation. In *Re P-B*, the local authority was only in a position to issue its placement order application two days into the final care hearing, but as everyone knew that adoption was the plan and a placement order application would be issued, there was no injustice in the placement application going ahead alongside the care order application.

This case illustrates the challenge of getting everything done within the 40 weeks of care proceedings, including:

- amassing the evidence to establish the threshold criteria

- carrying out all necessary assessments (including parents and extended family)

- reaching recommendations on the appropriate order and care plan[7]

- if the plan is for adoption, taking the case to Panel then obtaining the agency's 'best interests' decision

- preparing and issuing a placement order application.

This requires good organisation, a keen awareness of law and procedure and a constant eye on timescales.

16.1 – Placement and care orders

Leon is subject to a care order. No placement order is in place as the plan was for rehabilitation to his mother Melanie with adoption

---

5   *Re P-B (Placement Order)* [2006] EWCA Civ 1016 [2007] 1FLR 1106 Court of Appeal.
6   s18(2) ACA.
7   For an illustration, see the care planning scenario in Appendix 8.

as a contingency. Rehabilitation breaks down and, after considering the Panel's recommendation, the agency decides that adoption is in Leon's best interests.

The agency cannot place Leon for adoption until it has authority to place. If Melanie does not consent, the agency must obtain a placement order. If she does consent under s19 ACA, the agency is authorised to place Leon for adoption. But as she is not always reliable, the agency might decide to apply for a placement order anyway, although it can go ahead with the placement in the meantime.

Grounds

The link between placement orders and care orders is clear from the grounds set out in s21(2) ACA. An order can only be made if either:

- the child is subject to a care order (which might have been made minutes earlier);

- the threshold criteria are met even if there is no care order; or

- the child has no parents or guardians (a placement order is the only option as there is no one to give s19 ACA consent).

A placement order can only be made if adoption is in the child's best interests, but there is no need for an adoptive family to be identified at this stage. Indeed, a placement order can be made for a child who is difficult to place and for whom, in the end, it might prove impossible to find adopters. However, adoption must be the decided plan for the child. In a case where two children needed a therapeutic placement before anyone could know if they would ever be adoptable, it was premature for the court to make a placement order.[8] The court must therefore consider whether a child is suitable for adoption even if it may prove difficult or even impossible to find adopters.[9]

s1 ACA criteria

The court's paramount consideration is the child's welfare throughout his life and it must consider the welfare checklist and other factors set out in s1 ACA.

---

8   *Re T (Children: Placement order)* [2008] EWCA Civ 248 Court of Appeal.
9   *Re S-H (A Child)* [2008] EWCA Civ 493 Court of Appeal.

Parental consent

The court can only make a placement order if, for each parent with parental responsibility (PR), either:

- s/he consents unconditionally and with full understanding to the child's placement for adoption
- his/her consent should be dispensed with.

Dispensing with consent

The grounds for dispensing with parental consent are the same for placement orders and adoption orders. There are three possibilities:

- the parent/guardian cannot be found
- the parent/guardian is incapable of giving consent
- 'the welfare of the child requires the consent to be dispensed with'.[10]

It is possible for one parent to consent and the other's consent to be dispensed with, or for both parents to have consent dispensed with but on different grounds.

The first two grounds are familiar from the old law. The court will not accept that someone 'cannot be found' unless extensive efforts have been made to find them. It is sensible to list all the avenues pursued and seek the court's guidance as to whether anything further should be done.

A parent can be incapable of giving consent through mental illness or learning disability sufficiently profound to prevent her from understanding the issues, or through physical incapacity (such as a coma). In such cases, her interests are represented by the Official Solicitor.

The most common ground in practice, used where a parent opposes the adoption plan, is the 'welfare' ground. The Court of Appeal considered this ground in an appeal against the making of a placement order.[11] Wall LJ said that the language of the Act is straightforward: the court must consider whether the welfare of the child requires adoption. s1(1) ACA is pivotal. As in all other decisions relating to the adoption of a child, the child's welfare is the paramount consideration. The parent's consent can

---

10   s52(1)(a) and (b) ACA.
11   *Re P (A Child)* [2008] EWCA Civ 535 Court of Appeal.

only be dispensed with if the child's welfare 'requires' it. The Court of Appeal noted that 'requires' is a strong word, meaning that this must be what the situation demands, not something which is optional, reasonable, desirable or simply convenient. This ensures that the decision is proportionate, remembering that sanctioning a child's adoption against a parent's wishes is the most extreme interference with family life.

Where a parent opposes adoption, the real argument (indeed, usually the only argument) is at the placement order stage, not the adoption itself. By the final adoption hearing the child is settled in the adoptive family and the order is often practically a foregone conclusion. At the placement order stage, the child is not yet in his new family so the parents have an opportunity to contest the whole idea of adoption as a care plan. In opposing, parents could:

- repeat their case in the care proceedings:
  - denying significant harm and/or
  - denying responsibility for harm and/or
  - arguing for rehabilitation
- argue that, even if the child cannot return home, adoption is not the right order; for example:
  - the door to rehabilitation should be kept open
  - long term fostering would better preserve the child's sense of identity and contact with the birth family
  - a residence order or special guardianship order would be more proportionate
- argue against adoption in principle.

One case dealt with a mother's opposition to adoption partly on religious principle – she was a Muslim and adoption is not recognised under Sharia law.[12] Munby J held that a parent's religious belief can never be the deciding factor when considering a child's future. The mother's human right to freedom of religion (Article 9) was qualified by the child's right to a family life, albeit in a substitute family (Article 8). Although the mother's beliefs themselves were reasonable, her reliance on them to justify her refusal to

---

12   *Re S; Newcastle City Council v. Z* [2005] EWHC 1490 (Fam) [2007] 1FLR 861 High Court, a case heard at the very end of the old legislation but with an eye to the new Act.

consent to child's adoption was not. Applying society's current values, the advantages of adoption for the child were strong enough to override the mother's views.

Placement order application

The procedure for a placement order is similar to an adoption application except that the local authority is the applicant and the child is an automatic respondent. The authority must file a statement of the facts relied on in any application to dispense with parental consent. If the application is made alongside care proceedings, the court gives directions to deal with both applications together.

Contact

Before making a placement order, the court must consider and invite the parties to comment on any proposed contact arrangements.[13] On application by any of the parties or of its own accord, the court can make a contact order under s26 ACA alongside a placement order. ACA contact orders can later be varied or revoked by the court and contact can be suspended for up to seven days in an emergency, but generally agencies much prefer to be left with the discretion to arrange contact without being bound by a court order.

As a placement order comes before the child is placed – indeed in some cases an adoptive family may never be found – contact under a placement order may differ from that envisaged under an eventual adoption. Arrangements need to be flexible enough to adapt as the situation develops, and ideally any contact order should also reflect this.

16.2 – Placement and contact

Dean is six and his behaviour is challenging. The plan for him is adoption but it will not be easy to find a family. The plan is to scale down contact to a maintenance level, terminating direct contact if (and only if) a family is found so that Dean can say goodbye to his birth family before starting introductions to a new family. The local authority would like to be trusted to make suitable arrangements

---

13   s27(4) ACA.

without a court order, but if the court insists on an order the local authority must try to persuade it to incorporate into the order the plan to scale down and eventually end direct contact.

Effect of a placement order

Once a placement order is made:

- the agency is authorised to place the child for adoption

- the agency obtains PR for the child, shared with the parent(s) and (upon placement) with the prospective adopters, but the agency decides how PR is exercised

- the care order is suspended (not discharged)

- Children Act 1989 (CA89) contact orders and provisions are superseded by ACA

- no one other than the agency can remove the child from the placement.[14]

Duration of placement orders

A placement order is intended to be a step towards adoption, not a long term order. It therefore lasts until either:

- an adoption order is made, automatically discharging the placement order

- it is revoked

- the child turns 18 or marries under 18.

Placement orders can be revoked under s24 ACA, applying the s1 ACA principles. The local authority can apply if, for example, it becomes clear that an adoptive placement will never be found. A parent can only apply for revocation if the child is not placed for adoption and he can obtain court leave by showing a change of circumstances since the order was made. If a placement order is revoked, any pre-existing care order revives.

---

14   s34(1) ACA.

Changing names on placement

The interim period in which a child is placed for adoption but not yet adopted can be a delicate one. Adopters often want to start to call the child by their own surname, to claim the child as part of their family and to avoid compromising their confidentiality but the law is clear: while a child is placed for adoption, in the absence of written consent of parents with PR or court permission, no one can 'cause the child to be known by a new surname'.[15] In a case where surname change is particularly important, court leave should be sought at the placement order hearing.

The ACA does not mention first names, but the High Court considered the issue in a case involving two children whose first names were changed, one because the prospective adopters did not like the child's name, the other because the foster carers already had a child with the same name in placement.[16] The court was very clear that a child has a right to the name s/he is registered with. Adopters have no right to change a child's name until the adoption order is made, and foster carers are never entitled to do so. Local authorities should make this plain to carers at the outset. If there is a good reason to change a name the authority should consult parents and approach the court if necessary.

Parental consent to adoption

The issue of parental consent, already considered when the placement order was made, has to be dealt with again on the application for the adoption order itself. Unfortunately the wording of s47 ACA dealing with this crucial issue is very unclear and seems likely to be fertile ground for legal challenge.[17] The technicalities can be left to lawyers – suffice to say that it seems that the Act's intention is that an adoption order can be granted if there is either parental consent to adoption or the parents' consent can be dispensed with.

The grounds for dispensing with consent to an adoption order are the same as for a placement order. If consent has already been dispensed with at the placement stage, there seems little point going through the same

---

15   s28(2) and (3) ACA.
16   *Re D, L and LA (Care: Change of Forename)* [2003] 1FLR 339 High Court.
17   For a more detailed exploration of the author's view of defects in the drafting of the ACA, see L. Davis (2005) 'Adoption and Children Act 2002 – Some Concerns.' *Family Law Journal 35*, 294.

arguments again at the adoption hearing. The ACA recognises this by restricting a birth parent's right to contest the making of an adoption order where there is a placement order. S/he can oppose with court leave, only obtainable if 'there has been a change in circumstances since…the placement order was made'.[18]

This makes sense in practical terms but from the parents' position, and in human rights terms (the rights to family life and to a fair trial), it seems harsh. The parents are parties to the proceedings and want to oppose the permanent termination of their relationship with their child, but they are not allowed to do so. Test cases seem inevitable.

What kind of changed circumstances justify allowing a parent a second bite of the cherry? This question arose in a case where the child was thriving in an adoption placement after being made subject to care and placement orders.[19] In the meantime the parents successfully completed a residential assessment and were allowed to keep their second child. Naturally, they argued that their circumstances had changed and sought leave to oppose the first child's adoption.

The Court of Appeal decided that the first step is to see whether the change is sufficient in nature and degree to justify even considering the question of leave. If so, the second step is to decide whether to give leave, which, as 'a decision relating to the adoption of a child', is governed by s1 ACA making child's welfare throughout his life the paramount consideration. The Court of Appeal decided this could be determined on legal submissions without the need for evidence or cross-examination. In this case, nearly a year had passed and the care plan was working well. The judge was entitled to conclude that the child's need for security and permanence remained unchanged and the parents had no realistic prospect of successfully opposing the adoption order so they were refused leave to contest.

This is a very strong decision – reassuring for local authorities and adopters, but harsh on birth parents. It is difficult to imagine what changes a birth family could possibly make to warrant leave to oppose and there seems little point in parents being parties to the proceedings if they are not allowed to contest. Test cases in the House of Lords or Strasbourg seem likely. We wait to see whether changes in the prospective adoptive family (such as illness, death or separation) will justify giving leave to apply to

---

18   s47(7) ACA.
19   *Re P (Adoption: Leave Provisions)* [2007] EWCA Civ 616 [2007] 2FLR 1069 Court of Appeal.

revoke placement orders. We do know that a change in the child's circumstances may do so. In one case a child who was of very low weight actually declined in foster care and there was a very serious professional disagreement about the way forward.[20] It was no longer clear that the child was adoptable. In that case, the Court of Appeal agreed that this change in circumstances justified an application to revoke the placement order even though there was no realistic propect that the child would ever go home. If the placement order was ultimately revoked, the care order would revive, so the local authority would have to go back to the drawing board to determine the appropriate plan for the child.

Open adoption

The classic legal model of adoption envisaged a clean break between the child and birth family but today older children with memories of and attachments to their birth families are placed for adoption and we know more about children's need to understand their identity and origins. In consequence, adoptions have become increasingly 'open'. However, the term 'open adoption' has no legal definition and there is no common understanding about its use, which ranges from the mildest degree of information sharing to adoption with direct contact. To avoid misunderstanding, it is best simply to specify the arrangements for each case.

The child's needs for contact should be analysed before even searching for a family. An ideal placement may not exist, in which case some compromise has to be made between the child's conflicting needs for a permanent home and for ongoing contact. Proper efforts must be made first – in one case a local authority simply dismissed the likelihood of finding adopters amenable to an open adoption because there were none on the list at the time: that was not good enough.[21] In that case the child's needs for ongoing contact outweighed the disadvantages of disrupting the local authority's adoption plans.

Simon Brown LJ explained the benefits of contact continuing in adoption in some cases:

20   Re S-H (A Child) [2008] EWCA Civ 493 Court of Appeal.
21   Re E (Minor) (Care Order: Contact) [1994] 1FLR 146 Court of Appeal, which dealt with termination of contact under s34(4) CA89 because it was heard prior to the existence of placement orders.

contact may well be of singular importance to the long-term welfare of the child: first in giving the child the security of knowing that his parents love him and are interested in his welfare; secondly, by avoiding any damaging sense of loss to the child in seeing himself abandoned by his parents; thirdly by enabling the child to commit himself to the substitute family with the seal of approval of the natural parent; and fourthly, by giving the child the necessary sense of family and personal identity. Contact, if maintained, is capable of reinforcing and increasing the chances of success of a permanent placement, whether on a long-term basis or by adoption.[22]

Before making an adoption order, the court must consider existing or proposed arrangements for contact and obtain the parties' views.[23] Contact arrangements should be separately considered for each child remembering that plans may be different among children in the same family, or different contact may be appropriate for various members of the family. There should be no sense of a formulaic response.

The agency should be able to explain to the court:

- the purpose of contact

- the reasons for the type and frequency of contact proposed

- how long the arrangement is to continue, when and by whom it is to be reviewed

- what happens if contact is not taken up or if there are problems

- what happens if the child's needs change or he later wants more/less contact/none at all.

If direct contact is suggested the following should be decided:

- the venue

- how risks to the security of the placement will be managed.

If indirect contact is proposed the discussions should centre on:

- whether it should be through an intermediary

- whether it should be reciprocal or one way

- exactly what can be sent.

---

22   *Re E*, at pages 154–155 (see note 21 above)
23   s46(6) ACA.

There are many complex, sensitive issues to be worked out preferably before the adoption placement is even made. Decisions and reasons must be recorded in writing.

Contact orders

The court can make a s8 CA89 contact order at the same time as an adoption order, including imposing contact which is not proposed by the agency or adopters if it is in the child's best interests. Like any other s8 CA89 order it can later be varied or revoked, raising the spectre of possible subsequent court applications and undermining the permanence and security of adoption.

In practice, courts are generally reluctant to make contact orders in adoption. If contact is agreed, the court prefers to trust the adopters to meet the child's needs as time goes on, rather than impose an order, and this is of course consistent with the 'no order principle'.

The Court of Appeal confirmed that contact orders in adoption proceedings are unusual and the imposition of contact orders not agreed by the adopters is extremely unusual.[24] The court should be reluctant to make a contact order if the adopters reasonably object.

What if promised contact does not happen?

A court order is enforceable; an agreement for post-adoption contact is not. However, if adopters do not stick to an agreement for contact, an application for a contact order might be made later. No one in the birth family has an automatic right to apply (birth parents are no longer 'parents'), so court leave is needed and the tests under s10(9) CA89 apply.[25]

The Court of Appeal has said that adopters should always give reasons for altering an agreement made at the time of adoption and the court can consider whether those reasons are adequate.[26] In that case, adopters had reduced contact between their adopted seven-year-old and her 17-year-old sister from three meetings a year to one, with two-way indirect contact. This was because they felt the direct contact had an adverse effect on their

---

24   *Re R (Adoption: Contact)* [2006] 1FLR 373 Court of Appeal, a case heard at the very end of the old legislation.

25   See Chapter 4 for more detail.

26   *Re R* (see note 24 above).

child, and they worried about security as the sister retained links with the birth mother. The local authority viewed the stability of the placement as the priority. The 17-year-old wanted to apply to court to restore the original agreement but the court found the adopters' position was reasonable. If, however, they had completely gone back on their previous agreement, the application would have been allowed to proceed.

The message for practice is clear: adopters should never agree to – and should not be pressurised into agreeing to – any contact arrangement which they are not absolutely committed to keep. Contact must be a key part of the training and preparation of adopters and the significance of agreeing to any sort of contact must be clearly explained to them.

Points for practice

1. Whenever possible, seek a placement order at the same time as a care order.

2. Prepare with your legal team your arguments to justify adoption and dispense with parental consent for the placement order.

3. Carefully reason through plans for contact between the child and significant people both before and after an adoptive placement is found.

4. Make sure adopters are truly committed before any contact is offered.

Appendix 1A

Children Act 1989 Key Sections by Number

Section	Subject
1(1)	welfare principle
1(2)	no delay principle
1(3)	welfare checklist
1(5)	no order principle
2	parental responsibility (PR) – general
2(7)	ability of one person with PR to make decisions
3	PR – meaning
4	PR orders and agreements for unmarried fathers
4A	PR orders and agreements for step-parents
5	guardianship for orphans
7	welfare reports to court
8	residence, contact, prohibited steps and specific issue orders
10	right to apply for s8 orders
14A–G	special guardianship orders
17	children in need
17(10)	definition of children in need
20	accommodating children voluntarily
22	general duties to looked after children
23	accommodating and maintaining looked after children
23A–D	duties to young people aged 16+
24–24D	after care provisions
25	secure accommodation
26	independent reviewing officers
27	other agencies' duties to assist in providing services to children in need

Section	Subject
31	threshold criteria for care/supervision orders
31(9) and (10)	definition of 'harm'
33	effect of a care order
35	effect of a supervision order
37	reports to court where court suspects significant harm
38	interim care and supervision orders
38(6)	assessments under interim orders
39	variation and discharge of care orders
43	child assessment orders
44	emergency protection orders (EPOs)
46	police protection
47	duty to investigate child protection referrals
48	warrants etc. to assist with executing EPOs
91(14)	court's power to prohibit further applications
Schedule 2 part 1	services for families
Schedule 2 part 2	looked after children

Appendix 1B

Children Act 1989 Key Sections by Subject

Subject	Section
Accommodation	20
After care provisions	24–24D
Assessments under interim orders	38(6)
Care proceedings – grounds	31
Care order – effect	33
Child assessment order	43
Child protection investigation	47
Children in need	17
Children in need – definition	17(10)
Children in need – services	Schedule 2 part 1
Contact – child in care	34
Contact – private law	8
Discharge/variation of care orders	39
Discharge/variation of s8 orders	8(2)
Duties to people aged 16+	23A–D
Emergency protection orders	44
Guardianship (orphans)	5
Harm	31(9) + (10)
Independent reviewing officers	26
Interim care/supervision orders	38
Looked after children – duties	22, schedule 2 part 2

Subject	Section
Looked after children – maintenance	23
No delay principle	1(2)
No order principle	1(5)
Other agencies' duties to assist – child protection	47
Other agencies' duties to assist – children in need	27
Police protection	46
PR – exercise by one person	2(7)
PR – general	2
PR – meaning	3
PR orders/agreements – fathers	4
PR orders/agreements – step-parents	4A
Preventing future applications	91(14)
Prohibited steps orders	8
Report to court – suspected significant harm	37
Report to court – welfare	7
Residence orders	8
Section 8 orders – right to apply	10
Secure accommodation	25
Special guardianship orders	14A–G
Specific issue orders	8
Supervision orders – effect	35
Threshold criteria	31
Warrants etc. to assist executing EPOs	48
Welfare checklist	1(3)
Welfare principle	1(1)

Appendix 2

Residence, Special Guardianship and Adoption at a Glance

Residence	Special guardianship	Adoption
Children Act 1989 (CA89)	Children Act 1989 (CA89)	Adoption and Children Act 2002 (ACA)
s8 CA89	s8 CA89	whole Act
s1 CA89 applies	s1 CA89 applies	s1 ACA applies
Child's welfare is paramount (s1(1) CA89)	Child's welfare is paramount (s1(1) CA89)	Child's welfare throughout his life is paramount (s1(2) ACA)
Welfare checklist (s1(3) CA89) applies	Welfare checklist (s1(3) CA89) applies	Welfare checklist (s1(4) ACA) applies
Parents have automatic right to apply; anyone can apply with court leave	Parents cannot apply. Some have automatic right to apply, others need court leave	Only those approved by an adoption agency can apply; child placed by agency (subject to limited exceptions)
Court may request a welfare report	Court must consider a report by the local authority	Court must consider adoption agency report
Determines with whom the child lives	Appoints special guardian (SG) – SG decides where child lives	Appoints adopters – adopters decide where child lives
Confers PR shared equally with others	Confers PR shared but SG can exercise PR exclusively	Confers exclusive PR
Parent(s) retain PR, shared equally	Parent(s) retain PR subject to SG's right to act exclusively	Birth parents lose PR – only adopters have PR
Person with residence order does not become a 'parent'	SG does not become a 'parent'	Adopters are the child's only parents
Family relationships remain unchanged	Family relationships remain unchanged	All relationships with birth family end; new relationships are created with the adoptive family

Residence	Special guardianship	Adoption
No change to inheritance	No change to inheritance	Inheritance dependent on relationships change from birth to adoptive family
No name change without consent of all with PR or court order	No name change without consent of all with PR or court order	Adopters have the automatic right to change the child's name
No removal from UK for over one month without consent of all with PR or court order	No removal from UK for over three months without consent of all with PR or court order	No limit on removal from UK
Order lasts until child 16 (or 18 for non-parents)	Order lasts to 18	Order lasts for life
Can be revoked by court on application – parents have automatic right to apply	Can be revoked by court – parents cannot apply without showing change in circumstances	Irrevocable
s8 CA89 contact order can be made	s8 CA89 contact order can be made	s8 CA89 contact order can be made but very rare
Local authority has discretion to provide financial support (non-parents only)	Local authority has duty to assess support needs and devise package including possible financial support	Agency has duty to assess support needs and devise package including possible financial support

Appendix 3

Contact *Aide-mémoire*

Guiding principles

- The child's welfare is paramount (s1(1) CA89).
- The welfare checklist applies (s1(3) CA89).
- Delay is likely to be harmful (s1(2) CA89).
- Contact must be safe.
- Everyone's right to family life must be respected (Article 8) and competing rights balanced.

Starting point

If the person concerned has a presumption of contact such as:

- statutory presumption of reasonable contact for parents of children in care (s34 CA89)
- principle that children should have contact with their parents

start your reasoning at unrestricted direct contact and add necessary restrictions/limitations until you reach the right point for the case.

Give reasons at each step.

1. Informal arrangements

Can contact be left free and unrestricted? If not, consider to what level of detail it must be prescribed.

2. Direct contact

Can the child have face to face contact? Consider:

Staying contact

- frequency
- length of stay
- special arrangements for Christmas/other festivals, school holidays.

Visiting contact

- frequency
- length
- venue
- special arrangements for birthdays, Christmas/other festivals, school holidays.

Conditions/safeguards

Are conditions needed to make contact work? What and why? Consider:

- who can attend (parent alone or new partners, extended family, etc.)
- contact handover arrangements
- venue (parent's home or a neutral venue)
- pre-conditions (e.g. parent not to be drunk on arrival)
- supervision:
    - why
    - by whom (social work professional/community centre/family member/trusted friend)
    - what level of supervision (close supervision or periodical monitoring)

3. Indirect contact

As well as or instead of direct contact, consider:

Type of contact

- telephone calls
- text messages
- letters
- emails
- cards
- presents
- photographs
- progress/school reports.

Frequency

Times

Duration

Special arrangements for Christmas/other festivals, birthdays, school holidays, etc.

Conditions/safeguards

Are conditions needed to make contact work? What? Why? Consider:

- limitations on type of contact
- reciprocal or one-way
- monitoring/censoring content
- confidentiality of addresses/phone numbers/school details
- value and frequency of gifts.

4. For all contact

Consider:

- how contact fits in the child's life as a whole (taking a short and long term view)
- when and by whom arrangements should be reviewed
- what happens if there is a problem.

Appendix 4

Care/Accommodation at a Glance

In care	Accommodated
s31 CA89	s20 CA89
Child subject to care order made by court	No court involvement – purely voluntary arrangement
Local authority has PR	Local authority has no PR
Parent(s) retain PR but local authority can limit their exercise of PR when necessary in child's interests	Parent(s) retain full PR but may delegate some aspects to local authority
Lasts until child is 18 unless care order discharged by the court	Lasts as long as parents require
Parents cannot remove child from placement	Parents with PR can remove child from placement at any time without notice
s8 or special guardianship orders ended by care order	s8 or special guardianship orders remain in force
Contact is regulated by s34 CA89	Contact is regulated by s8 CA89
Child is 'looked after'	Child is 'looked after'

Summary of Duties to 'Looked After' Children

Welfare

Safeguard and promote welfare (s22(3)(a) CA89).

Services

Use any services available to children living with their own parents (s22(3)(b) CA89).

Consultation

Ascertain the wishes and feelings of the child, parents, anyone else with PR and any other relevant person before making any decision about a looked after child (s22(4) CA89). Give these due consideration (s22(5) CA89).

Religion, culture, etc.

Give due consideration to the child's religious persuasion, racial origin and cultural and linguistic background in making any decision for a looked after child (s22(5)(c) CA89).

Placement

Provide accommodation for a looked after child by placing him with local authority foster carers, in a children's home or with family members or friends (s23(2) CA89).

Arrangements can be made for an accommodated child to live with a relative or friend (s23(6) CA89), discharging him from accommodation.

Where appropriate placement should be near the child's home and with any siblings (s23(7) CA89). Accommodation for disabled children should be 'not unsuitable' (s23(8) CA89).

Follow the requirements of the Arrangements for Placement of Children (General) Regulations 1991 SI 1991/890.[1]

For foster care (including approval of carers, making, monitoring and ending placements) follow the Fostering Services Regulations 2002 SI 2002/57.[2] Friends or family members must be approved as foster carers within six weeks of an immediate placement.

If a child in care is placed at home with parents follow the requirements of the Placement with Parents etc. Regulations 1991 SI 1991/893.[3]

Secure accommodation

Child can only be placed in secure accommodation for more than 72 hours with a court order under s25 CA89 and following the Children (Secure Accommodation) Regulations 1991 SI 1991/1505.[4]

Reviews

Conduct reviews of each child's case following the Review of Children's Cases Regulations 1991 SI 1991/895 within four weeks of placement, then within three months, then six-monthly.[5]

Appoint an independent reviewing officer for the child following the Review of Children's Cases (Amendment) (England) Regulations 2004 SI 2004/1419.[6]

1   Available at www.opsi.gov.uk/si/si1991/uksi_19910890_en_1.htm, accessed 14 August 2008.
2   Available at www.opsi.gov.uk/si/si2002/20020057.htm, accessed 14 August 2008.
3   Available at www.opsi.gov.uk/si/si1991/uksi_19910893_en_1, accessed 14 August 2008.
4   Available at www.ops.gov.uk/si/si1991/uksi_19911505_en_1.htm, accessed 14 August 2008.
5   Available at www.opsi.gov.uk/si/si1991/uksi_19910895_en_6.htm, accessed 14 August 2008.
6   Available at www.opsi.gov.uk/si/si2004/20041419.htm, accessed 14 August 2008.

Contact

Arrange contact:

- for child in care – for anyone with a presumption of reasonable contact (s34(1) CA89) or a contact order (s34(2) or (3) CA89)

- for accommodated child – for anyone with a contact order (s8 CA89).

Promote contact between child and parents, anyone with PR and any relative, friend or other person connected to him unless not practicable or consistent with his welfare (Schedule 2 para 15 CA89).

Arrange independent visitor for child who has infrequent/no visits (Schedule 2 para 17 CA89).

Informing parents

Inform parents and others with PR of child's address unless child is in care and giving information would prejudice his welfare (Schedule 2 para 15(2) and (4) CA89).

Leaving care/accommodation

Advise, assist and befriend all looked after children to promote their welfare when they are no longer looked after (Schedule 2 para 19A CA89).

16- and 17-year-olds

For 'eligible' children (16- and 17-year-olds looked after for at least 13 weeks after the age of 14 and continuing beyond the age of 16):

- assess needs for advice, assistance and support while being looked after and thereafter

- prepare and keep under review a pathway plan[7]

- provide a personal adviser while he is looked after (Schedule 2 para 19B CA89).

For 'relevant' children (young people aged 16 or 17 who were 'eligible' but are no longer looked after):

---

7   In accordance with Children (Leaving Care) (England) Regulations 2001 SI2001/2874, available at www.opsi.gov.uk/si/si2001/20012874.htm, accessed 14 August 2008.

- keep in touch
- appoint a personal adviser
- assess needs for advice, assistance and support
- prepare and keep under review a pathway plan
- safeguard and promote welfare including maintaining him, providing accommodation, and providing assistance for education, training or employment (s23B CA89).

18–21-year-olds (and beyond if still in education)
For former relevant children (i.e. over-18-year-olds who were previously 'relevant' or 'eligible'):

- try to keep in touch
- provide and keep under review a pathway plan
- provide a personal adviser
- assist with expenses for employment, education or training
- give other assistance for his welfare (s23C CA89).

Advice and assistance
For under- 21-year-olds who were looked after at any time between 16 and 18:

- contact him as appropriate
- advise and befriend
- assist, including providing cash (in exceptional circumstances)
- contribute to expenses for employment, education or training.

Appendix 6

Emergency Protection Order
Aide-mémoire

1. Take legal advice

2. With your lawyers, analyse the grounds for emergency action

- Exactly what significant harm do you believe the child will suffer if action is not taken?

- How pressing is the risk – is it imminent?

- How serious is the risk – is the child in danger?

- Is there evidence to substantiate your belief?

- Is there any other way to manage the risk?

- Is it a true emergency? What would happen if there were a delay of one to three days (to allow care proceedings to start)?

- What are the implications of (a) taking or (b) not taking emergency action for the human rights of:

  ° the child (Article 2 – right to life; 3 – protection from torture etc.; 8 – family life)

  ° the parents (Article 6 – fair trial; 8 – family life).

3. Consider notice to the parents

- Start with the presumption they should be given notice.
- Is there a compelling case to proceed without notice?
- Exactly what do you believe will happen if you give notice?
- What is your evidence to justify that belief?

4. Application

- Seek legal representation.
- Present the court with detailed and precise evidence.
- Present the court with copies of any relevant documents (assessments, reports, letters, Case Conference minutes, etc.).
- Ensure the evidence is accurate, balanced and fair.
- Ensure the court is fully and fairly informed of the applicable law.
- Keep a full note of the hearing.
- Make any other necessary applications – exclusion requirement, warrant to enter and search premises, warrant to search for other children or warrant for police to assist.

5. Serving the order

- Serve the order as soon as possible.
- Give parents a copy of all documents presented to court.
- Give parents a note of the evidence and submissions presented to court.

6. Acting on the order

- Consider whether implementing the order is necessary and justified.
- Review the case daily.
- Arrange reasonable contact for the child and parents.

Appendix 7

Care/Supervision Orders at a Glance

Care order	Supervision order
Threshold criteria (s31 CA89) must be satisfied	Threshold criteria (s31 CA89) must be satisfied
s1 CA89 applies	s1 CA89 applies
Child's welfare is paramount	Child's welfare is paramount
Welfare checklist (s1(3) CA89) must be considered	Welfare checklist (s1(3) CA89) must be considered
Local authority has PR	Local authority does not have PR
Parent(s) retain PR shared with local authority. Authority can limit parents' exercise of PR	Parent(s) retain full PR
Local authority responsible for child's accommodation and maintenance	Local authority to advise, assist and befriend child
Local authority decides where child lives	Parent(s) decide where child lives
Parents cannot remove child from placement	Parents can move child where they like
Local authority can move the child from placement (including placement at home) at any time without notice	Local authority cannot move the child from home without fresh legal authority
Order lasts until child is 18 unless discharged by court	Order lasts one year. Can be extended to maximum three years
Order continues unless ended by court	Order ends unless extended by court
Child is a 'looked after' child	Child is not a 'looked after' child
s8 orders are incompatible with care order	s8 orders can exist alongside supervision order
Contact regulated by s34 CA89	Contact regulated by s8 CA89
Can be discharged or replaced by a supervision order	Can be discharged. Cannot be replaced by a care order – fresh care proceedings needed

Appendix 8

Care Planning Scenario

Carly's case

Carly

Aged 12 months, mixed racial heritage, profound hearing loss.

Mother – Maria

Aged 18, mixed heritage – white British and black Nigerian parents. Was in care due to physical and emotional abuse. Difficult care history, including absconding, involvement in petty crime, drug and alcohol abuse and suspected prostitution.

Father – Fred

Aged 21, white British. Had a stable upbringing, but 'went off the rails' in his teens, becoming involved in crime, including a short spell in a young offenders' institution. Short-lived relationship with Maria ended acrimoniously. Has now returned to live with his parents, distanced himself from his former associates and is undertaking an apprenticeship. Unaware of the pregnancy or Carly's birth until informed of care proceedings by Social Services.

Paternal grandparents – Gladys and George

Aged late 50s. Respectable working people in good health. Have brought up five children, Fred being the youngest – other four have had no problems and all have careers and families and remain in close contact with their parents. Live in an exclusively white area and have no experience of people from other ethnic groups or people with disabilities.

Foster carer – Rita

Aged 52. Single carer. Two adult daughters with young children of their own. Highly experienced and well-respected foster carer for young babies, with experience both of moving babies back to birth parents and on to adoption.

Approved prospective adopters – Andrew and Anthony

Late 20s. Andrew – white British mother, black Jamaican father. Anthony – white British. Anthony's sister is profoundly deaf – he and his whole family fluent in British Sign Language. Together as a couple for three years. Registered civil partnership. Both from happy, supportive families. Approved agency adopters.

The story so far

Carly's name was placed on the Register as an unborn baby due to Maria's history. Maria accepted little ante-natal care. Carly was born prematurely and spent some time in special care. Maria visited infrequently and paid little interest in Carly. Care proceedings were commenced at birth, and Carly was placed with Rita. Fred agreed that Maria should be considered as primary carer, and accepted contact once a week.

Maria formed a good relationship with Rita and with her encouragement started visiting regularly and proved attentive, caring and capable on contact. Maria successfully applied for a placement at a residential unit together with Carly. Fred decided not to take up contact while Carly was living with Maria.

The residential placement started well, but after three months the unit served notice. Maria spent unauthorised time away from the unit, returned smelling of alcohol, started to neglect Carly's basic physical needs and showed no interest in learning about Carly's hearing difficulties. She became abusive to staff trying to advise her.

The local authority decided to end the placement and return Carly to Rita's care.

The final care hearing is approaching. Carly has now been back with Rita for four months. Maria has been attending contact regularly for one hour three times a week. Contact has been of good quality. Maria and Rita continue to have a good relationship. Fred has resumed his contact once a week, and usually attends with his parents. The contact is of good quality and Rita gets on well with Fred and his family.

The parties' positions

Maria – wants another chance to care for Carly. She accepts she needs help and suggests she could move in with Rita and the baby until she is ready to live independently. If she cannot look after Carly, she wants her to stay with Rita and to have as much contact as possible.

Fred – does not think that Maria should care for Carly. He accepts that, as a young, single, working man, he is not in a position to care for her himself, but he wants to maintain contact with her wherever she is living. He supports his parents as carers.

Gladys and George – put themselves forward to care for Carly. Gladys will give up work to look after her. They will co-operate with the authorities in any training they need. They will be guided by Social Services as to what contact, if any, Maria should have, but they will not allow this to take place in their home as they consider her a bad influence.

Rita – has become very attached to Carly and would like to care for her permanently. She does not think that Maria is able to care for Carly, but is happy to promote contact in her home for Maria and for Fred and his family.

Local authority – considering all the options including the possibility of adoption, and is aware of the list of approved adopters including Andrew and Anthony.

- What options are available?
- What factors must be considered in each case?
- What legal grounds apply for any order?
- What arguments will each party raise?

Commentary

MARIA

Maria will have difficulty arguing against the threshold criteria. She must concentrate her opposition on the care plan. If she seeks another chance at rehabilitation, she could try to argue for a further interim care order with a care plan of a mother and baby placement with Carly in Rita's home, but given the failed residential placement, her hopes of success are limited. Her main arguments are therefore likely to be focused on the care plan rather than the care order itself, seeking to support ongoing placement with Rita, opposing any application by Gladys and George for residence or special guardianship or by the local authority for a placement order. If a placement order is applied for, she must show that Carly's welfare does not justify her (Maria's) consent being dispensed with. As a last resort, she will seek ongoing contact even if a placement order is made. She will inevitably plead her Article 8 rights to a family life with Carly.

FRED

Fred has no argument against the threshold criteria. His argument is against any care plan other than placement with his parents. He should seek a parental responsibility (PR) order alongside the other applications before the court to ensure that he has a full role to play (including the requirement to give his consent or have it dispensed with) in any placement or adoption order application. He is also keen to preserve his rights to contact if the plan is to place Carly with anyone other than his parents, so he may seek a contact order. He too will plead Article 8.

GLADYS AND GEORGE

They must be assessed by the local authority, and if that assessment is not favourable they may ask the court for an independent assessment. In the interim period they need to apply for as much contact as possible to build up their relationship with Carly. Their strong points are the blood relationship with Carly, the guaranteed preservation of Carly's links with her birth father and their parenting experience. They will argue that their lack of knowledge of ethnic minorities and disabilities can be remedied. The authority may be concerned about their attitude to Maria and their ability to bring Carly up with a positive image of her mother; even if a placement with Gladys and George is approved, careful consideration needs to be given to contact arrangements with Maria and whether these should be secured by a contact order. They will also plead Article 8 and will remind the court that the issue is not to compare them with theoretical ideal adopters but to see if there is any reason why they cannot provide a good enough home for Carly.

They could care for Carly as foster carers under a care order – this could even happen in the interim period if the authority approve the placement – but they are more likely to want the local authority out of their lives and to seek residence, special guardianship or adoption. A residence order brings with it the disadvantage of sharing PR with Maria, and an adoption order would distort family relationships, so their preferred option may well be a special guardianship order which would give them the power to overrule Maria. They may seek leave to change Carly's surname.

RITA

Rita is not an automatic party to the proceedings and will only be allowed to become one if she persuades the court that she has a separate case to make. She must ask the local authority to assess her as a permanent carer for Carly, whether as a long term foster carer or an adopter. This requires reassessment even though she is already an approved carer – permanent care raises different issues. Rita's strong points are her existing relationship with Carly, her good relationship with both parents and grandparents and her parenting experience. Question marks may arise over her age and her single status and whether, if Carly is not to remain within the birth family, she is really the best option available for Carly.

If the local authority does not agree that Rita is the best long term placement for Carly, she might seek an independent assessment. Otherwise, Rita has no automatic right to apply for an adoption order as she has not had Carly in placement for a year, nor can she apply for leave to seek a residence order against the authority's wishes for the same reason. The court could, however, make a residence or special guardianship order of its own motion if it considers Rita to be the best option for Carly.

ANTHONY AND ANDREW

The option of adoption can only be considered by the authority if and when family placements have been ruled out. If other options are unsuitable for Carly, adoption is likely to be the plan of choice given her age as it will give her life-long security. As care proceedings are under way and not completed, the authority must apply for a placement order if adoption is the plan. The placement order application should be heard at the same time as the care order – meaning that the case must have been taken to the Panel and an agency 'best interests' decision made first. The court will consider Maria's consent (and Fred's if he has obtained PR) which must be given to the placement order or dispensed with on the grounds that Carly's welfare demands it. Contact issues must be considered.

Anthony and Andrew have already been assessed as suitable adopters in principle and provide a good match in terms of racial, cultural and disability issues. The fact that they are a gay couple is irrelevant – it would not be an acceptable reason for Maria or Fred to oppose the making of an adoption order.

If a placement order is obtained, Carly can be placed with the couple and after ten weeks they can launch their adoption application. Maria and Fred (if he has PR) are parties but will not be allowed to contest unless they can show a change of circumstances since the placement order was made. The question of ongoing contact to Maria and Fred as well as Gladys and George and possibly Rita must be considered by the court before making any adoption order.

List of Statutes

List of Cases

Index